BURN SCARS

Burn Scars

A DOCUMENTARY HISTORY OF FIRE SUPPRESSION,
FROM COLONIAL ORIGINS TO THE RESURGENCE
OF CULTURAL BURNING

Edited by Char Miller

Oregon State University Press   Corvallis

Cataloging-in-publication data is available from the Library of Congress.

ISBN 978-1-962645-20-1 paperback; ISBN 978-1-962645-21-8 ebook

∞ This paper meets the requirements of ANSI/NISO Z39.48-1992 (Permanence of Paper).

© 2024 Char Miller
All rights reserved.
First published in 2024 by Oregon State University Press
Printed in the United States of America

Oregon State University Press
121 The Valley Library
Corvallis OR 97331-4501
541-737-3166 • fax 541-737-3170
www.osupress.oregonstate.edu

Oregon State University Press in Corvallis, Oregon, is located within the traditional homelands of the Mary's River or Ampinefu Band of Kalapuya. Following the Willamette Valley Treaty of 1855, Kalapuya people were forcibly removed to reservations in Western Oregon. Today, living descendants of these people are a part of the Confederated Tribes of Grand Ronde Community of Oregon (grandronde.org) and the Confederated Tribes of the Siletz Indians (ctsi.nsn.us).

Contents

Acknowledgments ix

Fire Breaks: An Introduction. 1

Michael Connolly Miskwish, "Aaw e'Hunn (Good Fire)" (2023) 19

PART 1 – COLONIAL SUPPRESSION

A Land of Smoke 29

Juan Rodríguez Cabrillo and Bartolomé Ferrelo Expedition (1542) 31

Sebastián Vizcaíno Expedition (1602) 32

Juan Crespí, Diary (July 20, 1769–October 17, 1769). 33

Captain Fernando Rivera y Moncada, Diary (October 3, 1774). 37

Fernando Rivera y Moncada, Diary (April 24, 1776). 38

José Longinos Martínez, Journal (1792). 39

José Joaquín de Arrillaga, Fire Proclamation (May 31, 1793) 40

Missionary Questionnaire (1798) 42

Fermín Francisco de Lasuén (1801–02). 43

Nineteenth-Century Settler-Colonial Observations 45

R. W. Wells, from "On the Origin of Prairies" (1819) 47

Alfred Robinson, from *Life in California* (1831). 49

Duflot du Mofras, from *Travels on the Pacific Coast* (1841) 50

California Statutes: First Session (1850). 51

California, An Act to Prevent the Destruction of Forests by Fire
  on Public Lands (1871–72) 52

John W. Powell, from *Report of the Arid Lands of the United States* (1879). 53

Franklin B. Hough, from *Report on Forestry* (1882). 55

Joaquin Miller, Address (1887) 60

William H. Mills, Testimony about Fires in the Yosemite Valley (1889) 61

PART 2 – LIGHT BURNING AND ITS DISCONTENTS

First Smoke, 1899–1919 67

Gifford Pinchot, from "The Relations of Forests and Forest Fires" (1899) 69

Marsden Manson, from "The Effect of the Partial Suppression
of Annual Forest Fires in the Sierra Nevada Mountains" (1906).......... 73

Charles Howard Shinn, from "Work in the National Forests—No. 5:
Holding Down a Mountain Fire" (1907) 75

George L. Hoxie, from "How Fire Helps Forestry: The Practical vs.
the Federal Government's Theoretical Ideas" (1910)................... 79

F. E. Olmsted, from "Fire and the Forest—the Theory of 'Light Burning,'"
(1911).. 84

Warren E. Coman, from "Did the Indian Protect the Forest?" (1911) 87

Joseph A. Kitts, from "Preventing Forest Fires by Burning Litter" (1919)....... 89

Fire Fight, 1920–1924 93

Henry S. Graves, from "Graves Terms Light Burning 'Piute Forestry'" (1920) .. 95

Stuart Edward White, from "Woodsmen, Spare Those Trees! Why Fire
Protection Does Not Really Protect Our Remaining Timber" (1920) 98

William B. Greeley, from "'Piute Forestry' or the Fallacy of Light Burning"
(1920)... 104

Aldo Leopold, from "'Piute Forestry' vs. Forest Fire Prevention" (1920) 109

Charles E. Ogle, from "Light Burning" (1920)............................. 112

Paul G. Redington, "*Hic Jacet* (An Epitaph): Light Burning" (1923).......... 115

Donald Bruce, "Light Burning—Report of the California Forestry
Committee" (1923) 116

"Suggests Indians Manage National Forests" (1924) 121

PART 3 – BRINGING FIRE BACK

Southern Backfires 125

Charles Lyell, from *Second Visit to the United States of North America* (1849)... 127

Ellen Call Long, from "Notes on Some of the Forest Features
of Florida" (1888)... 128

Herman H. Chapman, from "Forest Fires and Forestry in the
Southern States" (1912).. 131

Roland M. Harper, from "The Forest Resources of Alabama" (1913).......... 136

Eliza Frances Andrews, from "Agency of Fire in Propagation
of Longleaf Pines" (1917) 138

S. W. Greene, from "The Forest That Fire Made" (1931) 145

H. H. Biswell, from "Prescribed Burning in Georgia and California Compared" (1958) 150

E. V. Komarek, from "The Use of Fire: An Historical Background" (1962) 153

Herbert L. Stoddard, from "Use of Fire in Pine Forests and Game Lands" (1962) 156

Tall Timbers Audience Comment (1962) 161

National Reassessment. 163

R. L. Hensel, from "Recent Studies on the Effect of Burning on Grassland Vegetation" (1923) 165

Elers Koch, from "The Passing of the Lolo Trail" (1935) 170

Forest Service Chief's Circular Letter Announcing the Ten a.m. Rule (1935) . . 176

Allen Calbick to Gifford Pinchot (1940) 178

Emil F. Ernst, from "Vanishing Meadows in Yosemite Valley" (1949) 179

H. H. Biswell, from "The Big Trees and Fire" (1961) 186

From "Wildlife Management in the National Parks: The Leopold Report" (1963) 191

Rita P. Thompson, from "Are Land Managers Applying Our Current Knowledge of Fire Ecology?" (1976) 193

PART 4 – RETURN CYCLE

Return Cycle 199

"Tribal Forest Protection Act in Brief" (2004) 202

Bill Tripp, "Our Land Was Taken. But We Still Hold the Knowledge of How to Stop Mega-Fires" (2020) 204

Julie Cordero-Lamb, Jared Dahl Aldern, and Teresa Romero, "Bring Back the Good Fires" (2020) 207

California Senate Bill No. 332 (2021) 211

Katimiin and Ameekyaaraam Sacred Lands Act (2023) 214

Dawn Blake, "Cultural Burns Critical for Tribal Land Management" (2023) . . . 216

Index 219

Illustrations

1. Firefighting in the Wallowa National Forest, 1908 3
2. The Campo (Kumeyaay) Reservation fire truck stands guard over a prescribed burn on the Manzanita Reservation 18
3. Misión la Purísima Concepción de María Santísima (Mission of the Immaculate Conception of Most Holy Mary), founded in 1787 28
4. Yosemite Valley panorama, 1862) 44
5. Wallace, Idaho, destroyed by fire in 1910 and only slowly rebuilt 64
6. Pamphlet published by the California Board of Forestry in 1914 66
7. US Forest Service rail-adapted fire-patrol vehicle 92
8. Tall Timbers Research Station near Tallahassee, Florida................ 122
9. Results of annual, controlled burns, Tall Timbers Research Station 124
10. President Franklin Roosevelt accepting James Montgomery Flagg's fire prevention poster, June 10, 1937 162
11. Smokey Bear, the mascot of the Forest Service's fire suppression campaign 162
12. Annual, rotating two-acre burn on Junco Meadow on the Cleveland National Forest, early 2000s 196
13. Prescribed fire on Junco Meadow using diesel-fuel drip torches 198

Acknowledgments

Burn Scars was conceived, researched, and written in Tovaangar, the traditional, ancestral, and unceded territory of the Gabrielino-Tongva peoples, a landscape that encompasses the greater Los Angeles Basin and includes the village of Torojoatngna (now called Claremont, where I live and work). Two Tongvan elders, the late Julia Bogany and the late Barbara Drake, were vitally important mentors and teachers to many students, staff, and faculty of the Claremont Colleges. In their memory, a portion of *Burn Scars*'s royalties will be donated to the Tongva Taraxat Paxaavxa Conservancy. The conservancy is stewarding an acre in the foothills of Altadena, California, which was returned to the tribe in October 2022, making it the first land under its control since the early nineteenth century.

This collection of historic and contemporary documents has depended on the generosity of the editors of the journals, magazines, and newspapers where these texts originally appeared (each text is fully cited in the pages to come). I am especially grateful to modern Indigenous fire managers and analysts whose work graces these pages and for which they have been compensated. I have also been the lucky recipient of sage advice from other friends and colleagues, most especially Tilly Hinton, April Mayes, Steve Pyne, Doug MacCleery, and Paul Sutter. Ditto for the amazing folks at the Forest History Society, Jamie Lewis, Eben Lebman, Lauren Bissonette, and Steve Anderson, who have given me opportunities to speak about and provided an array of texts and images that illustrate *Burn Scars*'s narrative arc. Mike Wood and Raquel Romero of High Ridge Leadership have let me test out some of these ideas in the Forest Service's Middle Leadership Program. My next-door officemate, Preston McBride, was especially helpful with methodological and intellctual questions at a critical point in the book's development.

Burn Scars would not be in your hands without the ongoing support and editorial commitments of Kim Hogeland of Oregon State University Press; her colleagues at the press, including Tom Booth and Micki Reaman; copy editor Ryan Shumacher; as well as fire scholar David Carle and an anonymous external reviewer of the original manuscript.

No surprise, my students' engagement with these and other primary and secondary sources, and their agile and nuanced reading of this material, has helped me better understand these texts and their complicated contexts. At the Claremont Colleges Library, Lisa Crane, Jeanine Finn, Jennifer Beamer, and Kimberley Jackson, among others, have been essential to so many projects, *Burn Scars* not least.

Burn Scars is lovingly dedicated to the memory of my sister Kathy Miller Scogna (1949–2023), who lived in the oaked-studded foothills of the western flank of the Sierra Nevada through which the American River flows. During each fire season, especially the infernos that dominated the headlines in 2020–21, we would chat about about the extent of the defensible space around her home and the escape routes she might need to navigate if a blaze erupted nearby. In August 2021, we spent a smoke-filled afternoon outdoors rather than sit in the hospital waiting room jammed with Covid patients—one of many tough calls she made throughout her life. May her memory be for a blessing.

Fire Breaks: An Introduction

Burn Scars, a book about fire, was born of and by fire. Specifically, its inspiration came from the conflagrations that have swept across the western United States since the early 2000s. These megafires seem omnipresent in California, where I live and breathe. Eighteen of this state's twenty largest wildfires have erupted since 2003. More unnerving is that five of the seven largest fires lit up in August and September 2020. These blazes' speed, intensity, and size, the towns incinerated and lives lost, as well as the hundreds of thousands of residents who were fortunately and safely evacuated, were all unprecedented. For those who called the Golden State home during this moment, it was impossible to escape these fires' immediate residue: the smoke that burned our eyes, the acrid stench that inhibited our breathing, the white ash that twirled like snowflakes and clouded the sky. It is also no surprise that whatever their individual impact or collective consequences, these irruptions have generated an enormous amount of public comment and anguish. Each wave of fire that has engulfed the region has led me to rethink, rewrite, and reteach what I thought I had understood about wildfires past and present. *Burn Scars* has emerged from these reflections and engagements.

The larger cultural response, as reflected in digital, print, and electronic media, has been fascinated by and frightened of the clustering of this era's infernos; often, each significant outbreak has been dubbed with the ominous term "fire siege." What sparked them? Analyzing the sources of their ignitions has been site-specific—downed powerlines, vehicle sparks, arson, and even lightning. They are also global in origin. The warming of the planet, a consequence of the anthropogenic release of greenhouse gases, which began with the Industrial Revolution, has dried out large swaths of the US West. The decline in precipitation in the region has turned many forests and grasslands into kindling. They flare up partly because they are desiccated.[1]

---

1 The scholarly literature on fire in the United States is vast. Key works include Stephen J. Pyne's *Fire in America: A Cultural History of Wildland and Rural Fire* (Seattle: University of Washington Press, 1982), *The Pyrocene: How We Created the Age of Fire, and What Happens Next* (Berkeley: University of California Press, 2021), *Pyrocene Park: A Journey into the Fire History of Yosemite National Park* (Tucson: University of Arizona Press, 2023), and *To the Last Smoke: An*

Their increased vulnerability, many researchers argue, is also the result of a century-long suppression of fire on public and private lands. The key proponent of full-on suppression in the early twentieth century was the US Forest Service, then in its infancy. Its leadership, including first Chief Gifford Pinchot, argued that the practice of forestry, whose utilitarian purpose was to manage trees as a crop, required the protection of that economic good and thus its monetary value. Firefighting was the logical extension of the federal agency's mission. Yet announcing that mandate was not the same thing as implementing it successfully or fully. The Forest Service, and by extension other federal and state land-management agencies that followed its lead, did not have the budget, personnel, administrative infrastructure, or technology to accomplish its much-touted goal until after World War II. That was when these agencies secured the requisite funding, labor, and—not incidentally—surplus military bulldozers, chainsaws, and aircraft to battle wildfire across any terrain quickly, widely, and repeatedly. By this calculation, then, suppression qua suppression is but seventy years in the making.

That qualification notwithstanding, the Forest Service's aggressive commitment to fire suppression, as policy and prescription, as idea and intention, is critical to the narrative arc created by the documents collected in *Burn Scars*. The agency's announcement of its commitment to fire exclusion, as principle and precept, provoked its own firestorm. Centered in California and known as the light-burning controversy, the resulting debate pitted the federal agency against an assortment of Indigenous fire managers, timberland owners, ranchers, and other proponents of using fire to fight fire. These actors deployed cultural and controlled fire to burn forest underbrush to produce food, ritual and cultural materials, steward timbered assets, regenerate grasses for grazing, and clear areas for mining and other extractive uses. "Light burning" thus refers to these purposeful ignitions of fires; this concept now is often referred to as controlled or prescribed fires.[2] The Forest Service was strongly opposed to the use of any such conflagrations, and in the early twentieth century it fought hard to build an unassailable case against fire of any kind. Each side in the resulting twenty-year-long

---

Anthology (Tucson: University of Arizona Press, 2020); David Carle's *An Introduction to Fire in California* (Berkeley: University of California Press, 2021), and *Burning Questions: America's Fight with Nature's Fire* (Westport, CT: Praeger Publishers, 2002); Robert V. Cermak's *Fire in the Forest: A History of Forest Fire Control on the National Forests of California, 1898–1956* (Vallejo, CA: USDA Forest Service, 2005); Char Miller's *Natural Consequences: Intimate Essays for a Planet in Peril* (Santa Cruz, CA: Reverberations Books, 2022), 39–74, and *Not So Golden State: Sustainability vs. the California Dream* (San Antonio, TX: Trinity University Press, 2016), 127–160; and Lincoln Bramwell's "Understanding Wildfire in the Twenty-First Century: The Return of Disaster Fires," *Environmental History* 28, no. 3 (July 2023): 467–494.
2 Carle, *Introduction to Fire in California*, 11–12.

FIRE BREAKS: AN INTRODUCTION

Fig. 1. Special Agent J. T. Jardine fights a fire on the Wallowa National Forest in 1908. The fire is entering Ponderosa pine timber near Billy Meadow Ranger Station, Oregon. Credit: USDA Forest Service.

debate took to the media to make its case. A selection of these primary sources, and the points and counterpoints embedded within them, occupy the core of *Burn Scars* ("Light Burning and its Discontents"). Yet these sources must themselves be contextualized with reference to their historical antecedents in California and elsewhere in the nation ("Colonial Suppression"). Subsequent reassessments emerging in the Golden State and the West, and even more crucially in the South, led to a slow but significant shift in federal and state policies to reintroduce fire back into flame-adapted ecosystems throughout the country ("Bringing Fire Back"). The last word belongs to those who were on the ground first, and for whom fire was and remains a land-management tool of unparalleled significance—Indigenous nations ("Return Cycle").

RACE, GENOCIDE, AND FIRE SUPPRESSION

Embodying portions of each of these narratives about fire and its ecological import are the ghost trees that a young forester stumbled upon in the early 1970s while working on the Shasta-Trinity National Forest in Northern California. Because he was new to the region, Douglas MacCleery, who was then a timber-sale planner on the Hayfork Ranger District, made it a practice to familiarize himself with local forests; this led him to pounding "a lot of ground in pretty remote areas of the District." On one of these of these reconnaissance trips, he explored South Fork Mountain above the South Fork Trinity River, particularly "several hundred acres (maybe more) of about 120-year-old Douglas-fir forest." Tangled beneath the forest canopy, which soared one-hundred to one-hundred-and-twenty feet over his head, was a startling sight: a scattering of "live oak trees—a few still barely alive, but many dead." More astonishing than their presence was their size: "Many of the oak were huge—three-foot in diameter or more, often with large limbs spreading out relatively close to the ground. They had obviously spent their early life in an open grown condition."[3]

What had created these arboreal apparitions? How did this unusual ecological context emerge and what, if any, were its anthropogenic drivers? It was not until MacCleery met Tom Keter, then an archaeologist on the Six Rivers National Forest, which borders the Shasta-Trinity, that he gained a deeper understanding of the puzzling existence of these ghostly relics. Keter explained that "what I was seeing were the remnants of extensive areas of oak woodland and savannah that had been maintained by the Native peoples prior to them being displaced after the Gold Rush."[4] The Indigenous nations of Northern California (like those elsewhere) had used fire as a management tool to maintain the openness of the high ground that MacCleery had hiked through, as well as the valleys below.[5] By documenting the vegetation changes in southwestern Trinity County since 1850, Keter was able to confirm that fire had been used as a clearing agent in the area's grasslands and forests. Particularly pertinent to MacCleery's ghost trees was that between 1865 and 1980, oak woodland and savannah in the watershed of the North Fork Eel River had declined from covering 36 percent to 8 percent; conversely, Douglas-fir forests had increased from 11 percent to 47 percent.[6]

The implications of Keter's research, MacCleery recalled, was "a real revelation to me early in my career and substantially changed my perspective on the influence of native peoples in the pre-European landscape." Altered too was

---

3 Douglas MacCleery, email message to author, June 25, 2021.
4 MacCleery, email message to author, June 25, 2021.
5 Frank K. Lake, "Traditional Ecological Knowledge to Develop and Maintain Fire Regimes in Northwestern California, Klamath-Siskiyou Bioregion: Management and Restoration of Culturally Significant Habitats" (PhD diss., Oregon State University, 2007); M. Kat Anderson, *Tending the Wild: Native American Knowledge and the Management of California's Natural Resources* (Berkeley: University of California Press, 2005).
6 MacCleery, email message to author, June 25, 2021; Thomas S. Keter, "Overview of the Prehistoric and Historic Grasslands of the North Fork Basin of the Eel River" (paper presented at the 23rd Annual Meeting of the Society for California Archaeology, March 16, 1989), http://wordpress.solararch.org/wp-content/uploads/2021/02/Overview-of-the-Prehistoric-Historic-Grasslands-of-the-North-Fork-Eel-River-Basin-Trinity-County-CA..pdf.

the young forester's perception of those white settlers—miners, loggers, and farmers—who through violence and dispossession had disrupted the capacity of "Native peoples to be active managers of the landscape." In California, he concluded, "what happened to the Native Peoples would today be classified as genocide, plain and simple"[7]

He is not alone in that conclusion. Scholars and researchers—Indigenous and non-Indigenous alike—have confirmed what tribal communities have known for nearly three-hundred years: that the invasion that began with Spanish agents of colonialism in the mid-eighteenth century of what is now called California, which was amplified in the 1820s when Mexico claimed the former Spanish province and further intensified in the mid-1840s when the United States took control of the region, amounted to successive waves of genocidal assault. Regardless of the flag that flew over the various colonial outposts, whether mission compound, rancheria, or fort, or the languages these occupiers spoke, Spanish or English, the imperial objective in each case was to destroy the capacity of Indigenous people to live as they had lived for millennia. With deliberate intent, these settler-colonial empires struck at the independence of tribal communities and did so by challenging their ritual experience and cultural expression, their languages, foodways, and extended kinship relationships. The introduction of deadly diseases further decimated the once-robust Indigenous populations that inhabited the islands and coastal areas of California as well as its inland valleys and mountainous regions. Estimated conservatively at 300,000 on the eve of the Spanish incursion, the Indigenous population fell to roughly 150,000 by the end of the Mexican regime. This sharp decline was further accelerated during the first thirty years of American domination. Between 1846 and 1873, through state-sponsored eradication campaigns, which included the enslavement of children, forced removals, indentured servitude, and starvation, the Indigenous population plummeted to 30,000. Violence committed by non-Indians killed upwards of 16,000 Californian Indians during these years.[8]

---

7 MacCleery, email message to author, June 25, 2021.
8 Kari Marie Norgaard, *Salmon and Acorns Feed Our People: Colonialism, Nature, and Social Action* (Brunswick, NJ: Rutgers University Press, 2019); Anderson, *Tending the Wild*; Lake, "Traditional Ecological Knowledge to Develop and Maintain Fire Regimes in Northwestern California, Klamath-Siskiyou Bioregion," 272–273; Jean Pfaelzer, *California, a Slave State* (New Haven, CT: Yale University Press, 2023); Damon B. Akins and William J. Bauer Jr., *We Are the Land: A History of Native California* (Oakland: University of California Press, 2021); Benjamin Madley, *An American Genocide: The United States and the California Indian Catastrophe, 1846–1873* (New Haven, CT: Yale University Press, 2016); Brendan C. Lindsay, *Murder State: California's Native American Genocide, 1846–1873* (Lincoln: University of Nebraska Press, 2012); Jack Norton, *Genocide in Northwestern California: When Our Worlds Cried* (San Francisco: Indian Historian Press, 1979); Charles Sepulveda, "Our Sacred Waters: Theorizing

MacCleery's ghost trees offer another perspective on the comprehensive and destructive approach these invaders adopted in their individual and evolving attempt to dominate the region, literally to dislodge Indigenous landscapes and the people who had stewarded them. *Burn Scars* tracks the process by which the Spanish missionaries sought to limit—even fully suppress—the use of fire that had been key to the goods and services sustaining Indigenous lifeways. Controlling the land was critical to the control of people, Spanish military officers and Franciscan missionaries believed. That belief found legal sanction in 1793: Governor José Arrillaga issued a proclamation in which he ordered "*comandantes* of the presidios in my charge to do their duty and watch with the greatest earnestness to take whatever measures they may consider requisite and necessary to uproot this very harmful practice." This prohibition was essential, one missionary later declared, because fire was the tool of the "savage" and the heathen; suppressing fire was one way to "denaturalize" California Indians so that they could be more easily converted into "civilized" Christians. Racism and genocide were parts of a whole.

Like the Spanish, the US Forest Service was on a mission. Its staff was as zealous in its crusade to stamp out fire in the nation's grasslands and forests—with a special focus on California. Founded in 1905, by the 1920s the Forest Service managed more than one-hundred-and-fifty million acres of national forests, almost all of which were then located in the West; California was home to roughly twenty-million acres alone. The rapid growth of these newly designated federal lands directly impacted the Indigenous nations of the region, argues historian Theodore Catton. Between 1905 to 1909, for example, President Theodore Roosevelt, in collaboration with chief forester Gifford Pinchot, made frequent use of the General Allotment Act (first passed in 1887 and amended since) to shrink the size of reservations or dispossess individual Indians of their allotments. As the national forest system increased in size by an estimated ninety-seven million acres, Native American holdings shrank by eighty-six million acres. "The rise of conservation," Catton concluded, had dovetailed "with a national closeout sale on the Indians' landed heritage."[9]

In California, the situation was even more dire. Not only had the California Indian population been decimated by the mid-nineteenth century, Congress

---

Kuuyam as a Decolonial Possibility," *Decolonization: Indigeneity, Education & Society* 7, no. 1 (2018): 40–58; Ned Blackhawk, *The Rediscovery of America: Native Peoples and the Unmaking of U.S. History* (New Haven, CT: Yale University Press, 2023). Raising similar issues about race and the Forest Service in northern New Mexico in the twentieth century is Jake Kosek, *Understories: The Political Life of Forests in Northern New Mexico* (Durham, NC: Duke University Press, 2006), 142–227.

9 Theodore Catton, *American Indians and National Forests* (Tucson: University of Arizona Press, 2016). 40.

refused to ratify any of the eighteen treaties that the federal government nego-
tiated with 125 tribes in the state, which would have granted nine million acres
to a small number of Native polities. Without legal protections and because
in California, as elsewhere, those who secured some land through the allotment process often lost it through sales or theft, many of the state's Indigenous
peoples relied on "national forests and other public lands as their primary
traditional use areas."[10] This dependence did not mean they could use fire to
manage these landscapes as they had done for food and cultural and material
needs. Like the Spanish before them, federal foresters had determined that
because fire was the enemy of productive and profitable forest management,
those who advocated its use—like fire itself—must be suppressed. As Kari
Marie Norgaard notes, "The exclusion of fire from the landscape has led to
a dramatic reduction in the quality and quantity of traditional foods, negatively affected spiritual practices, threatened cultural identity, and infringed
upon political sovereignty."[11] To achieve that end, the Forest Service launched
a massive publicity campaign, which between 1910 and 1924 resembled a
scorched-earth attack: it demonized its challengers to such an extent that the
only acceptable resolution was for them to capitulate or convert.

One of the agency's tactics was to deploy a deeply troubling image of California Indians as part of its attempt at discrediting its white antagonists. When
those whites in favor of light burning linked their actions to the historic use
of fire by Indigenous people to sustain their resources and communities, the
agency and its allies mocked those claims with racist tropes. William Coman,
for one, scoffed at the argument Native people had for centuries burned the
forests: "To persons conversant with the Indian nature this is preposterous.
The Indians were nomads, who dwelt in skin tepees," and therefore had no
need for wood. Besides, systematic burning of the forests "would suggest a
desire by the redmen for the preservation of the trees for future use. But the
history of the Indians shows that they lived always in the present."[12]

The Forest Service denied another set of historical claims—Spanish missionary accounts, some of which are reproduced in *Burn Scars*—that corrobo-
rated active and deliberate Indigenous fire management. The agency's denial

---

10 Catton, *American Indians and National Forests*, 135; Robert B. Marks, "Dispossessed Again:
Paiute Land Allotments in the Mono Basin, 1907–1929," *Eastern Sierra History Journal* 4, no. 1
(2023), https://scholarship.claremont.edu/eshj/vol4/iss1/1/
11 Norgaard, *Salmon and Acorns Feed Our People*, 76; C. Eriksen and D. I. Hankins, "The Reten-
tion, Revival, and Subjugation of Indigenous Fire Knowledge through Agency Fire Fighting in
Eastern Australia and California," *Society and Natural Resources* 27, no. 12 (December 2014):
1288–1303.
12 Warren E. Coman, "Did the Indian Protect the Forest?," *Pacific Monthly*, September 1911,
300–306.

was based on a remarkable, if specious, assertion that Spanish missionaries and officers could not tell the difference between dried and burned grass. Strikingly, this argument remained in play well into the mid-twentieth century. In 1959, L. T. Burcham of the California Division of Forestry dismissed Spanish accounts while simultaneously impugning the existence of Indigenous fire management: "It appears highly improbable that the California Indians, lacking in manpower and physical facilities, and with but limited technological ability, would be able to burn on a systematic basis any but small tracts of land in which they were especially interested. Evidence is lacking that they made a concerted effort to burn major portions of their tribal holdings each year, or at intervals of a few years, as is sometimes contended." In other words, the Spanish did not know what they were observing.[13]

The Forest Service also derided traditional ecological knowledge and those who defended it. That was the thrust of a pair of letters that the journal of the California Fish and Game Commission published in 1916. The first, purportedly written by Klamath River Jack, opened with a stout defense of the continued use of fire as an ecological tool by Northern California Indigenous nations: "Fire burn up old acorn that fall on ground. Old acorn on ground have lots worm; no burn old acorn, no burn old bark, old leaves, bugs and worms come more every year. Fire make new sprout for deer and elk to eat and kill lots brush so always have plenty open grass land for grass." [14] Such flames produced food for humans and non-humans and a healthier forest; it was a sustainable process that the Forest Service fire-exclusion policies had interrupted to calamitous effect: "Now White Man never burn; he pass law to stop all fire in forest and wild pasture and all time he keep right on cutting out old wood on berry bush and fruit tree and cut brush off grass land and put medicine to kill worms and bugs."[15] In his rebuttal, forest ranger Jim Casey argued that *your fire is bad medicine* and was so because it destroyed the forest rather than protected it; it also stimulated the growth of thick brush that crowded out pine seedlings and made ranching near-impossible. Just as a fire-suppressed forest was being converted for colonial-settler logging and grazing, so too must Indigenous diets be altered: "there are other things that

---

13 L. T. Burcham, "Planned Burning as a Management Tool for California Wild Lands," unpublished report, California Division of Forestry, December 1959, 1–21.

14 The editor of the journal, in a prefatory comment about Klamath Jack's letter, raised a question about its source: "The Fish and Game Commission recently received an interesting letter, purporting to be written by an Indian in Del Norte County, which contained a plea for the burning of forest areas to destroy pests and renew growth." See Klamath River Jack and Jim Casey, "An Indian's View of Burning and a Reply," *California Fish and Game*, October 18, 1916, 194.

15 Klamath River Jack and Casey, "An Indian's View of Burning and a Reply," 194–195.

make better flour than acorns; why not plant some grain and vegetables and fruit trees on that flat back of your cabin? That's white man's grub, but its pretty good."[16] The condescension was integral to Casey's larger presumption—that Western foodways, like its technology, economics, and science—took precedence over all other ways of knowing.

At least Casey engaged with Klamath River Jack's ecological understandings, even if he rejected their contemporary applicability. The same cannot be said of W. W. Bergoffen, who worked for the Forest Service's Division of Information and Education. In the 1949 yearbook on trees for the US Department of Agriculture, this graduate of the New York State College of Forestry at Syracuse University offered an answer to the question of why "did the Indians start fires in the forests":

> Tradition says that they did so to drive game, but we have no positive proof that they did this as a regular custom over any area. The Indians had no matches and they used small campfires that they tended carefully; so, it is improbable that they set many fires. With the coming of the white man, and the cutting and clearing of timber, fires became more numerous and widespread.

By placing the query in the past tense, Bergoffen assured readers that Indigenous fires were a thing of the past; and, for want of modern matches, what burns they may have ignited had minimal impact (an amazing claim given that matches were only invented in 1840; which begs the question of how anyone created fire prior to that particular invention). His final sentence, which lays the onus of significant fire activity on the "white man," formally erases Native people as active agents on the land and in the historical record.[17]

THE LIGHT-BURNING CONTROVERSY

Although the Forest Service would not attempt to expunge white ranchers and loggers from the historical record for disagreeing with the agency's fire-suppression policies as they did Indigenous people, it nonetheless mounted a double-barreled attack on those who used controlled burning to sustain their extractive operations. The first shot was to lambaste these advocates as practitioners of "Piute forestry," a racialized slur designed to embarrass, if not

---

16 Klamath River Jack and Casey, "An Indian's View of Burning and a Reply," 195–196.
17 W. W. Bergoffen, "Questions and Answers," *Trees: The Yearbook of Agriculture, 1949* (Washington. DC: Government Printing Office, 1949), 26–27.

outright silence, anyone who doubted the Forest Service's expertise. Agency scientists in California, for example, were also strongly encouraged to produce data that would affirm the agency's fire-suppression arguments. Doing so, regional forester Coert duBois assured his research staff, would bring them into national prominence. "This work means big things. Those who contribute largely to it are going to be known in American forestry."[18]

In at least one case, these agency scientists literally cooked the results in service of the fire-exclusion cause. Because light-burning proponents usually cleared the areas around valuable timber before striking a match, Forest Service researchers S. B. Show and E. I. Kotok did the exact opposite: on a site near Snake Lake in the Plumas National Forest, they leaned large limbs and branches against several (already) fire-scarred pines and then ignited a fire.[19] The expectation was that the pines go up in smoke, thus "proving," as the two researchers noted in their widely read and cited 1925 study, that "light burning is a costly and dangerous practice" and that only "fire exclusion will promote real progress toward a fully productive forest property." Thirty years later, in an unpublished memoir, Show admitted what he had Kotok had done to ensure the "gratifying result that [the trees] burned down and became damage statistics."[20] Perhaps the most controversial aspect of the light-burning controversy, then, was the disconcerting tactics the Forest Service utilized to control public discussion and policymaking.

The climax of the long-running debate from the Forest Service's perspective had already occurred. Beginning in 1920, agency foresters participated in a multiyear, multiparty controlled-burning project near Yreka, California, to test the economic and environmental consequences of the use of light burning. Although the weather was either too wet or dry to conduct complete experiments, that did not stop the Forest Service from proclaiming victory three years later in the *Journal of Forestry*: "After three years of work the committee has not been able to find or to devise a fire protective system based upon the light-burning theory which seems more practicable and economical than that already in effect on the National Forests."[21] This resolution led regional forester Paul Redington to write an epitaph to the controversy for internal consumption: "The conclusions of the committee coincide with those reached by the

---

18 Coert duBois to D5 Supervisors, March 17, 1913, quoted in Diane M. Smith, *Sustainability and Wildland Fire: The Origins of Forest Service Wildland Fire Research,* FS-1085 (Washington, DC: U.S. Department of Agriculture, Forest Service, 2017), 16.

19 Smith, *Sustainability and Wildland Fire,* 28; S. B. Show and E. I. Kotok, *Fire and the Forest (California Pine Region)* (Washington, DC: Government Printing Office, 1925).

20 Show quoted in Smith, *Sustainability and Wildland Fire,* 28.

21 Donald Bruce, "Light Burning—Report of the California Forestry Committee," *Journal of Forestry* 21, no. 2 (February 1923): 133.

FIRE BREAKS: AN INTRODUCTION

Forest Service investigators three years ago," he noted in the regional newsletter. "The ghost of light burning is laid to rest."

This haunting conclusion had significant national implications, as was manifest in a series of congressional legislative initiatives. They first involved the Weeks Act (1911), which granted the federal government the power to purchase land from willing sellers in the upper reaches of river systems in the eastern United States. Over time, these sales added nearly twenty million acres to the Forest Service's inventory, which meant that these lands would be managed in strict in accordance with the agency's fire-suppression paradigm. One material symbol of this expansion of the Forest Service's efforts to fireproof the national forests in the East and South was the construction of fire-lookout towers that occupied mountains, ridgelines, and overlooks, a systematic approach then fully developed in California.[22] The second piece of legislation, the Clarke-McNary Act (1924), extended the fire-exclusion policy to state level; it did so by establishing the Forest Service as a conduit for federal dollars that would underwrite federal, state, and private collaborations for greater fire control, a financial incentive that recipients of this largesse found irresistible. And the third, the McSweeney-McNary Act (1928), poured millions of dollars into the Forest Service's research program, which, as historian James G. Lewis notes, gave the agency "a virtual monopoly over federal research on fire." A mark of this dominance was that the National Park Service, which was established in 1916, for the next half-century leaned heavily on the older agency's firefighting expertise, technologies, tools, and personnel.[23]

Another manifestation of just how dominant the Forest Service's fire-exclusion policy had become surfaced when researchers submitted articles that challenged the agency's position. In some cases, the writers self-censored their insights about fire as a regenerative force. Aldo Leopold, who in 1924 published an article about the positive role that fire played in establishing healthy ecosystems in what he called Arizona's brushlands, was careful not to extrapolate this claim to California, where fire exclusion dominated policy-making and implementation.[24] More direct challenges to the Forest Service's perspectives were often undercut when periodical editors attached disclaimers that rebutted the authors' arguments before readers encountered them.

---

22 Sally Atwater and Leighton Quarles, *Lookout: A History of Fire Control on the Southern National Forests* (Durham, NC: Forest History Society, 2023); Coert duBois, *Systematic Fire Protection in the California Forests* (Washington, DC: Government Printing Office, 1914).

23 James G. Lewis, *The Forest Service and the Greatest Good: A Centennial History* (Durham, NC: Forest History Society, 2005), 79–80; Hal K. Rothman, *Blazing Heritage: A History of Wildland Fire in the National Parks* (New York: Oxford University Press, 2007).

24 Aldo Leopold, "Grass, Brush, Timber and Fire in Southern Arizona," *Journal of Forestry* 22, no. 6 (October 1924): 1–10.

12   CHAR MILLER

That is what happened when S. W. Greene's essay, "The Forest that Fire Made," appeared in the pages of *American Forests*. "In this article, the author raises questions that will be warmly controverted," the editor noted—in italics, no less. "His conclusions that the longleaf forests of the South are the result of long years of grass fires and that continued fires are essential to the perpetuation of the species as a type will come as a startling and revolutionary theory to readers schooled to the belief that fire in any form is the arch enemy of Forests and Forestry." For good measure, the editor also indicated that Greene was not a forester and that the journal would not "vouch for the accuracy of Mr. Greene's conclusions."[25]

PUSHBACK

Over time, the Forest Service's paradigmatic control over the national conversation about fire control proved untenable—even in California. In fact, light burning there had never been entirely extinguished. Despite Forest Service prohibitions, for example, Indigenous people continued to use fire to manage resources, especially in remote Northern California.[26] Private landowners did, too, often abetted by a small number of sympathetic federal foresters.[27] Farther north, Indigenous and non-Indigenous foresters on the Klamath Reservation in southern Oregon and on the Colville and Spokane Reservations in eastern Washington were deploying controlled burning to regenerate ponderosa pine forests—and publishing reports of these fires' beneficial outcomes.[28] Moreover, academic and state-agency researchers and land managers were concluding that complete fire suppression, which the Forest Service took as Holy Writ, was having negative impacts on grasslands in Kansas and Arizona. From the southern longleaf pine forests emerged another set of critics. Among them was Herbert Stoddard, who, beginning in 1924, conducted extensive research on the role fire played in generating longleaf-grassland habitat for bobwhite quail in the Red Hills region of Georgia and Florida, pathbreaking work that would lead to the establishment in 1962 of the Tall Timbers Fire Ecology Conference.[29] In Montana in the mid-1930s, agency forester Elers Koch questioned

---

25 S. W. Greene, "The Forest that Fire Made," *American Forests*, October 1931, 584.

26 Lake, "Traditional Ecological Knowledge to Develop and Maintain Fire Regimes in Northwestern California, Klamath-Siskiyou Bioregion," 275.

27 Smith, *Sustainability and Wildland Fire*, 28–29.

28 Harold Weaver, "Fire and Its Relationship to Ponderosa Pine," *Proceedings: Tall Timbers Fire Ecology Conference* 7 (1967): 127–149, in which he describes learning to use prescribed fire while working on these reservations, beginning in the 1930s.

29 Herbert L. Stoddard, "Use of Controlled Fire in Southeastern Upland Game Management," *Journal of Forestry* 33, no. 3 (March 1935): 246–351; Albert G. Way, *Conserving Southern*

FIRE BREAKS: AN INTRODUCTION

whether complete suppression was the greatest good for some of forests in the Intermountain West.[30]

These many and varied challenges included internal researchers willing to discuss the damages resulting from a culture that stifled dissent. Among them was Inman Eldredge at the 1935 Society of American Forests annual conference:

> we foresters have fitted our practice always to the case in hand, but as regards fire, we have, for the main part, rallied behind the premise that the only way to manage any forest anywhere in the United States, from Alaska to Florida, is to cast out fire, root, stem, and branch, now and forever. We have, with closed ranks, fiercely defended this sacred principle against all comers and under circumstances and any forester who questioned its universal application was suspected of treason or at least was considered a dangerous eccentric.

If foresters refused to heed the recent scientific explanations of the multiple benefits from observed from controlled burning in the South, the consequences would be dire: "if these developments are ignored or misused there may be a widespread confusion and backsliding in forest practice and a consequent loss of public confidence in foresters, not only in the South but elsewhere as well."[31]

Thirty years later, Eldredge's insight into the Forest Service's culture of fire suppression above all else experienced an ironic upheaval. As early as 1960, agency leadership acknowledged the need for a critical reassessment of fire control at all costs. Its desires in this regard ran into a logjam of its own making, Herbert Kaufman reported. It "has taken considerably effort by the Forest Service leaders to overcome objections of some of their subordinates to 'controlled burning' as an effective and economical way of encouraging new growth in some kinds of forested areas," he wrote. "Even to experiment with the technique, the Forest Service had to engage in a large scale program of information and education for its own men, to sell them on the utility of at least *testing* it, and to overcome the overwhelming fear and hatred of fire

---

Longleaf: Herbert Stoddard and the Rise of Ecological Land Management (Athens: University of Georgia Press, 2011), 81–115; Leon Neel with Paul S. Sutter and Albert G. Way, *Art of Managing Longleaf: A Personal History of the Stoddard-Neel Approach* (Athens: University of Georgia Press, 2010).

30 Elers Koch, *Forty Years a Forester*, ed. Char Miller (Lincoln: University of Nebraska Press, 2019), 187–198.

31 Inman F. Eldredge, "Administrative Problems in Fire Control in the Longleaf-Slash Pine Region of the South," *Journal of Forestry* 33, no. 3 (March 1935): 244–245.

instilled in their in their training." Paradigms are difficult to break down, even for their creators.[32]

The dominance of Forest Service policy is one reason why, for Indigenous fire managers, bringing flames back to the land and scaling up the presence of flames has been a painstaking process. Another is that much of the once fire-adapted terrain in California has been fire-starved for so long—in the pre-colonial era between 4 and 12 percent of the state was annually burned, a proportion that would be impossible to replicate in an urbanized state that now has close to thirty million residents.[33] But the larger goal, in symbolic and real terms, is as much about politics as it is about ecology. The brutal infernos of August–September 2020 brought these historic and contemporary issues into sharp focus. As Don Hankins, a Plains Miwok fire expert and a pyrogeographer at California State University, Chico, put it: "In a perfect world, if the landscape of California was still stewarded continuously with Indigenous fire, we would definitely not see the same level of fires that we're seeing." Ron Goode, chairman of the North Fork Mono, was every bit as direct: "Removal of Native Americans from the land is the result of what we have today." Bill Tripp, the Karuk tribe's director of Natural Resources and Environmental Policy, shared Goode's insight and argued as well that fire as a tool is bound up with the (re)assertion of sovereignty. "If our Indigenous rights to burn would be recognized, and we could get some consistent and reliable funding mechanisms in place, then we could do it ourselves."[34]

Some of those barriers are beginning to collapse, though, a direct result of Indigenous activism and a related increase in legislative support for Native

---

32 Herbert Kaufman, *The Forest Ranger: A Study in Administrative Behavior* (Baltimore: Resources for the Future and the Johns Hopkins University Press, 1960), 82; Ashley L. Schiff in *Fire and Water: Scientific Heresy in the Forest Service* (Cambridge, MA: Harvard University Press, 1962), 115, notes that the agency's failure to heed warning such as Eldredge's was catastrophic: By "ignoring early caveats, the Service tragically slipped into a rut from which escape proved difficult and embarrassing. Thus had evangelism subverted a scientific program, impaired professionalism, violated canons of bureaucratic responsibility, undermined the democratic faith, and threatened the piney woods with ultimate extinction." By the 1960s, the National Park Service, which had followed the Forest Service's lead since its establishment fifty years earlier, began to adopt a more nuanced fire-management strategy; see Rothman, *Blazing Heritage*, 101–156.

33 Frank Kanawha Lake, "Indigenous Fire Stewardship: Federal/Tribal Partnerships for Wildland Fire Research and Management," *Fire Management Today* 79, no. 1 (January 2021): 30–39; Scott L. Stephens, Robert E. Martin, and Nicholas E. Clinton, "Prehistoric Fire Area and Emissions from California's Forests, Woodlands, Shrublands, and Grasslands," *Forest Ecology and Management* 251 (2007): 210.

34 All quotes from Ezra David Romero, "The Racist Removal of Native Americans in California Is Often Missing from Wildfire Discussions, Experts Say," CapRadio, September 16, 2020, https://www.capradio.org/articles/2020/09/16/the-racist-removal-of-native-americans-in-california-is-often-missing-from-wildfire-discussions-experts-say/; Lake, "Indigenous Fire Stewardship," 30–39.

FIRE BREAKS: AN INTRODUCTION

fire management from federal and state governments. The return of these Indigenous flames is rejuvenating such ecosystems as oak woodlands, upland meadows, and riparian habitat and reinvigorating the cultural resources and biodiversity they once sustained. They are also helping to incinerate some of the vestiges of a genocidal and racist past in which political repression, social erasure, and fire suppression have been fatally intertwined. To lay down cultural fires, in California and other fire-prone regions of the United States, has become and will remain an empowering act of sovereignty, restoration, and redemption.

A METHODOLOGICAL NOTE

Because there are no Indigenous written records of fire-management techniques and purposes from before the settler-colonial era, and because *Burn Scars* is centrally focused on the settler-colonial goals of fire suppression rather than detailed explorations of Indigenous burning practices, the documentary history portion of the book begins with Spanish-language diaries, journals, and correspondence. These texts, in which missionaries and military officials jotted down their impressions of Indigenous Californians' fire-management practices, provide indisputable evidence of the degree to which Indigenous people, from what is now San Diego north to the Bay Area, were putting fire on the ground. They were also training rising generations to do the same through a time-honored process of learning by doing. Even now, contemporary Indigenous fire managers relate that their first lessons were hands-on. Dawn Blake notes that she observed her grandmother used fire to generate basketry materials. Bill Tripp identifies his great-grandmother who, after watching him play with a book of matches, instructed him in the careful use of fire's potent force. The logical inference is that these elders also learned from their progenitors, a line of transmission—verbal and applied—that would have extended back into deep time.

The Spanish reports, then, represent the first literate representations of that reality; yet, their authors were not interested in collecting the oral histories that surrounded Indigenous fire use. That would be left to late-nineteenth-century American ethnographers like Stephen Powers. After interviewing tribal elders and white interlocuters in Northern and Central California in the early 1870s, he published a compendium of his observations under the imprimatur of the US Department of Interior.[35] Some of the stories Powers included in his

---

35 Stephen Powers, *Tribes of California, Contributions to North American Ethnography*, vol. 3 (Washington, DC: General Printing Office, 1877). The book is a revised and augmented version of seventeen essays the author published on Indigenous Californians for *Overland Monthly*.

book focused on the origins of fire, and at least one of them carried a cautionary message about the dangers that could result from its careless handling. I have chosen not to include these in *Burn Scars* due to ethical concerns about including oral histories gathered under colonial conditions. Powers's actions, in modern parlance, were a form of academic extraction: he took stories that were not his, published them, and was paid for his work, money he did not share with his interviewees.[36]

His transcriptions were also a form of social erasure. Pursuing his work on the assumption that Indigenous Californians—like other Native peoples of North America—would soon go extinct, Powers's transcriptions amounted to what he perceived as obituaries. Equally problematic is that Powers had no respect for the stories that California Indians shared with him, dismissing a Karuk "fable" about the origin of fire as a "very weak analogue to the Greek fire-myth of Prometheus."[37] Powers can only be considered an unreliable narrator.

Just as unreliable was Louis A. Barrett, an assistant regional forester in California. In 1924, while seeking confirmation of the agency's claims that Indigenous Californians did not use fire to steward their lands, he read Powers's 635-page tome. "In going over the book carefully one is struck by the fact that nowhere in it does the author intimate that the natives were in the habit of firing the valleys or the mountains even for the purpose of improving hunting conditions. Powers carefully describes the hunting practices of many tribes prior to and subsequent to the advent of the 'gold hunters,' but nothing is said anywhere to indicate that the Indians periodically burned over the country as many now contend." That led a gleeful Barrett to conclude: "Perhaps our present-day advocates of 'Piute Forestry' are not as well posted on early day Indian practice as they lead the public to believe."[38]

Had Barrett read more carefully, he might have reached a more tempered conclusion. Powers, for example, observed that the Yokut "used to fire the forests, and thereby catch great quantities of grasshoppers and caterpillars already roasted, which they devoured with relish, and this practice kept the underbrush burned out, and the woods much more open and park-like than

---

36 Adam J. P. Gaudy, "Insurgent Research," *Wicazo Sa Review* 26, no. 1 (Spring 2011): 113; Susan A. Miller, "Native Historians Write Back: The Indigenous Paradigm in American Indian Historiography," *Wicazo Sa Review* 24, no. 1 (Spring 2009): 25–45; Desi Rodriguez-Lonebear, "Building a Data Revolution in Indian Country," in *Indigenous Data Sovereignty: Toward an Agenda*, ed. Tahu Kukutai and John Taylor (Canberra: Australian National University Press, 2016), 254.
37 Powers, *Tribes of California*, 3:40.
38 Louis A. Barrett, "California Indians Not 'Light Burners,'" *California District News Letter*, November 7, 1924, 2.

FIRE BREAKS: AN INTRODUCTION

the present. This was the case all along the Sierra. But since about 1862, for some reason or other, the yield of grasshoppers has been limited. This is perhaps due to the effects of overgrazing by cattle and sheep."[39] Sometimes Powers got it right.

But only sometimes. That is why *Burn Scars* begins with a corrective: Michael Connolly Miskwich's overview of the history of Kumeyaay fire management in eastern San Diego County. It serves as an example of the cultural, environmental, and social import of Indigenous flames, then and now; and of the troubling impact of settler-colonial attempts to suppress them.

---

39 Powers, *Tribes of California*, 3:379. The use of fire to flush and roast insects, which had the associated advantage of clearing underbrush and regenerating grasslands that would attract another generation of grasshoppers, was extensive in California, notes M. Kat Anderson in *Tending the Wild*, 150–151, 167, 177, 260, 273.

Fig. 2. The Campo (Kumeyaay) Reservation fire truck stands guard over a prescribed burn on the Manzanita Reservation in eastern San Diego County. Credit: Stephen Fillmore.

Michael Connolly Miskwish: "Aaw e'Hunn (Good Fire)" (2023)

Fire is "aaw." For the Kumeyaay, a greeting starts with "haawka," from the fire within. Fire is both spiritual and physical. Fire destroys but also purifies; it kills but brings rebirth. Kumeyaay, as with most of the peoples from this place now called California, recognized and utilized fire as one of the most powerful and effective tools for ecosystem management.

For the Kumeyaay people, fire is one aspect of the interrelationship of plants and animals with humans, a reciprocal process that permeates their traditional lifeways. There is no single word we use to express this interrelationship, but some in the present day refer to the interrelationship as "e'Muht Mohay," or Love of the Land. In the practice of e'Muht Mohay, this relationship methodology is intertwined with understandings of cosmological balance and harmony. Some have even referred to it as a lifeway of ceremony. E'Muht Mohay also encompasses extensive wetland and riparian processes, groundwater-recharge enhancement, harvest methodologies, and plantings.

Fire was used for long-distance communications. Smoke signals were noted by members of the Serra expedition on their travel through the Kumeyaay lands in 1769. Later, Spanish military leaders commented on the signals back and forth during times of conflict. Fire was a tool to make other tools, hardening wood for tools or weapons. Fire altered the mechanical properties of stone that was used in creating grinding holes and shaping stone cutting surfaces. It plasticized sealants such as asphaltum and pine pitch.

Traditional Kumeyaay subsistence was varied and adaptive. The inconsistency of rainfall patterns meant that every year, resource use patterns could require readjustment to utilize alternative food sources. Acorns were a staple of the diet, but some years the oaks did not produce their usual bounty. Predator-prey population cycles could be greatly affected by climate swings. Yucca, agave, hollyleaf cherry, pine nuts, and other regularly used resources were subject to years of scarcity. At times this would necessitate fallback food sources such as manzanita seeds, scrub-oak acorns, and other less palatable plants.

Maintenance of the diversity of species required for traditional lifeways was primarily managed with fire. In the Kumeyaay Nation, this practice was used in differing ways for the habitats we now call the coastal sage, chaparral, oak woodland, and pine-cedar forest. In the coastal zone, fire was primarily a component of the traditional harvest of grasses. Fields were burned, and a portion of the seed harvest was broadcast by hand to seed the ground for the next harvest. The early Spanish colonialists observed this practice and referred to it as the Natives harvesting their "weeds" and setting fires.

The inland chaparral was subject to this traditional management, creating what is now referred to as the "fire mosaic." The many small burned areas created a multitude of transitional ecotones where various foods and medicines would grow in succession to the climax chaparral vegetation. The creation of the fire mosaic also allowed for a greater variety of plants to coexist in the many transitional ecotones. Additionally, the usual variability in rainfall patterns in the Kumeyaay region and the variability of plant populations meant a greater range of potential resources in case it was a bad year for any one specific species.

Many California plants need fire. Seeds need the scarification that comes with fire. Fire breaks down the protective coating of the seeds, allowing for germination. Natural fires can also serve this purpose, but excessive heat from natural fires may also destroy the seeds. The smaller scale of human-created fires encouraged a healthier ecosystem. Lower-heat fires also allow the roots of perennials to survive; their well-established root system, undamaged by fire, is key to the rapid regrowth of above ground shoots. These longer, stronger shoots provide much better material for baskets and cordage. They do not branch off as quickly as a plant that is just starting out. For Kumeyaay, basket grasses were generally subject to burns every three years to get the best productivity. Some of the plants, shrubs, and grasses that really like these kinds of transitional zones are chia, wild rye, sumac, deer brush, redbud, and deer grass. Some of these are for eating. Some are used for different types of basket weaving and other types of crafts. Medicinal and ceremonial plants also were enhanced by burned areas.

The margins of the ecotones were also attractive to deer, bear, mountain sheep, and other large animals. Smaller animals took advantage of the mosaic patterns by utilizing the woody climax vegetation as cover with proximity to the more open food sources within the burned areas. Going out into larger burned areas created a greater likelihood of becoming food for predators.

The oak woodlands were healthier and more productive under the fire regime. This was due to the reduction of fire-sensitive pests that might affect the trees or the competition from underbrush, which could also serve as a fire ladder, greatly exacerbating the effects of wildfires in unmanaged areas. The beauty and park-like appearance of oak woodlands were commented on by many visitors and migrants to Kumeyaay, as well as other California Native lands.

One important practice related indirectly to fire management was the use of rock-drop structures by the Kumeyaay. These structures are somewhat analogous to the dam structures created by beavers. At one time beavers were a significant factor in the creation of and sustaining wetlands in many parts of North America. In the drier areas of the country, including the Kumeyaay lands in what is now the California-Baja California region, humans supplemented that role by creating rock drops in stream channels with a corresponding beneficial enhancement of wetlands. Documentation of rock-drop usage goes back to the first Catholic mission in Baja California and is a documented part of the oral history of Kumeyaay. Modern practitioners have reintroduced this practice in many areas of the southwest. Recent documentation by Emily Fairfax of California State University, Channel Islands has shown a dramatic resistance to wildfires in the beaver created wetlands (Randall, 2021). Wetlands can also assist in the resiliency of the region by providing shelter for slower moving animals during the fire, thereby allowing a faster recovery afterward.

Long ago, as with people nowadays, Kumeyaay faced the issue of fire safety and thus had cleared areas around villages. Houses were highly flammable. Made of natural materials, they had designs suitable to different conditions. Kumeyaay had five general types of houses prior to European contact. One was made out of rock, but even this could have a thatched roof that would cover the top of it. The other homes were pyramidal, conical, A-frame, and dome-shaped. The most common house was a dome-shaped structure that was made using willow poles and thatching with whatever material was available. During the rainy season one of the preferred materials was tule. Tule was preferred because it expands when wet, providing protection from the rain, and shrinking when it dries out, so you would get good ventilation coming through your house. Unfortunately, it was also flammable. Other types of wood-frame construction might also substitute clay or other soils for thatching. Still, with the wood framing, it was only in exceptional circumstances that a fire would be inside the dwelling. To heat your home, you would bring in hot rocks from an external fire.

Fire maintained trails and village areas. Kumeyaay coexisted with mountain lions. At one time there were jaguars in their area. Grizzly bears were in San Diego County up until the 1930s, not to mention the five different kinds of rattlesnakes that might be sharing the path. Being able to see down the trail was an important thing.

In the land of the Kumeyaay, ignorance of the traditional relationships proved to be a restraining factor against the invading Spanish colonizers. "On all of New California from fronteras northward the gentiles have the custom of burning the brush," wrote José Longino Martínez in 1792. Father Crespí, who was part of the Portola expedition that brought Father Serra into California, noted in traveling from Santa Cruz to San Francisco twelve different cases of landscape burning.

The Spaniards commented that Kumeyaay people burned fields as soon as the harvest was complete, and they did not really understand the reasons why. In some writings, they described burning as a way of hunting rabbits. This was true, but rarely the main reason for burning; it was just a fringe benefit that came with it. Understanding the deeper meaning behind traditional burning was beyond their expectations of a population they deemed limited and inferior. They also remarked on the appearance the countryside, comparing it to a park, saying that God had cleared all the land for them. This was their explanation for the openness of the area under the canopy of the trees and the landscape.

Governor Fages of Monterey (1782–91) ended up prohibiting landscape burning. Although he acknowledged that the Indians were burning as a part of their harvesting of the grasses or the weeds as he called them, he still prohibited it. In 1793, Governor Joaquín de Arrillaga issued a proclamation that banned burning, which he characterized as childish behavior.

Without understanding traditional land management, the Spanish tried to introduce European agriculture and grazing. The European methods of agriculture (of course using many Native American crops) were mostly unsuccessful in Kumeyaay lands. This had a direct effect on the implementation of the colonial mission structure. In the missions, the preferred method of population control was to bring all of the neophytes under the direct control of the priests in the mission. In Kumeyaay lands this could not be done. Only a small portion of the converted population could live in the mission due to the lack of food production. Most of the villages of converts were allowed to continue living in a quasi-traditional manner, though burning was still restricted. This also aided the independent Kumeyaay in maintaining their control over the majority of their lands up to the coming of the American settlers in the 1870s and 1880s.

The Kumeyaay were successful in holding the Spanish presence to the coastal zone. It is these areas along the coast where the greatest impacts to the ecosystems occurred. Remnants of coastal sage habitat are now very rare. But at one time there was not only coastal sage habitat; there were also open areas where grasses were planted. There would be broadcast spreading of grass seeds, and following the harvest the area was burned. When the Spanish brought in their grains, they were adopted into the Kumeyaay practices.

Kumeyaay readily adapted to the introduction of European wheat by sowing and harvesting in the traditional manner. By the time the Spaniards had explored the more inland coastal areas north of San Diego they were surprised to discover wheat fields.

Conflict arose almost immediately after the introduction of European forms of agriculture and grazing animals into the ecosystem. Traditional harvest and burn techniques were not compatible with the use of the grasslands for pasturing. Still the desire to continue the practice of burning persisted even among the Christianized Indians. Eventually this resulted in Spanish proclamations and punishment for those who continued the practice.

After Mexican Independence in 1821, there was an increase in the establishment of ranchos by individuals (a few had been granted during the Spanish period). Most of these were clustered around the population centers. In 1833, there was passage of the Secularization Act, which resulted in the California government carving up extensive lands for grants to individuals. Under the act, 50 percent of the land was supposed to go to Native Californians and 50 percent to other Mexican citizens. In reality, the Indians received less than 10 percent of the rancho lands, and most of those went to Indians who were connected with the political power structure. But even with the creation of the ranchos, a large part of the state was still under the control of independent Indian people who were still doing their traditional practices. In the San Diego region, many ranchos were granted in the 1830s and 1840s; however, many never actually became fully functional. Widespread attacks from independent Kumeyaay forced their abandonment, with some being completely destroyed.

Diet for the inland populations of the Kumeyaay dramatically changed around 1900, as the Bureau of Indian Affairs (BIA) came in and started different programs on reservations, trying to shift people away from traditional foods. Wetlands were drained, and Kumeyaay were taught to use the plow and plant wheat, barley, and other mainstream crops. And, of course, fire was prohibited. For Kumeyaay, this was the opposite of the traditional view, which held wetlands and transitional ecotones to be productive inland habitats. Transitional ecotones were replaced by large acreages of plowed and planted crops. Oak forests were cut down to create more farmland and pasturage. The most productive lands for the traditional diet were replaced. One of the goals of the BIA was the creation of a cash economy through agriculture and ranching. Cash generated from tribal lands could be used to buy other foods and needed items. These were things like lard, beans, and salt, all of the foods that we think of as being part of the Western diet. As this diet began to take hold, the traditional Kumeyaay diet began to fall away, leading to increases in diabetes, obesity, and other ailments. The long-term effect on the wetlands was a gradual loss of water storage and fertility in the valleys. Oaks began to stress and die, and marginal cattle grazing became less and less viable.

Appreciation for the efficacy of traditional fire knowledge prompted an offer to aid the non-Indian community in the early twentieth century. An intertribal organization known as the Mission Indian Federation, headquartered in San Jacinto, sent a letter to President Calvin Coolidge in 1924, following a series of big fires in the San Gabriel and the San Bernardino Mountains. The Mission Indian Federation suggested to the president of the United States that they turn the national forests back over to the Indians. President Coolidge dismissed the suggestion, saying that the problems of the national forests required men of wide experience and training. Once again, as with the Spanish and Mexican governments, traditional knowledge and practices were seen as primitive and inferior, unworthy of understanding or emulation.

Can we reintroduce traditional land management? There are many opportunities to recreate elements of the fire mosaic. Some tribes cut and burn in piles under close scrutiny of firefighters. Others have been able to reintroduce a broader burn regime. Liability is a huge issue, which limits the scope of reintroduction programs, particularly in densely populated areas. On a more basic level, land-use planning itself must be modified to properly reflect the risk of building in fire-vulnerable corridors or slopes. There must be more emphasis on rural, village-style development that allows for broader swathes of undeveloped land where the mosaic can be maintained. The concepts of conservation need to include the variability and transitional nature of the habitat rather than attempt to hold habitats in static states. This understanding also needs to be incorporated into the planning for mitigation lands for endangered or threatened species. The reintroduction of traditional foods could also coincide, where possible, with the incorporation of traditional management techniques.

These are long-term strategies that may take many decades to implement and will probably need to be done incrementally. Success, however, will mean a much more sustainable strategy based on the contributions of traditional Kumeyaay fire-management knowledge and Western science.

References

Anderson, M. Kat. *Tending the Wild: Native American Knowledge and the Management of California's Natural Resources.* Berkeley: University of California Press, 2005.

Anderson, M. Kat, and J. E. Keeley. "Native Peoples' Relationship to the California Chaparral." In *Valuing Chaparral: Ecological, Socio-Economic, and Management Perspectives,* edited by E. C. Underwood, H. Safford, N. Molinari, and J. Keeley, 79–121. Cham, Switzerland: Springer, 2018.

Bird, R. Bliege, D. W. Bird, B. F. Codding, C. H. Parker, and J. H. Jones. "The 'Fire Stick Farming' Hypothesis: Australian Aboriginal Foraging Strategies, Biodiversity, and Anthropogenic Fire Mosaics." *Proceedings of the National Academy of Sciences of the United States of America* 105, no. 39 (September 30, 2008): 14796–14801.

Blackburn, Thomas C., M. Kat Anderson, and Ellen J. Lehman. *Before the Wilderness: Environmental Management by Native Californians.* Menlo Park, CA: Ballena Press, 1993.

Carrico, Richard L. *Strangers in a Stolen Land: American Indians in San Diego, 1850–1880.* Sacramento: Sierra Oaks Publishing Co., 1987.

Crespí, Juan. *A Description of Distant Roads: Original Journals of the First Expedition into California, 1769–1770.* Translated and edited by Alan K. Brown. San Diego: San Diego State University Press, 2001.

Crosby, Harry W. *Antigua California: Mission and Colony on the Peninsular Frontier, 1697–1768.* Albuquerque: University of New Mexico Press, 1994.

Cuero, Delfina, and Florence Connolly Shipek. *Delfina Cuero: Her Autobiography.* Ramona, CA: Ballena Press, 1991.

Godfrey, Anthony. *The Ever-Changing View: A History of the National Forests in California.* Vallejo, CA: USDA Forest Service, 2005.

Hohenthal, William D. *Tipai Ethnographic Notes: A Baja California Indian Community at Mid Century.* Novato, CA: Ballena Press, 2001.

Lewis, Henry T. *Patterns of Indian Burning in California: Ecology and Ethnohistory.* Ramona, CA: Ballena Press, 1973.

Manson, Bill. "Back to the Future: Campo Kumeyaays Relearn How to Revive Their Land with Ancient Tribal Methods." *San Diego Home/Garden Lifestyles,* May 2001.

Maxwell, Jessica. "The Campo Comes to Life." *Audubon,* May–June 1995.

Miskwish, Michael C., Stan Rodriguez, and Martha Rodriguez. *Learning Landscapes Educational Curriculum.* El Cajon, CA: Kumeyaay Diegueno Land Conservancy, 2016.

Miskwish, Michael C. *Kumeyaay –A History Textbook,* Vol. I, *Precontact to 1893.* El Cajon, CA: Sycuan Press, 2007.

———. *Maay Uuyow: Kumeyaay Cosmology.* Chula Vista, CA: Shuluk, 2016.

———. "Watersheds of the Southern Coast." Paper presented at 2009 California Tribal Water Summit, November 4, 2009, http://www.wrsc.org/sites/default/files/documents/pdf/watersheds_of_the_southern_coast.pdf.

Randall, Brianna. "Reviving Riverscapes." *Science News,* March 27, 2021.

Shipek, Florence Connolly. *Pushed into the Rocks: Southern Californian Land Tenure, 1796–1986.* Lincoln: University of Nebraska Press, 1987.

Part 1

Colonial Suppression

Fig. 3. Misión la Purísima Concepción de María Santísima (Mission of the Immaculate Conception of Most Holy Mary) was founded by Father Fermín de Lasuén, president of the California mission system, in December 1787. It was from this site that Fray Lasuén advocated tight controls over Indigenous use of fire. Much of the mission was destroyed in an 1812 earthquake, and a century later it lay in ruins. Credit: USC Special Collections.

Land of Smoke

The Spanish, intent on colonizing what they called Alta California, abhorred fire. What they abhorred about it was not its biochemical nature but its extensive use by the Indigenous people through whose territories the first Spanish entradas pushed in the mid-eighteenth century. Franciscan missionaries and military officers alike were surprised by the degree to which California Indians employed fire to manage various ecosystems and the services these fire-adapted landscapes generated. Although these outsiders, like Fray Juan Crespí and Captain Fernando Moncado, did not appreciate the beneficial outcomes of these routine, prescribed burns—initially they suspected that hunting and defense may have been their main purpose—in truth, Indigenous fire management was key to the production of food, clothing, and shelter, and an array of ritual and cultural materials. Give the Spanish credit, however, for seeing how often Native people inhabiting the coast and inland valleys burned their surroundings—and writing in their journals about the frequency of these burns and the mosaic-like patterns of areas charred and green. As ethnobotanist M. Kat Anderson argues in her seminal book, *Tending the Wild*, Indigenous fire management was "integral to the health and vigor of myriad species of plants and animals" and as such was "the basis of successful subsistence economies throughout the state."[1]

Disrupting these economies and the cultural fires on which they depended was central to the Spanish colonizing schemes. These involved an occupation by construction: the string of twenty-one missions, which were often associated with presidios and villas (towns), ran from present-day San Diego to the San Francisco Bay Area. Each was sited to take advantage of human and water resources. Each depended on Indigenous labor for myriad tasks: building churches, housing, and plazas; digging wells and irrigation ditches; and clearing, planting, and harvesting these communities' agricultural production.

To secure the necessary labor, missionaries and their military guards used force to convert Indigenous people and brutally treated Indigenous women,

---

1 M. Kat Anderson, *Tending the Wild: Native American Knowledge and the Management of California's Natural Resources* (Berkeley: University of California Press, 2005), 127.

the two actions being parts of a whole. Soldiers would set out from their encampments, Fray Junipero Serra wrote in 1773, to round up new labor, but when they were spotted Indigenous men and women tried to run away. "The soldiers, adept as they are at lassoing cows and mules, would lasso Indian women . . . who then would become prey for their unbridled lust." This rampant sexual violence in California, historian Antonia I. Castañeda asserts, "functioned as an institutionalized mechanism for ensuring subordination and compliance. It was one instrument of sociopolitical terrorism and control— first of women and then of the group under conquest."[2]

Another instrument was the 1793 Spanish prohibition of fire as a land-management tool that doubled as restriction on the California Indians' ability to maintain the land and the independence it provided. That is why José Joaquín de Arrillaga, then governor of Alta California, decreed that anyone caught violating his proclamation would receive the "most severe punishment." He hoped his proclamation finally would suppress what Fray Crespí earlier had observed: the ubiquity of fire-sculpted Indigenous landscapes.

---

2 Antonia I. Castañeda, "Sexual Violence in the Politics and Policies of Conquest: Amerindian Women and the Spanish Conquest of Alta California," in *Building with Our Hands: New Directions in Chicana Studies*, ed. Adela de la Torre and Beatríz M. Pesquera (Berkeley: University of California Press 1993), 15–29; Benjamin Madley, *An American Genocide: The United States and the California Indian Disaster, 1846–1873* (New Haven, CT: Yale University Press, 2016), 16–41.

Juan Rodríguez Cabrillo and Bartolomé Ferrelo Expedition (1542)[3]

On the following Sunday, the 8th of said month [October], they drew near to the mainland in a large bay which they called Bay of Los Furnas (Bay of Smokes),[4] because of the many smokes which they saw on [around] it.

---

3 Herbert Eugene Bolton, ed., *Spanish Exploration in the Southwest* (New York: Charles Scribner's Sons, 1916), 24–25.
4 This refers to Santa Monica Bay.

Sebastián Vizcaíno Expedition (1602)[5]

The Indians made so many columns of smoke on the mainland that at night it looked like a procession and in the daytime the sky was overcast. We did not land here because the coast was wild.

---

5 Excerpted from Bolton, *Spanish Exploration in the Southwest*, 79–80. The expedition anchored near the Coronado Islands off the coast of San Diego.

Juan Crespí, Diary (July 20, 1769–October 17, 1769)[6]

Thursday, July 20, 1769—We set out about seven in the morning, which dawned cloudy, and, taking the road straight to the north, we traveled by a valley about one league long, with good land, grassy, and full of alders. This passed, we ascended a little hill and entered upon some mesas covered with dry grass, in parts burned by the heathen for the purpose of hunting hares and rabbits, which live there in abundance.

Monday, July 24, 1769—We got up early this morning and broke camp at a quarter past six. Going north-northwest, we descended from the high hill on which we had stopped to a valley in the same direction. Before we left about nine heathens from a village in this valley allowed themselves to be seen. After traveling a short distance in it we came to two good villages, whose people were all very friendly. We greeted them in passing, and they made us their speech, of which we understood nothing. We traveled through this valley for about two leagues; it is of good land, but they had burned all the grass. From ridge to ridge it is about five hundred varas[7] wide. After two leagues' travel we turned to the northwest, veering considerably to the west, in order to climb a high pass through a range of grass covered hills;" and after traveling about a league over good mesas we descended to a pleasant arroyo, and a valley very full of large alders and live oaks, so that it looked like a fig orchard.

Sunday, July 30—After we two priests had celebrated Mass with all the people present, we started about seven and descended the hill, continuing to the north-northwest. We crossed the large plain, which has an extent of more than four leagues. To the west, far away, it seemed to communicate with the preceding valley, and in that direction some mountains were seen, with many trees at their base. Crossing the plain, we ascended a pass and entered a valley of very

---

6 Excerpted from Herbert Eugene Bolton, ed., *Fray Juan Crespí: Missionary Explorer on the Pacific Coast, 1769–1774* (Berkeley: University of California Press, 1927), 132, 137, 143, 197, 199, 214–16, and Juan Crespí, *A Description of Distant Roads: Original Journals of the First Expedition into California, 1769–1770*, trans. and ed. Alan K. Brown (San Diego: San Diego State University Press).

7 A vara equals roughly thirty-two inches. For a discussion of the vara, see Marcos A. Reyes-Martínez, "The Vara: A Standard of Length with a Not-So-Standard History," *Taking Measure* (blog), National Institute of Standards and Technology, October 11. 2019, https://www.nist.gov/blogs/taking-measure/vara-standard-length-not-so-standard-history.

34 COLONIAL SUPPRESSION

large live oaks and alders. We then descended to a broad and spacious plain of fine black earth, with much grass, although we found it burned.

August 5, 1769—This is a large valley that must be not less than six leagues in length from east to west; its width from north to south is not under three leagues; all of it very good, very grass-grown soil, though most of it had been burnt off; many patches however had not been, where grass still showed.

August 20, 1769—We went over land that was all of it level, dark and friable, well covered with fine grasses, and very large clumps of very tall, broad grass, burnt in some spots and not in others; the unburned grass was so tall that it topped us on horseback by a yard. All about are large tablelands with big tall live-oaks (I have never seen larger), and many sycamores as well. We have come across rose-patches in such great amounts that the plains here were full of them in many spots.

August 22, 1769— ...[I]n sight of the shore, over some low rolling tablelands with very good dark friable soil and fine dry grasses; in many places it had all been burnt off. It was all flat land, excepting only some short descents into a few dry creeks. If it can be dry-farmed, all the soil could be cultivated. Shortly after we left this point, the great live oaks at this spot dropped behind us.

August 29, 1769—We set out from the San Juan Bautista Village on a due northwest course, across level ground near the shore. We soon passed the second point, and made out still another afar off, making a sort of large bight. We went almost all the way over salt-grass, all very much burnt off by the heathens, with some descents to dry creeks. On going about a league and a half, we reached a stream [Honda Canyon] with a good amount of fresh water emptying into the sea, but no village nor soil of any worth upon it. The soldiers had scouted up to this point, and it was not a full day's march, nor was there grass for the animals, as it had all been burned off. ... On going about three hours in which we must have made about two leagues and a half, we came to a hollow where the heathens had said there were some pools of water, and although it had been burned off, there were spots that had not been and where there was good grass for the animals. ...

Thursday, September 28, 1769—We set out early in the morning, which was very cloudy, and followed the same valley and river by a level road, the grass all burned. As we approach the seacoast, the valley goes on widening, and in places the plain has a width of two leagues, in others still more. We traveled five

LAND OF SMOKE 35

hours, during which we must have made four leagues, and halted in the same plain of the valley in the midst of a grove of live oaks, which had a little pasture that had not been burned. Because the land had a whitish color it was called Real Blanco. Although we have come across many roads and paths beaten by the heathens, we have not seen one of them; some bands of antelopes were seen, but not within gunshot.

October 24, 1769—We set out at a quarter before nine in the morning from here at the small Saint John Nepomucene valley, course due northward—in company with four heathens belonging to this spot who came with us to show us the next watering places and villages—in view of the shore, over very big high ranges of knolls, all with very good soil and very grass-grown, though the grasses had almost all been burnt—everything being very bare of trees; only in the gaps between the knolls could be seen the white range of mountains in back, continuing still overgrown with pinewoods.

October 30, 1769—We set out at about nine o'clock in the morning from this stream and plain of the aforesaid Holy Apostles, following a northwestward course along the shore, packing wood with us from the stream belonging to this spot—where there is some—as the scouts had reported seeing no wood wherever they had explored. Close to the shore, there ran on some tablelands and rolling knolls with very good soil and very good grass, though the latter all burnt, since the heathens burn it all off in order for a better yield of the grass seeds that they eat.

November 7–10, 1769—[W]e went up a knoll and once again saw the inlet still continuing on down southeastward and southward, the same course that we had been bearing. It was all level land, seemingly of many leagues' extent, the entire plain being very good, dark, very grass-grown soil—although most of the grasses had been burnt off—and the entire plain much grown over with a great many large white oaks and live oaks.

May 7, 1770—we started from the San Juan Bautista de los Pedernales village and point here, keeping on a northwesterly course over very grassy level land near the shore. We shortly passed the point here, and in the distance made out another that formed still another bight. At once after setting out, we commenced to find the fields all abloom with different kinds of wildflowers of all colors, so that, as many as were the flowers we had been meeting all along the way and on the Channel, it was not in such plenty as here, for it is all one mass of blossom, great quantities of white, yellow, red, purple, and blue ones; many yellow violets or gillyflowers of the sort that are planted in gardens, a great deal of larkspur, poppy and sage in bloom, and what graced the fields most of all was the sight of all the different sorts of colors together. On going about a league and a half, we came down to a deep creek in a hollow where there is a good deal of grass and a good-sized stream of running water.... On this whole march, three leagues from the point of San Juan Bautista de los Pedernales, we have seen not a bush nor a single heathen.[8]

May 29, 1770: There is a great deal of fallen timber, half burnt, since the heathens burn off everything.

---

8 "These spectacular wildflower displays were seen in the very same area which Crespí had noted as having been burned the previous summer," observes Jan Timbrook, John R. Johnson, and David D. Earle, "Vegetation Burning by the Chumash," *Journal of California and Great Basin Anthropology* 4, no. 2 (Winter 1982): 167.

Captain Fernando Rivera y Moncada, Diary (October 3, 1774)[9]

There came a fire from the west that was burning the forage of the countryside, and as it neared the Presidio, the soldiers, servants and even I went out to fight it, not because of the danger to the houses but to preserve the grass for our animals. We managed to extinguish it. The heathens are wont to cause these fires because they have the bad habit, once having harvested their seeds, and not having any other animals to look after except their stomachs, they set fire to the brush so that new weeds may grow to produce more seeds, also to catch the rabbits that get confused and overcome by the smoke.

---

9 Quoted in C. Raymond Clar, *California Government and Forestry* (Sacramento: Division of Forestry, Department of Natural Resources, State of California, 1959), 7.

Fernando Rivera y Moncada, Diary (April 24, 1776)[10]

Having made beforehand in this Diary extensive report of this road, [and] given information about the villages of the Santa Barbara Channel, it has seemed to me [proper] not to repeat [this], since I have not had the least novelty in my [most recent] journey. I have experienced great drought [here], therefore some of the springs along the road I have passed [are] dry; this is something that has not happened to me since I entered these lands, and in the countryside [there has been] extreme need of pasture for the animals, which in some areas has caused me difficulty in staying overnight and even in stopping at midday, due to the horses and mules not having grass, all occasioned by the great fires of the gentiles, who, not having to care for more than their own bellies, burn the fields as soon as they gather up the seeds, and that [burning] is universal, although on some occasions it happens that it may be greater or less. . . .

---

10 Quoted in Timbrook, Johnson, and Earle, "Vegetation Burning by the Chumash," 168–169.

José Longinos Martínez, Journal (1792)[11]

In this part of the Santa Barbara Channel ... if a chief merely makes an attempt to pass through another's jurisdiction, fighting and quarreling result, so great is the distrust that these nations have of one another. ... Their wars are frequent and always originate over rights to seed-gathering grounds, or in disputes over concubines. ... The gentiles living between San Diego and San Buenaventura store up against the winter the plants that bear the most seeds. ... These nations [north of Santa Barbara] continually keep on hand small baskets of seeds and other foodstuffs. ... In all of New California from Fronteras northward the gentiles have the custom of burning the brush, for two purposes: one, for hunting rabbits and hares [because they burn the brush for hunting]; two, so that each first light rain or dew the shoots will come up that they call pelillo [little hair] and upon which they feed like cattle when the weather does not permit them to seek other food.

---

11 Quoted in Lesley Byrd Simpson, trans. and ed., *Journal of José Longinos Martínez: Notes and Observations of the Naturalist of the Botanical Expedition in Old and New California and the South Coast, 1791–1792* (San Francisco: J. Howell Books, 1961), 58–59.

José Joaquín de Arrillaga, Fire Proclamation (May 31, 1793)[12]

With attention to the widespread damage which results to the public from the burning of the fields, customary up to now among both Christian and Gentile Indians in this country, whose childishness has been unduly tolerated, and as a consequence of various complaints that I have had of such abuse, I see myself required to have the foresight to prohibit for the future (availing myself, if it be necessary, of the rigors of the law) all kinds of burning, not only in the vicinity of the towns, but even at the most remote distances, which might cause some detriment, whether it be by Christian Indians or by Gentiles who have some relationship or communication with our establishments and missions. Therefore I order and command all comandantes of the presidios in my charge to do their duty and watch with the greatest earnestness to take whatever measures they may consider requisite and necessary to uproot this very harmful practice of setting fire to pasture lands, not omitting any means that may lead to the achievement of the purpose which I propose in this order, to which effect they will publish it in their respective jurisdictions with particular charge to the corporals of the guard, commissioners, and magistrates of the towns that they exercise equal vigilance in trying to advise the Christian Indians and the Gentiles of the neighboring rancher as about this proclamation and impressing upon them that those who commit such an offense will be punished, and in case some burning occurs, they are to try immediately to take the most appropriate means to stop the fire, or failing that, to direct it into another direction which may result in less damage, apprehending the violators, of whatever class or sex, who would be punished in accordance with the degree of malice there may be on the part of the offenders; and in order that there may be no obstacle to the observance of this order, I beg and charge the Reverend Fathers, priests of the missions, that they do their part in instructing the Christian Indians not to commit such transgression. And in order that it come to the attention of all and that nobody may allege ignorance, I order that this decision of mine be published by proclamation in the presidios as well as the missions and towns

---

12 Quoted in Timbrook, Johnson, and Earle, "Vegetation Burning by the Chumash," 170–172.

of this province which is in my charge, making it be known to all classes of Indians, Christians as well as Gentiles, and repeating its publication annually, with the full understanding that whatever lack of observance may be noticed in this matter [which is] of such great interest will be worthy of the most severe punishment. Given in Santa Barbara, May 31, 1793.

Missionary Questionnaire (1798)[13]

After accusations from Fray Antonio de la Concepción Horra that Spanish missionaries mistreated Indigenous Californians, the viceroy directed Governor Diego de Borica to assess the situation. The governor submitted a questionnaire to presidio commandants, and after reading through the responses, he reported to his superiors that "generally, the treatment given the Indians was very harsh."

Question 12: What sorts of punishments are meted out to the neophytes? Differentiate for the sexes. For what sort of transgressions are they punished? Do the fathers have shackles, chains, stocks, and lockups, or whether they only make use of the means of punishment available to the members of the guard.

Answer:. . . The misdeeds for which we fathers chastise the Indians thus are concubinage, theft, and running away. When the transgressions are against the common good, like killing cattle, sheep, or firing pastures, which has occurred sometimes, the corporal of the guard is notified.

---

13 This text is drawn from answers submitted by Father Gregorio Fernández at Mission La Purísima, which was close to present day Lompoc and located in Chumash territory. This extract comes from Timbrook, Johnson, and Carle, "Vegetation Burning by the Chumash," 172. For context, see Lee M. Panich and Tsim D. Schneider, eds., *Indigenous Landscapes and Spanish Missions: New Perspectives from Archaeology and Ethnohistory* (Tucson: University of Arizona Press, 2014), 138.

Fermín Francisco de Lasuén (1801–02)[14]

1801: The uncultivated soil supports their manner of life, which differs little from that of the lower animals. They live on herbs while they are in season, and then gather the seeds for the winter, and as a rule, they celebrate the end of it by holding a feast dance. They satiate themselves today and give little thought to tomorrow. Here, then, we have the greatest problem of the missionary: how to transform a savage race such as these into a society that is human, Christian, civil, and industrious. This can be accomplished only by denaturalizing them. It is easy to see what an arduous task this is, for it requires them to act against nature. But it is being done successfully by means of patience, and by an unrelenting effort to make them realize that they are men.

June 16, 1802: There is no doubt that in all the pagan Rancherias heathen practices prevail. Who will remove the opposition which the Christians encounter, if they continue to live among their tribesmen at the very scene of those heathen customs? And who will prevent them at the same time from joining their tribesmen or even witnessing the orgies? Accustomed to their abominable feasts, and every hour finding their recollections revived, what place will they give to the catechism, and to the obligations contracted in Baptism which they have received? They possess no energy to apply themselves to what is conducive to a rational, social, and civilized life. Upon the vigilance of the missionaries and their incessant care it then necessarily depends that they observe what they have learnt; for it is indeed not only to this manner of life that the king wants the Indians to be brought, but to the Christian way. How will this royal and Catholic intention be carried out if the Indians are left to their wild freedom and in their Rancherias after they have been baptized?

---

14 Quoted in Panich and Schneider, eds., *Indigenous Landscapes and Spanish Missions*, 138–139.

Fig. 4. This Yosemite Valley panorama was first published in James Mason Hutchings's *Scenes of Wonder and Curiosity in California* (1862), a tourist guide to the remote valley. Note the open quality of the landscape, a result of Indigenous fire management.

Nineteenth-Century Settler-Colonial Observations

Indigenous fire-management practices, which the Spanish attempted to suppress, were well known to many non-Indigenous nineteenth-century settler observers across the country. Their observations add important context for framing the Forest Service's later insistence that the Indigenous people of California and the West had not regularly deployed fire as a land management tool. R. W. Wells would have scoffed at the agency's early-twentieth-century claim. In 1819, he asserted Indigenous people had intentionally used fire to create and maintain the vast midwestern prairies, and subsequent settler-colonial generations reaped the benefits of their ecological stewardship. In pre–Civil War California, another set of fire-dependent ecologies caught the attention of two travelers who kept extensive notes about these blazes' terrible and terrifying beauty. Alfred Robinson left an engrossing account of a fast-moving fire in the foothills above what is now called Ventura. Although published in 1831, his description of its growth, speed, and intensity—and its blackened aftermath—sounds strikingly familiar to reports of wildfires in the same coastal hills nearly two hundred years later. Duflot de Mofras's 1841 recounting of the behavior of wildfires in the central coast mountains north to San Francisco also seems fully contemporary. No less intriguing is his suggestion that the firefighting tactics that the Spanish missions utilized when confronted with wildfire no longer prevailed under Mexican rule.

No sooner had California become a state in 1850 than it passed legislation (and again in 1871–72) that sought to curtail Indigenous and settler use of fire, a prohibition with which some American scientists agreed.

John Wesley Powell and Franklin Hough would have been among them. In the late 1870s, Powell, then director of the US Geological Survey, believed that the major conflagrations that tore through the Rockies and Wasatch ranges were the result of Indigenous hunting practices. Protecting the forests and the white settlements that depended on the extraction of this resource led Powell to this simple equation: "The fires can . . . be very greatly curtailed by the removal of the Indians." Over at the US Division of Forestry, its director Franklin Hough was reaching a similar conclusion. Through a survey method that resembled crowdsourcing, he put out a call for white settlers in the region to write the bureau about the sources of the devastating fires that annually wracked the western region. Many of the correspondents blamed Native people for these damaging ignitions.

Not all settler-colonials agreed. Poet and raconteur Joaquin Miller was not alone in his belief that Indigenous fire-management practices benefited the forests of the West, protecting their health and resilience. William Mills concurred. During his service as a Yosemite Valley State Commissioner in the 1880s, he came to understand that the open pastures and park-like forest cover was a result of deliberate Indigenous use of fires to clear away the undergrowth and cultivate desired trees, shrubs, and tubers. If fire was excluded, as was happening already in Yosemite and much of the rest of the state, Mills warned, the results could be catastrophic.

R.W. Wells, from "On the Origin of Prairies" (1819)[1]

The probable cause of the origin and continuance of prairies has been the subject of much speculation among the learned and curious. The inquiry is interesting; and many theories have arisen; but although plausible and ingenuous, they are, in my opinion, unfounded in fact. R. W. Wells

... The writer of this having often visited and observed with attention the nature and appearance of the prairies of the Allegheny mountains, in the states of Ohio, Indiana, and Illinois, and having long been employed by the United States as a surveyor in the prairie country of the Missouri and Mississippi ... is of the opinion that the vast prairies and barrens, extending over the greater part of the western states, and over nearly all [of the] Louisiana [Purchase], was primitively occasioned, and have been since continued, by the *combustion of vegetables*[2], and that water has not agency in their creation. ...

Prairies are found only in those countries that are congenial to the growth of grass, and only where the soil is sufficiently rich to produce it luxuriantly— they are found commonly on high plains, sufficiently drained to prevent water from remaining on them the whole year; for it is by no means necessary that they should always be dry; only the contrary, if they are sufficiently level, to prevent the rains from running off immediately, the grass will grow thicker and higher—but they must be sufficiently dry to burn, at least once in two or three years, during the long dry season, called *Indian Summer*. It has been universally remarked that these seasons are much longer as we proceed westerly—commencing usually in October, and continuing a month and a half to two months, during which the vegetation is killed by the frosts, and dried by the sun; the wet prairies are also dried, and before the season has expired, the grass is perfectly combustible.

The Indians, it is presumed, (and the writer, from residence in their country and with them, is well acquainted with their customs), burn the woods, not *ordinarily* for the purpose of taking or catching game ... but for many other advantages attending that practice. If the woods are not burned as usual, the hunter finds it impossible to kill the game, which, alarmed at the great noise made in walking through the dry grass and leaves, flee in all directions at his

---

1 Extracted from R. W. Wells, "On the Origin of Prairies," *American Journal of Science* 1 (1819): 331–337.
2 Vegetables in this case refers to vegetation.

approach. Also, the Indians travel much in the winter, from one village to another, and to and from the various hunting grounds, which becomes extremely painful and laborious, from the quantity of briars, vines, grass, etc. To remedy these and many other inconveniences, even the woods were originally burned so as to cause prairies, and for the same and like reasons, they continue to be burned towards the close of the Indian summer.

Woodland is not commonly changed to prairie by one burning but by several successive conflagrations; the first will kill the undergrowth, which causing a greater opening and admitting the sun and air more freely, increases the quantity of grass the ensuing season; the conflagration consequently increases, and is now sufficiently powerful to destroy the smaller timber; and on the third year you behold an open prairie.

Ordinarily, all the country, of a nature to become prairie, is already in that state; yet the writer of this has seen, in the country between the Missouri and Mississippi, after unusual dry seasons, more than one hundred acres of woodland together converted into prairie. And again, where the grass has been prevented from burning by accidental causes, or the prairie has been depastured by large herds of domestic cattle, it will assume, in a few years, the appearance of a young forest. Numerous proofs of this fact can be adduced but a few shall suffice. The vicinity of St Louis and St Charles affords instances. Both these beautiful places are situated on what are termed first and second bottoms or flats—the former on the Mississippi, the latter on the Missouri; the second or upper bottoms, in both, are high plains that commence within a few hundred yards of the rivers and extend back many miles; all the old French inhabitants will tell you that the prairies formerly came immediately up to those places. Now, the surrounding country for several miles is covered with a growth of trees of four or five inches in diameter, near the towns where the burning first ceased, and gradually diminishing in size as you recede, until you at length gain the open prairies. So the barrens in Kentucky; many of the first settlers of that state distinctly recollect when many of those barrens were clear prairies, now partially covered with small trees. It is deemed unnecessary to offer more proofs, or additional arguments, in support of the opinion that the prairies were occasioned by *fire* and not by *water*. Indeed, one glance at the maps of those extensive prairie countries, surveyed by order of government, where the prairies and woodland are distinguished and correctly delineated, should carry conviction. The timber will be there observed to skirt the rivers; in the country near their sources a few solitary trees are seen, close on the banks, secure from the fires, and increasing in numbers as the rivers increase in size and the low grounds become more extensive. . . .

Alfred Robinson, from *Life in California* (1831)[3]

About this time, we were much alarmed in consequence of the burning of the woods upon the mountains. For several days the smoke had been seen to rise from the distant hills of San Buenaventura,[4] and gradually approach the town. At last it had reached the confines of the settlement and endangered the fields of grain and the gardens. Soon it spread low upon the hills, and, notwithstanding a strong westerly wind was blowing, the flames traveled swiftly to windward, consuming everything in their course. It was late at night when they reached the rear of the town, and as they furiously wreathed upwards, the sight was magnificent, but terrible. The wind blew directly upon the town, and the large cinders that fell in every direction seemed to threaten us with certain destruction. The air was too hot to breathe. The inhabitants fled from their homes to the beach, or sought the house of Señor Noriega, where prayers were offered, and the saints supplicated. The vessels at anchor in the bay were also much endangered, for their decks were literally covered with the burning cinders, and their crews incessantly employed in keeping them wet. During the entire night the ravages of the fire continued, and when daylight broke it had seized upon the vineyard belonging to the Mission. Here the green state of vegetation somewhat checked its progress, and it passed over to the mountains again, to pursue its course northward. On the uplands everything was destroyed, and for months afterwards the bare and blackened hills marked the course of the devastating element.

---

3 Alfred Robinson, *Life in California* (1846; San Francisco: W. Doxey, 1891), 109–110.
4 Today known as Ventura.

Duflot de Mofras, from *Travels on the Pacific Coast* (1841)[5]

Sometimes while traveling, one is amazed to see the sky blanketed with black and copper-colored clouds, to experience a stifling heat and to watch a fine rain of falling ash. The causes of these conflagrations in the forests and savannahs are the result of the negligence of Indians or whites, who, after lighting campfires, forget to extinguish them when they leave. These fires often last for several months and spread from one end of the province to the other, to the point of hindering travel. Woe to those who are caught in the flames in the valleys and plains, where the grass often rises to nine and ten feet, or in the woods, which have no marked roads! While traveling over the Santa Cruz Mountains to reach the Mission of Santa Clara, we spent several hours wandering in the middle of a burning forest, dodging falling branches and blinded by the ashes. The fire spooked the horses, which no longer recognized their route and were so frightened that they would have let themselves be burned on the spot. Bears, antelopes, deer run here and there, and we have seen the latter pursued by the fire on the eastern coast of the port of San Francisco, throw themselves into the sea without fear of sharks, and swim to the islands of the bay.

Under Spanish rule, as soon as a fire broke out, companies from the presidio and neophytes from the Missions arrived by the hundreds, armed with axes, and in a short time they managed to control the flames. Now the negligence is such that during our stay in Monterey, when a forest fire swept through the woods that dominate Point Pinos [now Monterey Peninsula], and which are but two or three hundred steps from the houses of this city, no one made the slightest attempt to extinguish the blaze.

Yet a burning plain is a magnificent spectacle. The flames run through the grasses of the savannah, envelop the wooded hillsides, and meander to the top of the trees, devouring the woody vines and other climbing plants. The ash trees, the sycamores, the oaks burn in their entirety, but the trunks of the pines, which would seem to be the first to be consumed, resist because of the thickness of their bark; one can only see long tears of transparent resin flowing down their trunks, while the fire projects a reddish glow, and the strong breezes from the northwest carry away clouds of ash and smoke.

---

5 Duflot de Mofras's two-volume account of his observations was first published in Paris in 1884. This extract is from Marguerite Eyer Wilbur, trans. and ed., *Duflot de Mofras' Travels on the Pacific Coast* (Santa Ana, CA: Fine Arts Press, 1937), 2:23.

California Statutes: First Session (1850)[6]

10. If any persons or person shall set the prairie on fire, or refuse to use proper exertions to extinguish the fire when the prairies are burning, such person or persons shall be subject to fine or punishment, as a Court may adjudge proper.

---

6 California State Statutes, First Session, Chapter 133, § 10:409.

California, An Act to Prevent the Destruction of Forests by Fire on Public Lands (1871–72)[7]

Section. 1: Any person or persons who shall willfully and deliberately set fire to any wooded country or forest belonging to this State, or the United States, within this State, or to any place from which fire shall be communicated to any such wooded country or forest, or who shall accidentally set fire to any such wooded country or forest, or to any place from which fire shall be communicated to any such wooded country or forest, and shall not extinguish the same, or use every effort to that end, or who shall build any fire, for lawful purpose or otherwise, in or near any such wooded country or forest, and through carelessness or neglect shall permit such fire to extend to and burn through such wooded country or forest, shall be deemed guilty of a misdemeanor, and on conviction before a court of competent jurisdiction, shall be punishable by fine not exceeding one thousand dollars, or imprisonment not exceeding one year, or by both such fine and imprisonment; provided, that nothing herein contained shall apply to any person who in good faith shall set a back fire to prevent the extension of a fire already burning. All fines collected under this act shall be paid into the county treasury for the benefit of the common school fund of the county in which it is collected.

---

7 California, An Act to prevent the Destruction of Forests by Fire on Public Lands Approved February 13, 1872, Laws of California, 1871–72, chapter 102, 98.

John W. Powell, from *Report of the Arid Lands of the United States* (1879)[8]

The protection of the forests of the entire Arid Region of the United States is reduced to one single problem—Can these forests be saved from fire? The writer has witnessed two fires in Colorado, each of which destroyed more timber than all that used by the citizens of that State from its settlement to the present day; and at least three in Utah, each of which has destroyed more timber than that taken by the people of the territory since its occupation. Similar fires have been witnessed by other members of the surveying corps. Everywhere throughout the Rocky Mountain Region the explorer away from the beaten paths of civilization meets with great areas of dead forests; pines with naked arms and charred trunks attesting to the former presence of this great destroyer. The younger forests are everywhere beset with fallen timber, attesting to the rigor of the flames, and in seasons of great drought the mountaineer sees the heavens filled with clouds of smoke.

In the main these fires are set by Indians. Driven from the lowlands by advancing civilization, they resort to the higher regions until they are forced back by the deep snows of winter. Want, caused by the restricted area to which they resort for food; the desire for luxuries to which they were strangers in their primitive condition; and especially the desire for personal adornment, together with a supply of more effective instruments for hunting and trapping, have in late years, during the rapid settlement of the country since the discovery of gold and the building of railroads, greatly stimulated the pursuit of animals for their furs, the wealth and currency of the savage. On their hunting excursions they systematically set fire to forests for the purpose of driving the game. This is a fact well known to all mountaineers. Only the white hunters of the region properly understand why these fires are set, it being usually attributed to a wanton desire on the part of the Indians to destroy that which is of value to the white man. The fires can, then, be very greatly curtailed by the removal of the Indians.

... The forests will be dense here or scattered there, as the trees may with ease or difficulty gain a foothold, but the forest regions will remain such, to be stripped of timber here and there from time to time to supply the wants of the

---

8 Excerpted from John W. Powell, *Report of the Arid Lands of the United States* (Washington, DC: Government Printing Office, 1879), 17–18.

people who live below; but once protected from fires, the forests will increase in extent and value. The first step to be taken for their protection must be by prohibiting the Indians from resorting thereto for hunting purposes, and then slowly, as the lower country is settled, the grasses and herbage of the highlands, in which fires generally spread, will be kept down by summer pasturage, and the dead and fallen timber will be removed to supply the wants of people below. This protection, though sure to come at last, will be tardy, for it depends upon the gradual settlement of the country; and this again depends upon the development of the agricultural and mineral resources and the establishment of manufactories, and to a very important extent on the building of railroads, for the whole region is so arid that its streams are small, and so elevated above the level of the sea that its few large streams descend too rapidly for navigation.

Franklin B. Hough, from *Report on Forestry* (1882)[9]

Forest Fires—Preliminary Considerations

(a.) Importance of the subject.

The importance of the injuries that are done to forests by running fires has led us to give particular attention to this subject, as directly relating to the maintenance of forest products within the United States. For the reasons stated under the following pages, we have collected, and in most instances condensed, the statutes of the different States and Territories relating to this subject, and after these the laws and regulations adopted in other countries, some of which might readily be adopted with great advantage in our own country. The whole series of these laws and regulations will afford ready assistance in the preparation of new laws upon the subject, or in the amendment of existing statutes.

These laws are followed by abstracts from replies of correspondents to local inquiries, and after these are presented various plans and suggestions that are regarded as valuable in measures for the prevention and control of these fires—the question of forest-fire insurance, as it stands at the present time in Europe, and such historical accounts as illustrate the terrible extent of these injuries, as they sometimes happen in hot and excessively dry seasons. The possibility of their occurrence presents the strongest possible motive for precautions, by which alone they may be prevented at times when the conditions threaten the greatest danger.

(b.) Advantages to be gained by following the Subject historically.

In following the successive steps of legislation upon a given subject, it may generally be expected that the earlier statutes embody the theoretical ideas of their authors, and the later ones, the modifications that these undergo when tested by experience. In a series of general statutes, therefore, the differences introduced by way of amendment, may be regarded as an evidence of an error to be avoided, a fault corrected, or an omission supplied. In this sense these earlier statutes, although obsolete, still have their value as showing the growth

---

9 Excerpted from Franklin B. Hough, *Report on Forestry, Submitted to Congress by the Commissioner of Agriculture* (Washington, DC: Government Printing Office, 1882), 128–130, 132, 197–200, 206–207, 224.

of ideas, and when compared with those of later date, they serve the useful purpose of indicating such provisions of law as have been tried and found wanting, and that therefore should be avoided. These considerations have accordingly led us to present, in the study of forest tires, as given in this report, so far as it could be done, the full history of legislation in the several States and Territories upon this subject.

(c.) Differences due to Soil, Climate, and other Conditions.

There can be no doubt but that differences of soil, of climate, and of circumstances, demand in some degree a modification of statutes to meet the wants presented in these variable conditions, and that therefore a universal law for the prevention of forest tires could scarcely be framed in such a manner as to be equally applicable to every section of the country. As a leading object, in presenting this subject has been to offer suggestions that have been thoughtfully devised, and carefully modified from experience, we have thought that this could be done in no way so effectually as by the statutes themselves. The information upon which they were founded has seldom been preserved, and the discussions that may have been had upon these projects, have for the most part been forgotten or lost. The laws themselves, however, unquestionably embody in every instance the views of those who enacted them, or at least the major part, and it may be fairly presumed that the earliest statute in the series of each State, not less than its subsequent amendments, represents the sum of experience and observation on the part of those who framed it.

(d.) The dangers are greater in new Settlements.

It is observed everywhere, that in the first beginnings of a settlement, whether in a forest region or upon the prairies and the plains, the dangers from running fires are greatest, and that they gradually diminish as the region becomes thickly settled and well cultivated. This partly results from the diminution of loose and inflammable materials, and partly to the increasing vigilance of the inhabitants, and the habitual care against accidents by those who have property to protect. The amendments to statutes may therefore in some cases be simply an indication of this change of conditions, and allowance should be made for these changes in estimating the propriety of the measures that sch statutes provide.

(e.) The improvident habits of Pioneers.

It is further to be remembered, that the earliest of the pioneers in a new settlement, are often those who do not make permanent improvements, but under a restless desire for change they seek a new field of enterprise long before the society around them has become permanently settled and well established. This unstable and transient class, the first beginners, are generally persons of slender resources, and have little to lose. They are accustomed to regard the world around them as open to their use, and in matters of pasturage for their stock, as well as forest products for their own supply, and often for such little industries as they can undertake upon a small capital or by their own labor, they often appropriate wherever it is most convenient. It is from this class of our population that we have the most to fear in the way of forest fires. Habitually careless and improvident, they do not hesitate, where there is a motive and an opportunity, to apply fires to lands not their own, for the purpose of improving and extending the range for their cattle, or to clear lands for cultivation, and sometimes to destroy the evidences of their own trespass and depredations. . . .

Local Inquiries Concerning Forest Fires

[Beaver County, Utah; Daniel Tyler, Beaver City]
No extensive forest fires have happened during the year. They are set by Indian and perhaps white hunters to drive out deer, and commenced this year about the middle of September, continuing some ten days. Perhaps one or two miles were burned over, chiefly in the canyons of the mountains east of Beaver City and within plain view. There is very little standing or green timber remaining, and the main damage was done to dry poles such as are used for fencing, some of which were standing and some down. These fires usually occur at a considerable elevation, and upon lands not fit for agriculture. They do not usually spread very far, and the only remedy that can be proposed would be to prosecute such whites as are proved guilty; but the evidence for this can rarely if ever be obtained.

[Kane County, Utah; R. W. Reeve, Duncan's Retreat]
A fire rarely occurs, except as set by Indians when hunting, and then sometimes it does great damage.

[Sevier County, Utah; W. Morrison, Richfield]
No fires have occurred in 1879–80, but in former years it was common for the Indians to fire the timber to drive out the deer. This is not practiced now, as they are less numerous and begin to depend more on farming than hunting.

[Fresno County, California; C. J. Davis]
A number of fires have occurred during the year, but none very destructive. They occurred in September and the first part of October, and usually were set by sheep owners to improve pasturage, or by Indians gathering pine nuts. No care is ever taken to check these fires, and they sometimes spread over considerable areas. The best remedy is private ownership. There is a considerable

amount of timber and grazing land in the county, but the timber suffers more from the sheep than from fires, as they destroy everything under from five to eight years old, and they should be prohibited from running at large, for at least ten consecutive years out of every fifty.

[Mendocino County, California; G. McCowen]
The lumbermen in the redwood belt annually set fires to clean out the limbs, tops, bark, broken trees and their splints, as well as to keep down the under-growth. The growing timber is seldom damaged, but the practice is very waste-ful, for all shivered, checked, or otherwise imperfect logs are burned up. In the grazing belt, fires are often started to burn the dense chaparral in the hills and in both cases, parties are usually prepared, and the damage is nominal, and more from the burning of dry feed than any other.

[Plumas County, California; M. Ball, Greenville]
Forest fires occurred to limited extent from about the middle of August to the 1st of October, caused by the carelessness of Indians, and may have burned over 10,000 acres in three several places. About a fourth part of the timber within the burned area was killed.

Summary of Opinions as to the Origin of Forest Fires

Correspondents, all reporting the causes that originate forest fires, must nec-essarily depend upon their opinions rather than upon certain knowledge; for in a great majority of cases the origin of these fires is to them unknown. They may have received their information from hearsay, and these rumors may have been purposely started in the wrong direction by the parties really guilty of the wrong to divert public indignation or avoid legal consequences.

Giving to each assigned or supposed cause an equal credit, the summary, in numerical form, is as follows:

Natural causes—lightning, 3

The direct or incidental act of man, 464

Of the latter, the Indians are charged as the originators in 21 cases, the remainder being ascribed to civilized man. The motive with the former is sup-posed in most cases to have been hostility to the whites, and a desire to harm them as much as possible. It will be remembered that these returns often refer back to a still recent period of Indian hostilities in Colorado, New Mexico, and the northern tier of Territories. In a very few cases their custom of burning to drive game, &e., is mentioned; while on the other hand, in Oregon, they are mentioned as having formerly scrupulously careful in the use of fires, least the feed for their horses should be destroyed, and that so long as they remained sole occupants of the country forest fires were unknown.

7. Fires in former times.

(a.) Prehistoric Fires: Indian Customs.

Forest fires within the present area of the United States are by no means limited to the period of European colonization, for we find, besides Indian traditions, abundant evidences of exceedingly widespread and destructive fires of very ancient date. It may be generally stated that wherever there is a uniform or nearly uniform growth of timber of any species or of any size the trees that compose it have sprung up upon a burned district. On the other hand, a great diversity of species usually indicates a certain degree of antiquity, for within certain limitations of temperature, humidity, and character of the soil each species appears to be seeking to perpetuate itself wherever the opportunity offers.

It can no longer be doubted but that our "oak openings" and "barrens" of the Western States, and in many instances the prairies, are the result of forest fires, which we may fairly presume have been annually set ever since the aboriginal races in possession at the time of European settlement have dwelt in the country, and perhaps for a much longer period. In fact, a portion of the treeless soil in Wisconsin, Michigan, and elsewhere was found filled here and there with roots that scarcely showed their presence above the surface, but which opposed a serious difficulty to the first cultivation. These "grub-lands," if let alone, would in a very few years make their appearance as young wood lands without any new seeding, and wholly without any need of a theory of spontaneous generation other than by the simplest law of budding from living roots and natural growth. The mesquite and other trees of the West and Southwest afford evidence by the size and abundance of their roots that their vegetation above ground has been time and again repressed, and for a very long period, by fires, while the gain in growth in the roots has been constantly maintained under great difficulties, but with marked result, under the protection of the covering soil.

Joaquin Miller, Address (1887)[10]

... It was my fate to spend my boyhood with Indians. They were the only true foresters I ever knew. In the spring after the leaves and grasses had served their time and season in holding back the floods and warming and nourishing the earth, then would the old [Indigenous women] begin to look above for the little dry spot of headland or sunny valley. And as fast as dry spots appeared they would be burned.

In this way the fire was always under control. In this way, the fire was always the servant *never the master*. And by the time the floods came again there was another coat of grass and leaves stronger and better than the one before because of the careful and temperate fire of the careful and wise old women. By this means the Indians always kept their forests open pure and fruitful and conflagrations were unknown.

I say then let the forests be placed in the hands of those who live in or near them and have some heart and some interest in their preservation. I say that the life and duration of this nation depend on her walls of wood, more than ever did that of Athens; and I say further that while we may plant our valleys, we must preserve our mountains.

Let the few remaining millions of forest lands be conceded to the States and then on down to counties, and even smaller divisions—school districts, for example. And then let the forester of plain, hard, common sense follow the Indian's simple method of preserving his property, and my word for it, neither New York, Louisiana, Michigan, nor California need fear flood or fire, drought or drowning rains. We would then be getting back near to Nature and Nature never betrays her own. Who ever heard of either flood or fire in the Indian's home until the white man came to make it his monopoly?

---

10 Excerpted from *Annual Meeting of the American Forestry Congress* (Springfield, IL: State Register Book and Job Print, 1887), 25–26.

William H. Mills, Testimony about Fires in the Yosemite Valley (1889)[11]

Mr. Mills: . . . [I]t was related to me that the Indians used to burn the valley for the purpose of making an open glade and pasture there, and it is my opinion that that was a very good practice.[12] You have also here under examination the Big Tree Grove. There was granted by the United States a large area, covered with *Sequoia gigantea*, which grows in Mariposa County. Some four or five years ago, when I visited the valley, I became thoroughly persuaded that the fagots which had fallen at the foot of those trees was endangering that forest. In early times that was burned over in such a way that a little fire did no harm; but fagots had piled up at the roots of those trees to the depth of four or five feet, and if a fire comes in that forest it will burn those trees up. These trees are the remnants of a past geologic age. They belonged to a species which disappeared from the earth hundreds and thousands of years ago. It will be necessary to remove those fagots and the fallen limbs and the bark from around those trees. None of that has ever been burned, and the result is an accumulation of undergrowth, which in the dry season is dry—and you have a dry season, the same as you have in the Sacramento Valley. Those meadows become brown, just about the time they do in the San Joaquin Valley, and those ferns and brakes. . . . There may be a few weeks difference, and it is only a question of a few weeks; those falls dry up entirely, and the only living water in the valley is Glacier Springs; and in some such dry season as that the Mariposa Grove of Big Trees will be burned. This has been the subject of serious consideration by the [Yosemite] Commission, as to how to prevent that. There is the removal of this stuff from around the foot of the trees, which would be a very expensive thing, and in my opinion the State will have to stand the expense to properly administer that great trust.

---

11 Excerpted from William H. Mills, Testimony about fires in the Yosemite Valley, in *Appendix to the Journals of the [California] Senate and Assembly* (Sacramento: State Printing, 1889), 8: 42-44.

12 Mills recalled that he had heard this from Yosemite promoter and hotelier James Mason Hutchings. For more on Hutchings, see Jen A. Huntley, *The Making of Yosemite: James Mason Hutchings and the Origins of America's Most Popular National Park* (Lawrence: University Press of Kansas, 2011).

Mr. Hook[13]: Can't they be raked away from the trunks of trees and then burned up?

Mr. Mills: Yes, sir; it can be, and is being done. The Commissioners have authorized that to be done repeatedly, and progress is made all the time in that direction; the removing of that stuff away from the roots of the trees, but leaving the Yosemite Valley to itself; with the grass growing up among this underbrush, and the configuration of the valley is very favorable to a conflagration. That would be admitted by any of you gentlemen, if you visited it. If a fire was built in the valley, by reason of the nearness of the walls, their precipitous character, and the great depth of the valley, there is a constant tendency to produce a great draft; and if a great fire should occur in that valley, it would make it a blackened ruin in a short time. This is a question which appears, in my mind, to be a reasonable apprehension, and therefore, from the very start, I was in favor of resisting that encroachment of undergrowth.

Mr. Tulloch[14]: In former times was it not customary, from what you have heard, for the Indians to burn the forests off the valley now and then, annually?

Mr. Mills: Yes, sir; the Indians do that all over California. I was recently in a portion of the coast country and saw a great fire in the mountains. . . . I was told that it was a universal custom of a remnant of a tribe of Indians to burn it and not allow it to grow up with . . . chaparral.

Mr. Tulloch: How is it that these tribes of which you speak, having very ancient origin, were not affected thereby and burned out thereby, and that they are not burned out now?

Mr. Mills: The difference would be in the accumulation of fagots, which would make a fire to burn them out. They burn it every year, and the accumulation of fagots is not sufficient to make a fire menacing the life of a tree. These trees are all blackened. You can see the evidence of past burning through this forest. Many of them are blackened and burned at the roots. The one that you see the picture of, where the stage goes through, was burned nearly through on both sides, and they simply morticed it at the heart of that tree. But there is evidence of former fires also in the valley. You will see, every now and then, a fallen tree or the trunk of a tree that shows that fires have run through this

---

13 Hook appears to have been a counsel for the investigating committee.
14 Tulloch also seems to have been a counsel for the senate committee.

valley in former times. I have always respected the ability of the Indians to manage that valley. . . .

Mr. Hook: You said just now that you believed in the Indian management of the valley?

Mr. Mills: Yes sir.

Mr. Hook: Do you think the untutored mind has a greater capacity for managing the valley than the cultivated mind?

Mr. Mills: The whole of the scenic grandeur of California was better when we first discovered the country than it is now. You take the forests of California they were vastly more beautiful than now and whenever you go into what is called the primeval forest you will find it much more beautiful. The utilitarian spirit of the age is destroying much of the scenic grandeur of this country. The forests of the Sierra Nevadas in what is called the Fredonia Pass are vastly more beautiful than they are where civilization has had a chance to make inroads upon them. The result is that where the Indians desire to make pasture they burn it out. You see as you pass through the Blancos of the Sierra Nevada Mountains on the western slope you will see marks of these fires upon the trees, and you will see a magnificent open appearance that was due entirely to running fires through these forests every year and burning up a moss that will accumulate and finally get as soft as a carpet. . . .

Mr. Hook: Mr. Mills didn't answer my question.

Mr. Mills: I wanted to get the question answered in your own way whether the untutored mind has a greater capacity for managing the valley than the cultivated mind. I find that the highest wisdom among men has been by accident. Nearly all the great discoveries have been made by accident and if the Indians accidentally struck a method of taking care of the bed of Yosemite Valley through the necessity of getting some pastureland for the game upon which they fed, I think that was a very good method of management. I am in favor of keeping the valley as much in appearance as possible of a park.

Fig. 5. Wallace, Idaho, was destroyed in the 1910 fires that swept through the region, killing more than eighty people. The town was only slowly rebuilt, as revealed in this 1915 photograph. Credit: Library of Congress.

Part 2
Light Burning and Its Discontents

CALIFORNIA STATE BOARD OF FORESTRY

THE GOVERNOR HAS PROCLAIMED
APRIL 18, 1914

FIRE PREVENTION DAY

—— A LESSON ——

WINTER AND SPRING WORK TO PREVENT SUMMER FIRES.

APRIL 18   1914

CALIFORNIA STATE PRINTING OFFICE

Fig. 6. This pamphlet, published by the California Board of Forestry in 1914, urged the public to recognize that "the greatest enemy of our forests is fire" and that they must act to prevent them. Credit: Library of Congress.

First Smoke, 1899–1919

Despite the enduring recognition of many nineteenth-century commentators of the key role that well-managed fire, as practiced by the Indigenous people in California and elsewhere, played in creating western forests and grasslands, the emergence of a corps of federal-government scientists began to contest the idea and reality of Native American fire management. Many of these individuals, like Gifford Pinchot, who in 1899 was head of the US Division of Forestry (and six years later would become the first chief of the US Forest Service), fully understood fire's ecological role in regenerating forests and grasslands. That fact is abundantly evident in the first article in this section, which Pinchot wrote for *National Geographic*. But it is also clear that Pinchot and his forestry peers privileged the politics of—and perceived need for—fire suppression over ecological realities. This was done to build consensus in support of the agency's managerial mission, which also included an economic argument: because trees were a crop, they argued, they must be protected from fire to ensure their continued profitability. Making forestry pay was not just a slogan, it was essential to the conservation agenda.

Not everyone accepted that emerging agenda. Some loggers and ranchers, who used fire to further their economic ends, pushed back. Their counternarrative challenged the putative scientific expertise that the first generation of foresters in the United States claimed justified their conviction that all fire was inimical to good forest management. They wondered, as did George Hoxie, whether the Indigenous use of fire might not be a smarter approach than the "theoretical" claims that fire must be excluded to create healthier forests. They suggested, as did Joseph Kitts, that using what he called "surface fires" as practiced by the Indigenous people of the Sierra Nevada, where his lands were situated, increased the health of his timber holdings, and thus benefited his bottom line.

The Forest Service could not accept Kitts's claims about fire boosting the value of his property, given its insistence that wildfire was a destructive force, full stop. Its position solidified after the brutal fire season in 1910, in which three-million acres were incinerated in three days in portions of Washington,

Idaho, and Montana. This trauma was embedded in W. E. Coman's rebuttal to Kitts assertion that Native communities had long utilized fire to sustain their lives and livelihoods. "The systematic burning of the forests by the Indians would suggest a desire by the redmen for the preservation of the trees for future use," Coman wrote in 1911. "But the idea that the Indians burned the forests at stated intervals to preserve them is derided by pioneers who have spent years with the redmen and who understand their ways and methods, and it is laughed at by old Indians today." This, then, marked the launch of a racist trope that those outside and inside the agency routinely utilized to denigrate critics of the Forest Service's mission. Agency officials tagged their opponents as practitioners of "Piute forestry," a derogatory term that in the early 1920s would become even more central to the Forest Service's more aggressive defense of full-on suppression of all fires, any time and everywhere.

Gifford Pinchot, from "The Relation of Forests and Forest Fires" (1899)[1]

The study of forest fires as modifiers of the consequences and mode of life of the forest is as yet in its earliest stages. Remarkably little attention, in view of the importance of the subject, has hitherto afforded to it. A few observers who have lived much with the forest, such as John Muir of California, have grouped fire with temperature and moisture as one of the great factors which govern the distribution and character of forest growth; but so little has been said or written upon the subject that the opinion of each man seems to have been reached independently and upon the single basis of personal observation. The documents upon the subject still reside, with very few exceptions, in the forest itself. It is unfortunate that our acquaintance with what might almost be called the creative action of forest fires should be so meager, for only through a knowledge of this relation and through the insight which such knowledge brings can there be gained a clear and full conception of how and why fires do harm, and how best they may be prevented and extinguished. . . .

That fires do vast harm we know already. Though just what the destruction of its forests will cost the nation is still unknown. Records compiled by the Division of Forestry indicate that the average direct recorded loss from this source is not less than $20,000,000 a year. To this figure must be added that vast direct loss unrecorded, together with the great but indefinite damage from the effect of forest destruction on water supply, the deterioration of the soil, the destruction of the young growth, and the loss of the increment which a healthy young forest would have been laying on year by year. . . . With further study a more exact statement of the grant total of the loss will be possible; but even now it is safe to assume that for the nation as a whole the loss is represented yearly by a sum much in excess of $50,000,000. That figure sufficiently proves that the destructive action of fire on the forest is a subject of the first interest and importance; but in the present paper this brief reference must suffice. The regulative action of fire on the forest is here more directly in question.

Fires determine the presence or absence of forest in a given region more generally than is often supposed. A very large part of the prairie regions of the United States is treeless probably because of fire. . . . The same course of

---

1 Excerpted from Gifford Pinchot, "The Relation of Forests and Forest Fires," *National Geographic*, October 1899, 393–403.

70   LIGHT BURNING AND ITS DISCONTENTS

reasoning applies to certain kinds of open glades of the prairie, well named "fire glades" by Mr. Frederick V. Coville, Botanist of the U.S. Department of Agriculture. In the Black Hills of South Dakota, for example, these glades, surrounded by forest-bearing land are almost exclusively confined to ground rich enough to support a crop of grass sufficiently dense to burn fiercely, which the timber is restricted to rough or stony land almost always higher than the glades and comparatively safe from fire because of the scantiness of the minor vegetation it is able to support....

Perhaps the most remarkable of the regulative effects of forest fires relates to the composition of the forest—the kinds of trees of which it is composed and the proportion of each. This effect depends on the action of fire in combination with the various qualities of resistance which trees possess. These qualities are of two chief kinds; one, adapted to secure the safety of the individual tree directly through its own powers of defense, the other to assure the continuance of the species, with little regard for the single tree. An example of the first kind is the western larch, whose enormously thick bark is almost fireproof, and so good a non-conductor that it protects the living tissue beneath it even against fires hot enough to scorch the trunk 50 to 75 feet above the ground. It is to this quality of its bark, as well as their marvelous vitality, that the big trees of California owe their power to reach an age of 3,000 or 4,000 years. The eastern pitch pine protects itself in the same way. So do many other trees, including the longleaf pine, which adds to this quality of its bark another method of protection that places it at the head of all the trees of my acquaintance in its capacity to resist fire.

Almost all trees yield readily to slight surface fires during the first ten or fifteen years of life. To this statement the longleaf pine is a conspicuous and rare exception. Not only do the young trees protect themselves in early youth by bark which is not uncommonly as thick as the wood (the whole diameter being thus two-thirds bark and one-third wood), but they add to this unusual armor a device specifically adapted for their safety when growing amid long grass, usually the most fatal neighbor to young trees in case of fire. It is to be noted that the vast majority of longleaf pines are associated with grass from the beginning to the end of their lives. During the first four to five years the longleaf seedling reaches a height of but four or five inches above the ground. It has generally been erroneously assumed that this slow growth made it especially susceptible to injury from fire; but while the stem in these early years makes little progress, the long needles shoot up and bend over in a green cascade which falls to the ground in a circle about the seedling. Not only does this barrier of green needles itself burn only with difficulty, but it shades out the grass around the young stem, and so prepares a double fire-resisting shield about

FIRST SMOKE, 1899–1919

the vitals of the young tree. Such facts explain why fire which has restricted the spread of evergreen oaks in parts of Florida, for example, has made a pure forest of pines in a region where reproduction of the oaks phenomenally rapid where the annual fires cannot run.

The second method of protection against fire is that which sacrifices the individual but secures the safety of the species. Perhaps the most striking example of this method is furnished by the lodgepole pine, which is being distributed over hundreds of square miles of the Rocky Mountain region by the action of fire. It is a fact that this thin-barked tree, which succumbs with the almost readiness to fire, is gaining ground by the action of its enemy, replacing over great areas thick-barked species like the red fir and the western larch. The device to which this curious device is due is similar to that of *Pinus attenuate* [Knobcone pine], to which John Muir long since called attention. It consists in the hoarding for several years of the ripe seeds in the cones. Fire rarely burns down the lodgepole pine, but in nearly every case simply kills the standing tree and leaves it to be blown down years after, when decay shall have weakened the roots. In the meantime, the hoarded winged seeds are set free by the opening of the cones, are distributed and germinate, and the new crop contains a larger proportion of lodgepole than the old. By the repetition of this process great stretches of burned land are finally covered with a pure, even-aged young growth where formerly the forest was composed of other and usually much more valuable species. The details of the process by which the more valuable species will undoubtedly in the end regain possession of the soil I do not yet know.

A somewhat less obvious, although not a less interesting, instance of distribution controlled by fire is that of the red fir in these portions of Washington (and presumably Oregon also) where it reaches its best dimensions and greatest commercial importance. Here the young seedlings are found in remarkable abundance on unshaded spots wherever the vegetable covering of the mineral soil has been burned away. An actual count and measurement of every tree on many hundreds of acres of fir timber in various parts of the Puget Sound region, and a study in the Olympics, combine to show them practically absent in the shade of their elders. In the latter region, as I had occasion to say in a report (dated January 26, 1898) to the Secretary of the Interior on the condition and proper management of the national forest reserves:

> Continuous stretches of miles without a break were covered with a uniform growth of Douglas fir (red fir) from two to three feet in diameter, interspersed with numerous rotting stumps of much larger trees bearing the marks of fire. The young firs were entirely unscarred, but

charcoal was found at the roots of some specimens which had been thrown by the wind.... Charcoal was found directly beneath a growing cedar tree four feet in diameter, under which a hole had been excavated in the course of lumbering operations. This mass of evidence acquires a crucial importance with relation to the forest from the fact that in my ten days' visit to the region I did not see a single young seedling of Douglas Fir (red fir) under the forest cover; nor a single opening made by fire which did not contain them.

In a word, the distribution of red fir in western Washington, where it is by all odds the most valuable commercial tree, is governed, first of all, so far as we know at present, by fire. Had fires been kept out of these forests in the last thousand years the fir which gives them their distinctive character would not be in existence but would be replaced in all probability by the hemlock, which fills even the densest of the Puget Sound forests with its innumerable seedlings. I hasten to add that these facts do not imply any desirability in the fires which now are devastating the West....

Marsden Manson, from "The Effect of the Partial Suppression of Annual Forest Fires in the Sierra Nevada Mountains" (1906)[2]

Prior to 1849 the forests and even the foothills of the Sierra Nevada Mountains were annually burned over by the Indians. This process effectively suppressed seedlings, and as it had manifestly been practiced for many generations, the forests were mainly composed of old trees, many badly burned at the butt. The scattered groves of Sequoias, with their hoary fire-scarred trunks and devoid of middle-aged and young trees, the clear floor of the Yosemite Valley, and the great forests of sugar and yellow pine, fire, spruce, red cedar, etc., without seedlings or young growth abundantly attest to the prevalence of this practices of annually burning off the leaves. These light fires gave open forests through which one could readily see for great distances.

So impressive were these forest vistas and so majestic were the great boles that poetic and impracticable natures at once accepted the Digger Indian[3] system of forestry as unquestionably the natural and correct one. This impression has been strengthened by two facts: first, the absence of a definite knowledge of what forestry really is; secondly, by the establishment of a far worse system than that of the Digger Indians,—namely, the ruthless cutting out of the trees and burning over the areas, designedly, to give better pasture to sheep, or, accidently, after a heavy growth of young trees had started.

The writer has been familiar with the forests of the Sierra for many years and has quite recently traveled through several hundred miles of forest areas which were previously known to him. In these trips it was distinctly observed that where forest fires had been suppressed, whether the area had been cut over or not, young trees of species not previously found as young trees were beginning to find foothold. This is notably brought out in the Tuolumne grove of sequoias. Here in early visits not a single specimen except full-grown, dead, or dying trees could be found. . . .

Observations here and in other parts of the Sierra showed vast thickets of young trees sprinkled over with young sugar-pines. The sequoia and sugar-pine

---

2 Excerpted from Marsden Manson, "The Effect of the Partial Suppression of Annual Forest Fires in the Sierra Nevada Mountains," *Sierra Club Bulletin*, January 1906, 22–24.
3 "Digger" is a racist term that whites in California routinely used to distance themselves from Indigenous Californians and deride their way of life.

are exceedingly tender and are killed by the slightest fire; other species are more resistant, and more abundant. The suppression of forest fires will restore two splendid species to the Sierra, and with either clear cutting or by leaving young and seedling or mother trees there will be no difficulty in preserving forever the forests of the Sierra. The Digger Indian system of forestry will not give timber as a crop; but it will give place to systematic forestry which will admit of either cutting close or reseeding with valuable timber such as sugar-pine or sequoia or both; or by cutting only mature trees, leaving growing timber and seedlings for future generations. The observations of the writer lead conclusively to the opinion that the recuperative powers of Sierra Nevada forests are so great that to preserve them only fire protection and cutting our superabundant young growth is necessary.

To aid the extension of the best species two systems should be followed: First, inferior species should be cut out before seeding, and superior species should be allowed to seed and be planted; second, in regions near the upper limits of superior species they should be systematically extended and aided, as all species are naturally reaching out toward higher elevations. The situation is by no means as black as it has been painted, and only requires systematic and sustained protection and aid to maintain the Sierra Nevada forever as a source of wealth both of timber and water.

Charles Howard Shinn, from "Work in the National Forests—No. 5: Holding Down a Mountain Fire" (1907)[4]

... [N]ow that there is a stillness under the giant sugar pines of Ellis Meadow, I can write down some of these as yet unsaid matters about our mountain fires. And, first of all, let me emphasize the importance of saving every tree, large and small, that we can save from fire, at any cost of time and money.

Would it surprise you, my reader, to be told that any one of a dozen of these sugar pines contains something like ten thousand feet of salable lumber? One was cut up here last August that contained 35,000 feet! Some of these pines began to grow before Spenser wrote his Faery Queen, or Raleigh cast his embroidered cloak at the feet of stately Elizabeth, or the baby Shakespeare opened his eyes on English daisies.

For trees such as these, and for their children's children, clear down to the last year's seedlings, plain mountain men are more than content to crawl on hands and knees under spurts of flame in red hot gulches, in some life and death struggles toiling all night long, like Titans lent to us from some greater planet. To spoil such work with praise were a shabby use of words; let us take the results, rejoicing that such things are; and let us confidently lean upon this primal fact, that the field men of the Forest Service are learning to take hold of their work.

Out here with the steady trade winds, the rainless summers, the immense accumulation of dry and resinous materials, the constant travel all through the Forest—Indians, lumbermen, miners, cattlemen, tourists—one certainly lives on the wavering edge of trouble between June and December. The whole country fills with smoke from stubble fires in the San Joaquin Valley, and from brush fires in the foothills outside of the Forest.

Suddenly this dull haze thickens, blurs, and threatens, or it begins to glow with dark and troublous red.

Somewhere, in some canyon, there is fire, which must be found by sight or smell, or by news from some traveler. If you can discover and reach it in an hour two men can handle the fire at a cost of less than fifty dollars; one man even may hold it in check till help comes. But if three hours are lost before

---

4 Excerpted from Charles Howard Shinn, "Work in the National Forests—No. 5: Holding Down a Mountain Fire," *Forestry and Irrigation*, December 1907, 637–547.

76 LIGHT BURNING AND ITS DISCONTENTS

the place is spotted by the rangers, "we the people of America" may lose fifty thousand dollars in timber alone—or may even witness in helpless regret one of those never-to be-described over-head fires which have sometimes wiped out the timber resources of whole counties.

Beyond question the greatest enemy of the forest is—fire. Where a great fire has run, the soil itself may be ruined beyond restoration for many decades, the "old burns" remain most ghastly places. Where even a little fire has passed, the reproduction is checked, the brush creeps in, the insect enemies flourish and multiply. And it is the little neglected fires which in the aggregate do the largest amount of harm to the forest. Stubborn, ignorant, or careless people who leave camp fires burning, or set brush fires in their own fields, or toss cigar butts and cigarette ends in the brush as they ride along the trail—these are the real enemies of our work. Out of a hundred fires, I think that ninety-nine are simply due to stupid ignorance and foolish carelessness of men whose interests are really bound up in the welfare of the forests. Habits are hard to change, as we all know, and this fire-scattering habit of Americans is hard to remedy.

I have known respectable people in San Francisco, whose money was invested in mountain communities, wholly dependent on the lumber industry, to go far up in the Sierras for a Fourth of July, and shoot off no end of rockets from their camp in the tall timber. The poor Indian [women] who start a fire to smoke out wild bees and wasps, the mountaineer who burns a troublesome log that lies across the trail, have some excuse for what they do, but the man who carries a hundred dollars-worth of fireworks to his Sierra camp (as I once knew of) is something very near to a criminal.

I have always felt an interest in what may be termed the Piute system of forestry. It has often reached the dignity of print; it has even found distinguished (and vituperative) advocates. When I came here to the Sierra Reserve, every one, without exception worth noting, argued openly that fires did no harm at all: but rather did good by opening up the brush thickets, by increasing the feed for livestock, and by destroying dead and fallen timber, pine needles and the worthless bear brush (*Chamaebatia foliosa*). Rising to the main point, this theory further holds that fire in all the forest each year is wholly beneficent; in brief, that Piute forestry is the only scientific method. Stripped of the non-essentials, it is thus held that because the Indians used to burn the whole country every summer this was mighty good practice for white men to adopt.

Those short-sighted neighbors of mine who believe this forget, or do not know, that the Indians who first set fires in our Sierras were broken Piutes of whom tradition relates that they were cast forth and driven helter-skelter out of Nevada into the mountain fastnesses some hundreds of years ago, becoming the Monos of today. It grieves me to say it. but we have no evidence that these Indians were really trained foresters or even practical lumbermen. I hate to mention it here—but they were not American homebuilders, the planters of gardens, the fencers of fields, the users of wood lots. They were children of Nimrod; they desired clear spaces under the great pines in order to aim their obsidian-tipped arrows. For that, and that only, they flung wide their fires in the forests of the Sierras.

The mountaineers in this region have almost wholly ceased to swear by Piute forestry methods. They prefer to have timber, mills, towns, prospective railroads, and all that. I know one lordly pioneer who long declared, sitting like a white-haired god on his front fence, that "the Indians knew more than all you forest people, and if there was any nerve left the whole Sierra would be burned over from end to end." There came a fire one summer on adjacent private lands that caused him a loss of several thousand dollars before the rangers could handle it. Everyone noted that the old lion ceased growling and fought fire desperately. It only half converted him, but it took most of the snap out of his tirades. . . .

As for the Brush Problem—which the ignorant Piute foresters bequeathed us by their system of destroying the young timber, it seems to me that we have to consider a number of items such as these: soil, exposure, elevation, rainfall, natural growth, possibilities of slowly changing brushland into woodland, and woodland into real forest. I am absolutely sure that the yellow pine is extending westward towards the foothills, in many places on this Forest. I think that this is primarily due to the "care and protection" afforded by the methods of the Forest Service, especially in regard to grazing and fires.

But there are large areas of dense "chaparral" where this peaceful extension of the forest ceases. Less "brush," more rainfall, some seed-trees—and the scale would slowly turn. It is far too expensive to cut or pull the chaparral and then seed the ground. Can the scattered oaks and pines be protected from destruction, while the chaparral is burned in strips, taking perhaps three years to clear the whole surface? How many men and what kind of organization will make such work safe and effective? Is it not possible that experiments on a large scale may show that the remedy for the evil done by Piute forestry is simply the intelligent use of a match box in the foothills, below the line of "tall timber?"

It is easy to object that when you burn you destroy the soil-cover and the humus. You certainly lose a lot. But if the oaks increase and the pines come in you more than get it back. The humus-producing value of the annual crops of grasses and "weeds" which take the place of the chaparral in this climate can hardly be over-estimated. Oak leaves make a better seed bed than chaparral leaves do. The leaves of our ceanothuses, manzanitas, etc., are very coriaceous, lasting many years; oak leaves decay the first season. If one can get the brush out of the way, the trees move down, especially when the two or three "wet seasons" of a California climate happen to come together.

Really, I do not know of any greater forest problem than this one—thus briefly stated: Can we make fire our servant and helper in changing chaparral to woodland and in changing that woodland into timber region? It is a problem of the semi-arid West; it is the largest and the most fascinating of all our field problems. Sometimes when I talk it over with a little man, fresh from the lecture room, he says, "utterly impossible." The large man, who loves nothing half so well as to see impossible things done, says, "It is worth study and experimentation." Let us leave it there—the fundamental problem of foothill forestry in many places in California.

George L. Hoxie, "How Fire Helps Forestry: The Practical vs. the Federal Government's Theoretical Ideas" (1910)[5]

Practical foresters contend and can demonstrate that from time immemorial fire has been the salvation and preservation of our California sugar and white pine forests. The white man found these forests to his liking five hundred to two thousand years after they sprang from the soil and it is admitted that the Indian for centuries, for his own convenience, no doubt, fired the forests at periods of about three years . . . that is to say, he burned certain forest areas one year and certain other areas another, and so on, to the end that the burnings were about three years apart.

The practical forester invites the aid of fire as a servant, not as a master. It will surely be master in a very short time unless the Federal Government changes its ways by eliminating the theoretical and grasping the practical.

Just a few pertinent questions:

Were the Federal Government's present theories in vogue covering a period of the age of our California forests of say, five hundred to two thousand years?

Is it not very much the exception to find as much as one acre in a very large forest area (unless on logged-over or partially logged-over ground) *destroyed by fire*?

What percentage of the forest areas of California was rejected and set aside as not worth the price on account of the ravages of fire? The Federal Government's plot books covering timbered areas make no specific record of elimination on account of the ravages of fire. In fact, such areas are so limited as to be of little consequence.

Yet the evidences of fire running at will are to be found in all of our California forests. Yet how keen has been the speculative spirit to acquire these burned over forest areas—so much so that the Federal Government saw fit to take a hand and withdraw them from sale and incidentally raise the price of stumpage to more than double that for which private owners of timbered areas would be glad to sell their stumpage, and this in the face of the fact that private holdings are subject to state and county taxation. The Federal Government

---

5 Excerpted from George L. Hoxie, "How Fire Helps Forestry: The Practical vs. the Federal Government's Theoretical Ideas," *Sunset Magazine*, July 1910, 145–151.

pays taxes only when the timber crop is harvested and the cash for the same in its coffers.

I have said that fire always has been and always will be the salvation and preservation of our California sugar and white pine forests, and no doubt the forests of many other states. In a manner, however, fire running at will is *master*. This is not the practical aspect. It is the intention to deal herein with fire as a servant, whose coming is to be prepared for in advance. This preparation can be undertaken successfully in the summer months and the servant fire can be put to work in the fall months, or after the first rains, when it would require aid rather than otherwise in its good work of destroying decayed logs and off-fall, the accumulation of a year or two or more; more than that, fire also destroys the destructive insects such as beetles, which are, it is declared by experts, by reason of the Federal Government's theoretical ideas of keeping fire out of the forests, becoming very much more destructive; their ravages have become very notice able and in effect are the same as girdling.

Naturally the question is asked by the theorist: "How will the fire be kept from the standing live timber; how save that from the awful ravages of fire deliberately turned loose in it?" The answer is: *In itself it won't burn*, as an all wise nature has given it protection in the form of bark that is a nonconductor of heat; but that all-wise nature does not prevent a dead tree from falling or rolling against a live one and subjecting it to unusual and unnecessary hazard. The practical simply proposes to remove these extra hazards in advance of the servant fire. Should the extra hazard be a log, cut out a section of it immediately against the living tree and roll the cut-out portion a safe distance from the particular tree endangered, or clear away limbs, as the case may be, and in this manner prepare for the servant fire; perchance, this may mean trimming, cutting down, and piling for subsequent firing, of extra hazard in the shape of thickets of small trees.

It is claimed by the theorists that fire, even passing through forest areas previously prepared for it, will destroy young trees and that the damage on this account would he irreparable. The claim will also be made by the theorists that the vegetable mold or forest carpet is subjected by this enemy fire to total destruction. The practical answer to this is that in the forests described an average from say five to fifteen trees (very much oftener the former number) is all an acre will sustain. In nature it is simply the survival of the fittest, so that in mature forests the fittest control and, in effect, stunt and make dormant the younger growth by depriving it of the life-giving light and heat. And this younger growth will never make any considerable headway until the parent tree is removed, as can be readily demonstrated by cutting any of the trees subjected to the conditions described and counting the yearly rings. The

FIRST SMOKE, 1899–1919

writer has cut trees growing under the conditions described, not exceeding two inches in diameter, and found them to be upwards of fifty years of age. Had conditions of light and heat been favorable, these same trees would have been at least twelve to fifteen inches in diameter in this period of time. The horticulturist knows that for the same reasons it is extremely difficult to grow a young fruit-tree in an old orchard.

The practical answer to the destruction of the vegetable mold or forest carpet is that during even the driest period of the year it is protected by green growths of varied kinds that in themselves will not burn. These growths include what is locally called bear clover, snow-brush, squaw carpet, elk grass, manzanita, white thorn, and deer brush, lupine, and natural grasses, such as thrive at high altitudes with a limited amount of sunlight, usually a species of bunch-grass. But the forest cover or carpet has been wet by the first fall rains, before the practical subjects the forest areas to fire and the only portions of forest carpet that would be even damaged would be those portions directly under a pile of brush, previously placed for burning, or under decayed logs, and a search-warrant will be necessary to find these burned spots a season or two after the burning.

The damage by fire to forest trees of all kinds will be noted almost universally to have occurred at the butts and on the uphill side of the particular tree damaged—evidence that extra hazard in the shape of accumulated inflammable matter, drifting down hill, was the direct cause.

It is a mistaken idea that fire in the California forest areas climbs green trees and destroys them. It is also an undeniable fact that the greatest fire hazard is that portion of the forest area situated on the slopes of mountains, as such slopes conduce more or less of a draught that does not exist on the level or mesa portions of forest areas. For this reason, these slopes should receive the greatest amount of attention in preparing for the servant fire. This would include filling in, with earth, depressions immediately at the foot of trees damaged by fire, to prevent the creation of draught and to eliminate thereby in a great measure damage that might otherwise result from subsequent fires.

These conditions would seem to direct that in practical forestry fires should be started at the proper time of year on the summits of the timbered areas selected to be cleaned by the use of the servant fire, as this would tend to eliminate the draught created by the fire itself on the slopes.

The theorists say at time of harvesting the forest crop of logs sufficient seed trees must be left to insure and perpetuate the forest growth. The practical knows that in the California forest areas at least, the season following milling operations (unless it be the purpose of the owner to fight the new growths) a hundred, perchance a thousand or more, little forest trees will spring up where one parent tree was re moved. Then in a few years the danger of fire is *real*, for a thicket condition exists and total destruction by the master fire is unavoidable, unless the cutting down and thinning of these new forest growths is resorted to in advance of the servant fire. Yet even if these thicket conditions were permitted to continue nature would work out her own salvation in the very slow process of the survival of the fittest; the fittest would in time smother the less vigorous by towering above them and depriving them of the light and heat and normal forest conditions would ultimately exist by reason of the slow decay of the smothered growths.

The practical realizes that nothing but a miracle will keep fire out of the forest areas, for, to accomplish this, even lightning must be eliminated; further, it is realized that if the theoretical continues for a few years longer there will be no hope of saving these areas from useless unnecessary and enormous damage, as the accumulated fallen limbs and unusual and unnecessary hazard is many times greater in five or ten than in two or three years, for in the nature of things forest trees drop their lower limbs annually and others are broken by snow, falling timber, or otherwise.

The practical says, "Let the fire at the proper time of year run at will," in the forest described, rather than not at all, as it can be clearly demonstrated that the class of forests named is greatly benefited rather than injured by this manner of treatment. The proof is abundant: magnificent virgin forests of the class described that have been subjected to fire at will, and not at selected favorable periods of the year, for the past five hundred to perhaps two thousand or more years.

For instance, the writer has had an opportunity of observing the holdings of a company in which some friends and himself are associated. We hold and own about twenty-eight square miles of forest area in the sugar and white pine belt of California; and the ideas embodied herein have been observed in the timber district of which these holdings form a part, as well as in other areas of like timber in this state. Within the past ten years fire has run at will through portions of the holdings mentioned and in each instance such burned over area was and is improved by reason of the burning, so much so that we look with special pride on one particular area so burned, as it is absolutely free from inflammable matter and the live timber is uninjured and the forest cover or carpet is perfect. These fires occurred in the summer months and not as the practical would choose to have them, as no advance preparation was supplied. Still, as I have said, better to have fire at will than not at all, and the periods of such burning should need exceed three or four apart, oftener would be better.

These described holdings form a part of a three-million-acre forest reserve. The percentage of privately owned forest lands in this vast area is as a drop in the bucket compared with the holdings of the Federal Government in this reserve.

Under these conditions the very serious question arises as to how private owners can follow on lines of practical forestry, as the administrative power of the Federal Government is equally rigid so far as the privately owned tracts are concerned, because these are part and parcel of the forest reserve itself and come under the ban of the Federal Government's theoretical forestry whims.

There would seem to be, under this condition, only one avenue of escape for the private owners of timbered properties in forest reserves, and that is to attempt at least to educate the directing hand of federal forestry affairs away from the theoretical and into the practical, and there is no question of doubt but that the federal forest rangers—or at least many of them—know that the present theories are ruinous and calculated to insure unnecessary and great damage to the forest areas by the master fire if continued. . . .

F. E. Olmsted, from "Fire and the Forest—the Theory of 'Light Burning'" (1911)[6]

The present and intense question of the forest-fire question is decidedly valuable because it is sure to result in a determined effort all along the line to lessen both the fire risk and the fire damage. Public discussion of the matter has brought to light, among other things, the fact that some people still believe in the old theory of "burning over the woods" periodically to get rid of the litter on the ground, so that big fires which may come along later on will find no fuel to feed on. This theory is usually accompanied with reference to the "old Indian fires" which the redmen formerly set quite methodically for purposes of the hunting of game. We are told that present virgin stands of timber have lived on and flourished in spite of the Indian fires. Hence, it is said, we should follow the savages' example of "burning up the woods" to a small extent in order that they might be burnt up to a greater extent by and by. Forest fires, it is claimed, are bound to run over the mountains in spite of anything we can do. Besides, the statement is made that litter will gradually accumulate to such an extent that when a fire does start it will be impossible to control it and we will lose all our timber. Why not choose our time in the fall or spring when the smaller refuse on the ground is dry enough to burn, the woods being damp enough to prevent any serious damage to the older trees, and burn the whole thing lightly?

This theory of "light burning" is especially prevalent in California and has cropped out to a very noticeable extent in Idaho and Montana.

The plan to use fire as a preventative to fire is absolutely good. Everything depends, however, upon *how* it is used. The Forest Service has used fire extensively ever since it assumed charge of the public timber lands of California. We are selling 200,000,000 feet of timber and on all the lands on which we have logged we see to it that the slashings and litter on the ground are piled up and burned. This must be accomplished, of course, in such a way that no damage results to the younger tree growth, such as seedlings, saplings, thickets, and poles of the more valuable species. If we should burn without preparing the ground beforehand, most of the young trees would be killed. . . .

---

6 Excerpted from F. E. Olmsted, "Fire and the Forest—the Theory of 'Light Burning,'" *Sierra Club Bulletin*, January 1911, 42–47.

What "light burning" has done on private lands in California, accompanied by preparation of the ground beforehand, shows that wherever the fire has actually burned, practically *all* young trees up to fifteen years of age have been killed absolutely, as well as a large part of those between the ages of fifteen and forty years.

The operation, to be sure, has resulted in cleaning up the ground to a considerable extent and will afford fairly good protection to mature trees in case they are threatened by fire in the future. If a fire comes along it will naturally not have as much rubbish to feed upon and may not be so hot as to injure the larger tree growth. In other words, a safeguard has been provided for timber which may be turned into dollars in the immediate future. With this advantage has come the irreparable damage to young trees. It has amounted, in fact, to the almost total destruction of all wood growth up to the age of twenty years.

This is not forestry; not conservation; it is simple destruction.

That is the whole story in a nutshell. The private owner of timber, whose chief concern is the protection of trees which can be turned into money immediately and who cares little or nothing about what happens to the younger stuff which is not yet marketable, may look upon the "light burning" plan as being serviceable and highly practical, provided the expense is reasonable. On the other hand, the Government, first of all, must keep its timber lands producing crops indefinitely, and it is wholly impossible to do this without protecting, encouraging, and bringing to maturity every bit of natural young growth. Any attempt to artificially reproduce the area of government forests as a whole would be impracticable from the standpoint of expense and has also proved very uncertain of success. Forest organizations the world over rely chiefly upon a natural regrowth to take the place of the old timber, and planting and sowing are resorted to only in cases where the natural regrowth has failed or is exceedingly hard to obtain; in such cases, of course, planting is indispensable.

The experimental "light burning" has cost approximately 75 cents per acre. Therefore, to clean up and burn the government lands in California even partially and most unsatisfactorily, coupled with a most serious loss of young growth (which in itself would prohibit the operation), an expense something like a million and a quarter dollars a year would be necessary, provided we repeated the process every three or four years, as deemed necessary by those advocating this theory.

As for the "old Indian fires," in California alone they have reduced over 2,000,000 acres of valuable timber lands to non-productive wastes of brush; they have damaged the mature stands of timber which we now have to the extent of reducing their original volume by at least thirty-five percent; and they have practically eliminated most of the young growth in their paths up to thirty years old. This is a fact fully sustained by the most casual observation on the ground....

Another argument is that if the ground is kept clean by "light burnings" we shall never have "crown" fires, and the frightful conflagrations in Montana and Idaho during the last summer [1910] are pointed to as examples of criminal negligence on the part of the Forest Service.[7] It is said that if we had burned over the ground lightly from time to time such fires would never have occurred. As a matter of fact, no amount of "light burning" would have made any difference whatever. If we had burnt the ground until there was nothing upon it but bare earth the same disastrous results would have followed. The flames were in the *tops* of the trees, advancing in solid masses of flames. The condition of the ground had absolutely nothing to do with it. The top-fires resulted, in the first instance, from many small and scattered ground fires which the inadequate force was unable to get to, control, and put out at the start. Then came the hurricane, which carried these fires up into the crowns of the trees. If the small fires had been properly put out at the very first there would have been no ground fires. If there had been men enough, telephones enough, roads and trails enough, they could have been extinguished and we should have had no "crown" fires.

The theory of "light burning" is sound. The Forest Service uses it in practice, and has done so for years, and will continue to do so. "Light burning" cannot be considered, however, unless it is preceded by such thorough preparation of the ground as will insure complete protection to young growth when the fire comes along. At present this preparation cannot be made effective except at an expense which is wholly out of the question. If it could be done at a reasonable cost, we should gladly and immediately extend our fire cleanings as practiced on lumbered areas on all uncut forests.

---

7 The Great Fires of 1910 burned an estimated three million acres in Idaho and Montana in three days, a fire siege that had a formative impact on the fledgling US Forest Service and its call for full-on fire suppression; see Stephen J. Pyne, *Year of the Fires: The Story of the Great Fires of 1910* (Missoula, MT: Mountain Press Publishing Company, 2008).

Warren E. Coman, from "Did the Indian Protect the Forest?" (1911)[8]

This is the time of year for forest fires. Through the acrid haze overhanging all this vast Northwest the sun rises a disc of angry crimson and sets with face still ruddier—like an old toper rising from a past debauch to stagger through another round of yet deeper potations, to fall at last to his couch, more ingloriously drunk than ever.

How many millions are going into the making of that haze this season? Will improvements in methods of prevention, greater vigilance, larger forces for the fire war, check the dreadful yearly waste?

The statisticians will tell us when the fall rains and upland early snows knock out the last timber blaze in 1911.

What is the best method to preserve the forest from fire?

One somewhat vociferously advocated is that of annual burning to destroy the undergrowth and the fallen leaves and twigs. The proponents of that system of forest preservation point, as one of their principal arguments, to the face (as they claim) that the Indian has been accustomed for centuries to burn the forests, in order to preserve them in their pristine state.

To persons conversant with the Indian nature this is preposterous. The Indians were nomads, who dwelt in skin tepees, and banded together in tribes, whose interests were always individual and tribal and never collective, as a nation or an association of tribes.[9]

The systematic burning of the forests by the Indians would suggest a desire by the redmen for the preservation of the trees for future use. But the history of the Indians shows that they lived always in the present. If they wished fuel, a tree on the ground was much easier to cut than one which they had to fell, and an Indian is not looking for hard work. They had no need to provide lumber for habitations, for their dwellings were covered in skins of animals and not with products of the mills. They were, however, conversant with the ways of the beasts of the forest and the manner by which nature reproduced her

---

8 Excerpted from Warren E. Coman, "Did the Indian Protect the Forest?," *Pacific Monthly*, September 1911, 300–306.
9 Counter-arguments include David J. Strohmaier, *Drift Smoke: Loss and Renewal in a Land of Fire* (Reno: University of Nevada Press, 2005), 35–43, and Nancy Langston, *Forest Dreams, Forest Nightmares: The Paradox of Old Growth in the Inland West* (Seattle: University of Washington Press, 1995), 46.

species. They knew after a fire was started, the deer, bear, and other animals would frequent the vicinity of the blaze, not in the path of the flames, but on the sides and on the burned-over ground where the smoke kept off the swarms of flies and gnats that tormented them in the open, and the Indians also knew that if they burned the grass in the forest one year, that the next year there would be better grazing for their ponies. They likewise knew that if, for any reason, the grass was not good where they were, they could pack their tepees on their ponies and go where it was better. But the idea that the Indians burned the forests at stated intervals to preserve them is derided by pioneers who have spent years with the redmen and who understand their ways and methods, and it is laughed at by old Indians today.

On the contrary, the use of fire to preserve the forest is a modern idea, and the beneficial results from flames among the trees in earlier days was accidental rather than designed. The nature-lover walks amongst the trees and the soughing of the zephyrs among their branches brings him peace and contentment. The dense growth of underbrush and fern, the green turf underfoot the climbing vine delight him with their beauty. A thick mat of dry grass tempts him to rest his limbs, while he ponders the wonders that Nature has provided for his entertainment. A mass of cones from the pine tree heaped high above its base adds its part to the picture as the nature-lover sees it.

The woodsman, however, looks at it a different way. The dense undergrowth and fern and climbing vine are to him a menace. The thick mat of dry grass on which the nature-lover reposes, is an insidious enemy, and the heap of pinecones at the base of the tree are an immediate source of danger. He realizes the disaster a match or a cigarette, carelessly dropped, might cause. . . .

There are two methods of fire protection for forests: One is that of annual burning, and the other is the patrol system. Some persons maintain that the first is the *only* way; others maintain that the second is best under present circumstances . . .the only practical plan under present conditions is the patrol system, whereby a corps of efficient men is kept in the areas to be protected, whose duty it is to keep a lookout for fires, and extinguish them if possible, or summon assistance if necessary.

Such a system can be maintained at its fullest efficiency where the Federal Government, the State forces, and the private owners work in a systematic manner and on a definite plan. . . . Such concerted, systematic efforts will result in the preservation of the timber at the lowest cost. A well-trained patrolman can direct a large number of laborers. By concerted action on their part, what would otherwise become a disastrous conflagration could be extinguished in its incipiency.

Joseph A. Kitts, from "Preventing Forest Fires by Burning Litter" (1919)[10]

Forest fires in the United States destroy, year by year, more than the forest yield. Fire destruction increases as forest litter increases. The stand of timber is being cut at a rate not less than 3.5 percent per annum. It is evident that we must not only save the yield, but also augment natural reproduction by planting, in order to insure a future supply. Fire has been the most difficult problem of the forests and the situation is now so critical that engineers should earnestly seek a solution.

Forest fires are of three types in effect. Surface fires that spread over the surface of the forest floor, fed by the litter; ground fires consuming the humus and sometimes the roots of trees; and crown fires, which destroy the entire forest cover. The crown fire is an extension of the surface fire into the tree crowns and the litter must be very heavy, dry and inflammable to cause and sustain it. Tree crowns will not burn of themselves. The humus must be very dry to sustain a ground fire.

On my homelands, in California, I have practiced, for the past 28 years, a method of prevention of destructive forest fires learned in principle from the Sierra Nevada Indians. This method, which is a natural one, has proven thoroughly practicable, considering cost of application and betterment of the forest, and is here offered as a solution of the fire problem in the coniferous forests.

Briefly, the method is as follows: Surface fires are employed, during and at the end of the wet season to remove the litter, the cause of crown fires. A fraction of the forest area is burned over each year in rotation. The period of rotation is varied from five to 50 years depending upon the local rate of litter accumulation; i.e. from one-fiftieth to one-fifth is cleaned of litter each year. This is the employment of the backfire principle, before summer fires occur, to form fire barriers. The litter is not allowed to accumulate in any area in proportions sufficient to cause and sustain crown fires. The litter is so damp, at this season of the year, that it is barely able to sustain a surface fire; thus, the surface fires do no harm to the live trees and there is no danger of crown or ground fires. The method will be outlined in detail in a succeeding paragraph.

---

10 Excerpted from Joseph A. Kitts, "Preventing Forest Fires by Burning Litter," *Timberman*, July 1919, 91–92.

That the Indians practiced a periodic practice of burning over the forests is well known.... In other words, he used the surface fire often enough to prevent the litter from accumulating into crown fire proportions. This was the natural and only method available to him. The Indian may not have been very scientific from a silviculturalist's point of view, but we must admit that his methods of preservation and natural reproduction were highly successful when compared with our results. Although the first growth trees are fire-marked throughout the Sierra Nevada forests, the indications of crown fires prior to the coming of the Americans are in small proportion and so indistinct as to point to destructive fires very remotely in the past, if at all. This aboriginal practice accounts for the survival, for thousands of years, of the oldest living beings, the Big Trees. The conifer trees naturally create conditions which make fire inevitable: the Indians used a natural agent, fire, to prevent these inevitable fires from causing destruction. The pioneers found these forests clean and open; today, they are so encumbered with fallen trees and other litter that complete destruction is the usual result of a summer fire.

Crown fires are unknown in the densely planted coniferous forests of France because the people gather the litter for fuel. It is not economically possible, of course, for us to go fagoting through our forests and we must dispose of the litter in some other manner....

Any engineer, forester, or woodsman experienced in forest fire fighting may safely use the following rules for surface fire control and ground fire prevention.

- Burn the forest litter, by means of surface fire spreading over the forest floor, during and at the end of the wet season, in intervals of from five to 50 years, depending on the local rate of litter accumulation. Standing dead snags, fallen trees, limbs, cones, leaves, needles, underbrush and weeds should be included as litter.
- Do not fire the forest litter when the humus becomes dry. A wet humus serves as an index to the safe burning season and prevents ground fires.
- Do not light fires when a high wind is prevailing.
- Fire the "snags," dead trees, in mid-winter when conditions are most unfavorable for fires.
- Fire the lodgments of litter when conditions are unfavorable for surface fires.
- Light the first fires over the areas of least litter and least density of stand.
- Backfire from the barriers (toward the wind). These barriers may be roads, trails, canals, barren and cultivated areas, recently burned over areas, bodies of water, ice and snow, and barriers scrapped for the purpose.

- Burn over the southerly slopes while the snow is on the north slopes. Burn downward from the tops of the slopes.
- Fire the ridges before the slopes and the slopes before the ravines, forming a succession of barriers.

In initiating fire control, the order of burning should be as follows for a five-year rotation:

- First year, snags and lodgments
- Second year, ridges
- Third year, southerly slopes
- Fourth year, northerly slopes
- Fifth year, ravines or bottoms

These rules will require a logical interpretation to suit the local conditions.

The cost application of this method is practical as it involves little more than lighting fires and allowing them to spread over the forest floor, observing and controlling their progress. . . .

Fire is a natural silvicultural agent in the coniferous forests provided that these fires are confined to moderate surface fires as would be possible if this method were used. Fire is an aid to reproduction as it creates favorable conditions for the germination of the seeds by removing competition, preparing the seed bed, allowing the sun to reach the soil, releasing seeds by opening closed cones, temporarily driving away seed-eating rodents, and removing insects and fungus. Fire serves to keep a forest clean and thrifty by removing the insect pests and fungus diseases which have their origin in rotting litter of the forest floor. A surface fire renders the forest immune to crown fires at all seasons of the year and for at least five years. The use of fires is a natural silvicultural method particularly adapted to the coniferous forests because of the great fire resistance of the conifer tree, and the more valuable species have the greater resistance.

This use and control of the surface fire, the natural agent, is the solution to the fire problem in the coniferous forests.

Fig. 7. Among the technological innovations that the US Forest Service developed to accelerate its rangers' ability to spot and fight fires, was this rail-adapted fire-patrol vehicle. Credit: Library of Congress.

Fire Fight, 1919–1924

It became increasingly difficult for those like Joseph Kitts, who believed that fire was a critical tool for good forest management, to make themselves heard. That is because, beginning in the late 1910s, and accelerating through the mid-1920s, the US Forest Service noisily proclaimed that the suppression of all fire was the only acceptable policy. It pressed its case through every available medium, sending out reams of publicity to newspapers and magazines across the country. Whenever the opposition published an article, as with Stuart Edward White's in *Sunset*, the Forest Service submitted a rejoinder (a back-and-forth that after two or three rounds left the agency with the last word). Federal researchers joined the fray, developing data about the exorbitant costs of "light burning"—some of it manufactured—that reinforced the Forest Service's conviction that forests must be protected from fire. Two chiefs of the agency, Henry Graves and William B. Greeley, declared their allegiance to this cause, and their arguments and the evidence on which they are based are so parallel and consistent that they seem templated. As chief, Greeley squashed internal dissent: "Face the facts," he wrote Roy Headley, a member of the agency's Washington staff, after learning that his subordinate had questioned the thrust of pro-suppression research emanating from California.[1] Even Aldo Leopold, who later would emerge as a critic of the agency, adopted this framework in his contribution to Forest Service's all-hands-on-deck approach to managing public discourse.

California was the epicenter of the battle to control the debate. *Sunset*, which favored the use of light burning, was located in San Francisco, as was the Forest Service's regional office. Under the direction of regional forester Paul Redington, agency staff, publicists, researchers, and rangers churned out articles—professional and popular—that reinforced the party line. They amplified the use of the term "Piute forestry" to demean their opponents (apparently operating on the assumption that the worst thing one white person could call another was an Indian) and conducted historical research that purported

---

1 Diane M. Smith, *Sustainability and Wildland Fire: The Origins of Forest Service Wildland Fire Research*, FS-1085 (Washington, DC: USDA Forest Service, 2017), 29.

to show that Indigenous people in the state had not used fire to manage the land and that the Spanish missionaries were mistaken when they recorded copious examples of fire-tended terrain. After the California Forestry Committee reported in late 1922 that it had successfully proven that light burning was more expensive than fire suppression and therefore was an unacceptable forest-management tool, Redington declared victory.

This was a Pyrrhic victory, however. Those in favor of controlled burns had argued since the late-nineteenth century that excluding fire from western forests would increase the danger of runaway conflagrations. Just as the light burning controversy simmered down in the mid-1920s, the Angeles and San Bernardino National Forests, which overlay the Southern California mountains, experienced a series of large fires. As a result, the Mission Indian Federation wrote to President Coolidge in 1924 urging that the land be returned to its original stewards. The Department of Agriculture ignored in its reply the implied claim that Indigenous people knew best how to manage these fire-prone landscapes and it would be decades before the federation's assertion that traditional ecological knowledge should take precedence over western science gained traction, it is telling that these principles were announced at the very moment when the Forest Service's fire-suppression policy appeared ascendant. Paradigms at their birth contain the seeds of their undoing.

Henry S. Graves, from "Graves Terms Light Burning 'Piute Forestry'" (1920)[2]

Without attempting any exhaustive statement on the subject, I wish to give the readers of *The Timberman* just what the issue is which has been raised by the advocates of light burning in California. I do this with a great deal of conviction, because I feel that the plausible theory of "Piute forestry" strikes at the very roots of the whole system of forestry protection, which the timber owners and states in your region have built up with such admirable results, upon which so much money and effort have been expended and for which such a splendid backing in public sentiment and support has been secured. We are now told in subtle words that, as to the pine lands of the western states, this system of forest protection is unnecessary and that we substitute for it a cheap and easy method of "touch'em off and let it burn."

Light burning advocates assert that by firing pine forest every few years the woods will be kept clean of inflammable debris without injury to the merchantable stumpage, even without injury to the young growth. The constant cleaning out of small stuff, underbrush, and litter supposedly would thus protect the woods from serious conflagrations. It has even been claimed that pine forests protected by this system will not burn, and the whole thing is to be dome at a cost of a fraction of a cent an acre.

As a matter of fact, it is the repeated firing of the woods which has steadily eaten up the pine forests of California. Our national forests in that state today contain close to two million acres of brush patches, which were once heavily timbered. Wiping out the forests on these areas in the national forests alone has cost the timber resources of California, on the basis of average figures, around 37 billion feet of stumpage, and probably $75,000,000 in value at the present time. This loss is not the result of a few large conflagrations. By and large, it has come about from one ground fire after another extending over a total of 50 or 100 years. Not only does each of these ground fires destroy much of all the young growth; the butts of the old timber are eaten out, inch by inch. After every burning a few more of the old trees topple over in the wind. The ultimate result is a brush patch.

---

2 Excerpted from Henry S. Graves, "Graves Terms Light Burning 'Piute Forestry,'" *Timberman*, January 1920, 35.

To me it is an absurd proposition that we can now go into the pine forests and large areas deliberately at a negligible cost per acre, which is one of the main claims of the advocates of the system, without continuing the same process of graduate but irresistible destruction. The "light burning" is supposed to be controlled. In practice the control apparently amounts only to choosing the time of year when the woods are fired. The Forest Service has studied every area which it was able to learn about where intentional light burning has been practiced. Its effects have been substantially the same as those of the unintentional ground fire in the California pine forests. In every case at least a large part of the young growth has been killed. In every case more or less injury has been done to old timber, except where large trees have been protected by costly methods, such as raking debris from the butts or piling earth around them, methods so costly that the light burners have abandoned them.

The Forest Service has no young growth to burn up. Neither has it any merchantable stumpage to sacrifice to the theory of protection which is essentially destructive. Hundreds of thousands of acres of national forest lands in the Western pine belt, which has been protected successfully for 12 or 15 years, now furnish a practical demonstration of what these forests can be made to produce under a genuine system of fire protection. Their brush patches are disappearing in thickets of pine saplings. The net growth per acre has been tremendously increased. The timber which the whole country will need when our virgin forests are depleted is now being produced. The Forest Service must oppose with the utmost vigor any system of protection which will wreck these growing forests or which will make it impossible to produce similar forests in the Western pine belt generally.

The issue is not simply one between protecting old timber and growing young timber. The plausible arguments advanced in support of light burning make this proposal exceptionally dangerous to our whole protective system. It weakens the confidence of the public in a genuine system of fire protection. It weakens the united effort which all forestry interests in the Northwest have made for the prompt protection and suppression of forest fires, for the close control of the use of fire and for developing a public sentiment alert at all times to keep fire out of the woods. It weakens the support given by timber landowners to joint and organized protective efforts. . . . It encourages incendiarism on the part of anyone who for his own personal ends wants to have the woods burned. It tends to block progressive fire protection legislation in the western states. I regard it as a challenge to the whole scheme of efficient forest protection., in which the Pacific Coast has taken such fine leadership and which is absolutely fundamental to any progressive development in forestry.

I, of course, recognize fully the utility of fire, properly controlled, as an agent of forest protection. The burning of slashings, in the manner best adapted to the type of forest and its natural process of regeneration, is good forestry. But I can admit no argument on the basic premise that the conception of forest protection which must underlie all of our efforts must be a conception of forests so protected that they will be perpetuated. Anything else is purely a makeshift, which at its best is simply a part of a process of timber mining. Our difficult problem of forest protection in the Western states must be worked out in harmony with this basic conception of our goal. It must underlie our state legislation as well as all activities and efforts of the federal government. It is because of the light burning theory is a direct attack upon that conception that I have desired to define the issue in unequivocal terms.

Stewart Edward White, from "Woodsmen, Spare Those Trees! Why Fire Protection Does Not Really Protect Our Remaining Timber" (1920)[3]

Fifteen years ago, the people did not realize they possessed National Forests; or, if they were aware of that fact, they were rather inclined to resent it. There was too much interference with grazing and lumbering and camping and independence of the Freeborn to suit them. A Forest Ranger was about as popular as a crutch. But now, thanks to the devotion and loyalty of a group of these ill-paid men, we know we own the forests, we use them and are proud of them and interested in their preservation and maintenance.

That result has come about because of a campaign of education carried on both in print and by object lesson in the field. Cattlemen and sheepmen, formerly hostile, are now happy and satisfied in the regulated rights that have been substituted for the raids and wars of the old days; lumber sales have been worked out on a practical basis until both Government and operator have agreed on methods acceptable to both sides; the wonders of the mountains have been opened up by trail, road, and sign; by proposed camp-site and reserved horse feed to the great public on whose good will in the final analysis all these things depend. The beginnings were crude and many of the earlier theories ridiculous, but the Forest Service has worked steadily toward its two ideals, Use and Preservation; and it has in general held an open mind and felt its way toward perfected knowledge. Its willingness to abandon or modify its tentative ideas as new facts intervened has been the strength of its youth. In education of the public toward these ideals of Use and Preservation, by far the most emphasis has been on the prevention of fire. Fire has been considered the most destructive of all agencies.

Nevertheless, there is a more destructive agency now at work, increasing in violence and capable at its worst of destroying a full one hundred per cent of any forest in which it is allowed to run unchecked. It is a little beetle, about a quarter inch long, and he kills trees ten feet through, often in a single season.

---

3 Excerpted from Stewart Edward White, "Woodsmen, Spare Those Trees! Why Fire Protection Does Not Really Protect Our Remaining Timber," *Sunset Magazine*, March 1920, 23–26, 108, 110–116.

FIRE FIGHT, 1919–1924

These are your forests; you are at last taking some pride and interest in them; and you must stand one paragraph of pure statistics just to impress you with the fact that your property is in danger.

In the Black Hills of South Dakota this beetle has destroyed over one billion feet of timber and has stopped only where there was nothing left to destroy. In valleys and canyons of the Tuolumne of California near Hetch Hetchy, he has killed ninety-five percent of the mature trees.

On the Tongue River Indian Reservation[4] the authorities cut down 11,017 trees in an attempt to stop its ravages. In two and one-half months on about thirteen hundred acres a lumber company lost 1,845,000 feet of pine lumber. That is enough of statistics from widely separated localities. They could be repeated at any length you please. On both government and private timber, the infestation is epidemic, and where not controlled is increasing in deadliness. No fire has destroyed utterly a billion feet of mature pine trees; no fire has ever killed ninety-five per cent of pine trees in any considerable area; no fire known has swept pine lands as destructively as in the tracts above named, or in a thousand others.

Are the guardians of our forests alive to this menace? The Forester realizes the deadly nature of the danger, but only partially its extent. The same may be said of a great many of the subheads. Unless they have personally inspected large areas of infested forests, they can be only partially informed. And for this reason:

The Ranger and the Guard, on whom naturally they must depend for their statistics, are well trained in most ways, but not as regards tree-killing beetles. They can spot a fire and locate it and fight it expertly; they can handle sheep trespassers, timber sales, tourists, and especial uses. But they do not know an infested tree unless it is so far gone in dissolution that any child could spot it. Until three years ago there were just two men in the Forest Service of California who could tell a "bug tree" in its early stages—and that is the effective time to get busy. I do not believe there are many more now—certainly not in the rank and file of the field men. It is more important than his ability to handle fires, and it is more technical. He cannot learn it by going out to take a look; he must be taught by a competent expert.

One result of his ignorance of method is higher official ignorance of the situation. The Forester writes the District Forester a letter of inquiry and the District Forester commands a report from his field men on the situation. The Rangers ride about conscientiously enough but they fail to see ninety per cent of the indication for the simple reason that they have not the technical training

---

4 Now the Northern Cheyenne Indian Reservation.

to do so. The result is an official statement that the "alarmist reports are greatly exaggerated." Proof of this? Many of them on request, but one instance will suffice. The Head Ranger of one California forest reported officially—and honestly—that in a certain region "beetle infestation is nil." On one section only in that region we counted thirty-seven infested trees—all doomed and, what is of more importance, all centers for spreading infestation to their healthy neighbors.

Nor is this ignorance confined entirely to the field men who could not be expected to know about such things without especial training. Certain of the Government entomologists, some of them highly placed, have been betrayed by human nature into false doctrines. The whole question of tree-killing beetles in relation to the forests is comparatively a new one. A certain amount of excellent laboratory work had been done and also a certain amount of too-hasty field work, when certain theories that should have been advanced as tentative hypotheses were put forward as final conclusions. There is where the human nature comes in. Once having committed themselves, these scientists were reluctant to back water. They abandoned the scientific for the polemic; they were more interested in procuring facts to bolster their expressed theories than in refitting their theories as fresh facts came to attention. This is a serious statement and is meant to be.

. . . [T]here is another and bigger aspect to this subject. We must as an emergency measure control this epidemic before it destroys our property. We must also examine into its possible causes in order to prevent its future occurrence. And in that process, we find ourselves in a way to discuss another of the so-called destructive agencies—Fire.

Fire, however applied, kills beetles. In the ordinary control work of peeling and burning described above, it is the fire that does the trick—mere felling and peeling is no good. Fire running through the forest also kills the beetle, unless there is so much débris that the resultant conflagration is hot enough to sour the sap. Note that phrase *unless there is so much débris*, for we will return to it later. Just why fire kills beetles in the trees is not as yet quite clear. It certainly is not the heat, for sufficient heat to reach them under the bark would destroy the trees themselves by souring the sap. Perhaps the smoke gets the emerging swarms; perhaps the smoke may even penetrate the porous bark; perhaps the insects refuse a new host that has itself been thoroughly smoked. At present the theory is not clear nor conclusive. But the *fact* is well established. Three years ago . . . I advanced the idea as a hypothesis to be proved. My return to the forests this year has furnished that proof. Of seven hundred acres lightly burned over in 1915 we found in 1916 no infected trees; in 1917 one; in 1918 none; in 1919 two; a total of three. On the adjoining seven hundred acres of exactly the same timberland there were in 1917 twenty-eight; in 1918 six; in 1919 ten; a total of forty-four. Statistics are dull, so I offer this as a striking example. I have reports of eighteen similar instances. To the complete satisfaction of every practical woodsman outside of the Forest Service, and secretly to a great many inside it, the hypothesis has been proved—Fire kills bugs.

There remains to examine this remedy, to determine whether or not it is worse than the disease. The Forest Service tells us that it is, and the general public, educated for twenty years by the Forest Service, reacts blindly and instinctively against any suggestion of fire. Nevertheless fire—a bad master—is an excellent servant. There are good fires and bad fires. Let us not too blindly condemn one for the misdeeds of the other. To begin with, let us divest our minds for the moment of all thought of modern forest conditions and revert to the natural forest before man began either to cut or to protect. These forests were burned over periodically by fires that ran unchecked until the rains put them out. There is not a mature stand of forest in existence that does not show indications, not of one, but of many forest fires. Not one. Last year lightning started 851 fires out of a total of 1862 reported! Indians used to burn regularly. The actual tree destruction from these repeated fires was practically nothing, for at the present time the mature timber stand is as heavy as the soil will support. This is shown by the fact that until ripe timber is cut out the young growth remains stunted and worthless.

. . . It may be stated, and the real facts honestly examined will bear out the statement, that destructive fires in pine lands are practically impossible, either in large or small growth, without kindling to make them burn. You cannot burn a green log in a fireplace without kindling. Nor can you in a forest. You cannot even burn green pine branches in a forest thicket without superheating the air, generating gasses, and generally producing especial conditions. If you do not believe this, go into the woods with a gasoline torch and try it.

We leave now the "natural" forest and come to the forest as influenced by civilized man. He has made destructive fires by furnishing the kindling. This he has accomplished in two ways: by use and by preservation.

Nobody is unfamiliar with the huge and destructive fires that have ravaged some of the northern states and some parts of our mountains in the Northwest. Few are unfamiliar with the old-fashioned "slashing" that followed bad lumbering methods and furnished the materials from which many of these great conflagrations sprang. That is a cause and effect plainly remediable and need not concern us here.

But few are equally familiar with the conditions that result from rigid protection against all fires, beneficent and maleficent, over an extended period of time. The principle of rigid fire exclusion has come from a false interpretation of the forest methods in use abroad. Our forestry system was at first patterned pretty closely on a Prussian model. The forests of Europe are kept clean by hand labor; fallen branches, twigs and other débris are picked up and made into faggots, the brushy growth is kept down, the infected trees are extirpated the moment they show. There the forest floor is as clean as the back of your hand. It is a good system for them, but it is not applicable to us. No flight of the imagination could cover our immense and tangled forests with hand labor! Nevertheless, hand labor as a cleansing agent is the only substitute for the natural cleansing agent of fire. We have taken that away, but we have substituted nothing in its place.

The result is that we are painstakingly building a fire-trap that will piecemeal, but in the long run completely, defeat the very aim of fire protection itself. Rigid fire exclusion accumulates kindling, and when you get enough kindling you get a fire that you cannot exclude.

... I have seen assertions that "had it not been for surface burning California forests would now have from forty to sixty billion feet more timber." This is merely wild assertion based on unscientific surmise without a fact to support it, but it reads well, and it has its effect on the public. Barring lumbering, the destruction by fire where fuel has been allowed to accumulate, and small denuded areas due to one cause or another, the timber-bearing soil of California has until recently been carrying about its full crop. You cannot grow more trees to the acre than the soil will support even if you can find small openings here and there. As for several large open areas where "formerly forests stood," there is no evidence that these were even occupied by trees. You have to have soil, climate, altitude, and a few other things beside space.

Furthermore, what happened in the hot fires mentioned a few paragraphs ago is going in the long run to happen to the rest of the protected forest. By educating the public, by vigilance, by expert methods, one may prevent fires for five, ten, twenty five, fifty years. But one cannot eliminate all carelessness, all cussedness, all natural causes. More and more people are going into the National Forests on business and pleasure. They make camp fires, they smoke. The lightning continues to strike twice in the same place, proverbs to the contrary notwithstanding. Hundreds, perhaps thousands, of fires are started every year and are corralled before they get going, but sooner or later one out of a hundred of these little blazes—or one out of a thousand, it does not matter— does get going and then you have a big fire that deserves front pages in the papers. The longer the forest has been "protected," the more kindling and fuel have accumulated; the more fuel, the hotter the fire and the more difficult to confine. Instead of a cleansing, beneficent fire at the right time of year, we have a destructive maleficent fire at the wrong time of the year. It is the perfect example of the vicious circle.

... As a matter of fact, examination of a great many destructive August fires has fairly well convinced me that the April price would be low. The hottest fires—remember I am referring always to pine forests—at the worst times are not nearly as fatal as seems at first.

... Now, in conclusion, I wish to appeal for a fair scientific attitude toward these things. Forestry in this country is something that is pretty new. Our conditions here are not at all the same as those in other countries. We are feeling our way toward knowledge. Our danger is that we will become bureaucratic and hidebound and inclined to the closed mind. The Forest Service has no sincerer friend than myself and no more ardent admirer in most things. ... But in this one matter of fire in forests, the Forest Service has unconsciously veered to the attitude of defense of its theory at all costs. It is time to examine that theory. Practical woodsmen, intelligent men who are capable of observation and deduction and who have been in the woods all their lives, are a solid unit behind the ideas I have expressed in this article. There is nothing new in them. The facts are solidly there for the intelligent examination of whomever will divest his mind of all theory and examine for himself. It is a matter of thorough and open-minded examination and experiment. That examination and experiment should be made—*thorough and open-minded*. We cannot conclude them such when we find isolated facts stated out of context, partial suppressions, omissions, and half statements. There is no conscious dishonesty but there is plenty of human nature. Most of these woodsmen who are genuinely interested in these subjects have read and digested the standard textbooks in use at the forestry schools and colleges. It would astonish you to discover how conversant with the academic theories these "rough old lumbermen" are. The graduates of the forestry schools do not represent so exclusive a body of expert opinion on these subjects as they imagine. But the practical woodsmen have in addition two advantages—an open mind and wide experience. The private owner of forests has no pet theory. He holds no brief for light burning, nor, on the other hand, has he a four years' course of education as to fire exclusion to defend. What he wants is to preserve his forests. Most scientists or experts have a contempt for laymen. But in this case, it is not justified. The layman, if one can call them such, are not speaking from ignorance of the "experts'" reasons or reasoning. They speak from the teaching of the schools as tested rigidly, *for results*, in the forests themselves.

William B. Greeley, from "'Piute Forestry' or the Fallacy of Light Burning" (1920)[5]

For nearly 20 years a drive has been made in the western states to put an end to the destruction of forests by fire. This effort has been backed by many timber owners and by state and municipal agencies with a fine spirit of cooperation. From year to year it has received more widespread support in public sentiment.

The goal of this effort has been to keep fires out of the forest. It has sought to make the woods as fireproof as practicable through the disposal of slashings; to reduce the number of man-caused fires by state control of the use of fire and by creating a public sentiment wide awake at all times to keep fire out of the woods; to detect small fires quickly by patrols and lookout stations; and to put fires out by the systematic organization of all the forces available in an emergency.

In a large measure the effort to stop destructive forest fires in the western states has been successful. Millions of acres of both private and public forests have been efficiently protected. Thousands of small fires have been put out before doing serious damage. Many thousands more have been prevented through law enforcement and the educational campaign which has enlisted the support of the hunter, the camper, the logger, the railroad operator, the herdsman and the settler. The effort has not prevented all conflagrations in seasons or localities of extreme drought. It has not solved certain problems in protecting forests which are still inaccessible stretches of wilderness or which are still undermanned, or which are subject exceptional hazards by reason of local climate or local social and industrial conditions.

Bad fires still occur in European forests which have been under systematic protection and management for 200 years. We can expect no less in the inaccessible and thinly populated portions of our western states, which are exposed to climatic fire hazards as extreme as exist perhaps in any portion of the world. To condemn the methods of protecting the western forests because they have not prevented all fires would be as sensible as to condemn the fire-prevention work of our large cities because of the occasional Baltimore, San Francisco, or Chelsea fire. The protection of our western forests from fire, in which work timber owners and associations have taken a leading part, is one of the finest

---

5 Excerpted from William B. Greeley, "'Piute Forestry' or the Fallacy of Light Burning," *Timberman*, March 1920, 38–39.

accomplishments in forestry yet witnessed in the United States. One of its best features is that it has been brought about largely by the people of the western stares themselves, and that its greatest asset today lies in the public sentiment of the West to keep fires out of the woods.

It would seem unnecessary to uphold the protection of our western forests as a work commanding the support of every foreseer and timber owner in the United States, but a propaganda is now being preached which subtly strikes at the very roots of it. The advocates of light burning, or "Piute forestry," assert that fire should not be kept out of the pine forests, by all odds the most extensive in our western states. Instead of keeping fire out of the western pineries, the advocates of this system propose to burn them regularly every few years. They claim that a succession of light fires will keep these forests clean of inflammable material without injury to the merchantable stumpage. The frequent burning up of small growth, underbrush and litter supposedly would thus protect the woods from serious conflagrations.

It is even claimed that pine forests protected by this system will not burn, that their young trees will not be seriously injured, and the whole thing is to cost but a fraction of a cent per acre. This system is advocated by the Southern Pacific Railroad, which, because of its enormous federal land grants, is one of the two or three largest timber landowners in the United States. It is supported by other large timber-owning corporations particularly in California. Light burning has been preached in articles appearing in *American Forestry* and in various lumber journals. It is, in fact, a substitute offered to the people of the western states for the present system of forest protection which has hitherto made such splendid headway.

The light burners claim that their scheme was practiced by the Indians in various western pine forests long before the advent of the white man, asserting that the noble redskin fired the forests regularly, not so much to facilitate his hunting or protect his dwelling as because his nature lore taught him that this was the way to prevent the "big" forest fire. Their scheme means nothing more or less than a continuation of the frequent ground fire which, whether started by Indians or by lighting, swept over many of our western pineries at frequent intervals prior to the coming of the early hunters, prospectors, herdsmen, and settlers.

The light burners proposed to "control" the destructiveness of the deliberate firing by burning the woods in the spring or fall when sufficiently moist to prevent the fire from seriously injuring either old timber or young trees. A careful study of the area where this system has been intentionally practiced shows that such control amounts to little or nothing. The light burners ignore certain basic facts about fire conditions in our western pineries. They ignore the rapidity with which evaporation under intense sun light in warm weather heats up the litter in the pine woods. A south slope will be so dry as to make any fire exceedingly hot and destructive before a north slope will burn at all. Areas which will burn but lightly and irregularly early in the morning, will flare up and consume in the most approved fashion by mid-afternoon. The moisture following light spring or fall rains often disappears so rapidly that the period of "safe" burning is a matter of hours, not of days. Actually, to burn the western pineries, as the advocates of this theory propose to burn them, would, if it could be done at all, entail a cost for effective control many times greater than the cost of an efficient system of fire detection and suppression.

Light burning, in actual practice, is simply the old ground fire which has been the scourge of the western pineries, under a new name. Its use means a deliberate continuation of the destructive surface fires which were steadily and irresistibly eating up the pine forests of our western states until they were placed under protection. In every western state without exception, the pine forests have been thinned out, cut down in area, replaced here and there by brush or grass land, have often become diseased, and have lost much of the young growth which normally they should contain, as the result of fire. This has not been brought about by a few large conflagrations. It is the cumulative result of one fire after another extending over a period of 50–100 years. Every time a fire runs over these areas, a few more old trees are hollowed out at the base so that the next high wind topples them over, a few more fine logs become infected with rot through surface scars, and more of the young growth by which nature constantly seeks to recover lost ground is crowded out by brush. If surface burning is not stopped, the end is total destruction, a destruction which, though less spectacular, is just as complete and disastrous as when a forest is consumed in a crown blaze that kills everything at once.

The total destruction of pine forests has actually been caused by repeated firing in many parts of the West. The National Forests of California alone, where light burning is most strenuously advocated, contain nearly two million acres of pure brush patches which formerly were heavily timbered. These brush patches cover nearly 14 percent of the timber belt in the National Forests of that state. That they were once pine forests is fully attested by the occasional snag or half dead tree still left standing, by the charred stumps, by tree roots half rotted in the ground. Those brush patches represent a loss to the forest resources of California today which we can safely put at 37 billion feet of standing timber with a value of probably $75,000,000; and that loss will go steadily on if light burning of the pine forests is permitted. In many other pine areas, the stand of timber is not only much less than it should be because of frequent surface fires but has been reduced in volume and quality by disease which follows in the train of the fire. Incense cedar is one of the important trees in the California pine forests, but its timber is so defective that the lumberman has often been unable to log it at all. An intensive study of sample areas has shown that 84 percent of the rot in incense cedar is traceable directly to fire scars. A large proportion of the loss in volume and quality of pine stumpage, which is a normal thing in practically all western pine camps is due to the same cause.

Aside from the gradual wiping out of the mature timber in these virgin forests, the system of ground burning effectively cleans them of young tree growth. If all the seedlings and saplings are not destroyed in the first or second fire, the third or fourth fire completes the job. It is absolutely impossible to ground burn large areas repeatedly and save any young growth on them. The actual fires of the light burner prove this, whatever he may claim. As a matter of fact, the light burner does not want young growth. It is part of the inflammable debris which he would get out of the forest as to render a "serious" conflagration impossible. When the mature timber in a light-burned forest is cut, the forest is at an end. Its productivity ceases. It becomes a brush parch.

This is the real issue which has been raised by the advocacy of light burning. ... In other words, let us recognize frankly that light burning is simply part of the game of timber mining. To the gutting of heavy cutting it adds the gutting of total destruction to young growth. To cheapen the protection and utilization of old timber, it deliberately transforms the forest into a brush patch.

The issue raised by light burning is not what its advocates claim—the utility of fire properly controlled as a means of forest protection. Everyone recognizes the utility of fire, if properly controlled. ... The issue raised by light burning is rather whether our forest protection in the West is to be the kind of protection which conserves and promotes tree growth, or whether it is to be simply an adjunct of timber mining. It is for this reason that I stated with conviction at the beginning of this article that light burning strikes at the roots of our forest protection effort in the western states. The people living in and near the western pineries have been caught to believe that fire must be kept out of the woods. To a surprising degree they have recognized the truth of that slogan. They have supported state legislation and private associations based upon that principle. They have come to believe that fire and forest growth do not go together. Their support of a genuine system of forest protection has been not only to save their virgin stumpage but also to perpetuate their vast pineries which mean so much so the economic future of the West.

Now comes an insidious doctrine telling everyone that this system of fire protection which has been built up with so much effort is unnecessary; that all we need to do with our western pine forests is to "touch 'em off." The plausible arguments advanced in advocacy of light burning make this proposal exceptionally dangerous. It weakens the confidence of the general public in real fire protection. It weakens the support given by timber landowners to organized protective efforts such as state and federal agencies and many associations have been successful in bringing about. It tends to block progressive fire legislation in the western states. It tends to encourage incendiary fires by the settler, prospector, or stock grower who has reasons of his own for wishing to clear the woods. It is a direct challenge to a national policy of forestry for it strikes unmistakably at the effort to keep timber lands productive rather than permit them to become waste. . . .

We should no more permit an essential destructive theory, like that of light burning, to nullify our efforts at real forest protection than we would permit sure cures of tuberculosis to do away with sanitary regulations of cities, the tuberculosis sanitaria, fresh air for patients, and the other means by medical and hygienic science for combatting the white plague.[6]

---

6 The irony of this analogy is that contemporary medical science was no more able to "combat" the "white plague" than the Forest Service in the 1920s was able to stamp out wildland fire.

Aldo Leopold, from "'Piute Forestry' vs. Forest Fire Prevention" (1920)[7]

Southwestern mining men and southwestern foresters have many common interests. The National Forests supply timber and water used by miners, while the mines are one of the important sources of prosperity in the National Forest communities. For this reason, southwestern mining men may be interested in a new problem which now confronts the administrators of the forests, namely, the propaganda recently started by the Southern Pacific Railroad and certain timber interests in favor of "light-burning," or the so called "Piute Forestry."

"Light-burning" means the deliberate firing of forests at frequent intervals in order to burn up and prevent the accumulation of litter and thus prevent the occurrence of serious conflagrations. This theory is called "Piute Forestry" for the alleged reason that the California Indians, in former days, deliberately "light-burned" the forests in order to protect them against serious fires.

Foresters generally are strenuously opposing the light-burning propaganda because they believe that the practice of this theory would not only fail to prevent serious fires but would ultimately destroy the productiveness of the forests on which western industries depend for their supply of timber.

The whole principle involved may be put in a nutshell by stating that under certain conditions mature forests are not killed outright by light-burning, and can be kept alive in spite of surface fires, provided, however, that no other actual drain is made upon their productive capacity. In other words, certain forests will withstand light-burning provided they do not have to withstand anything else. But this proviso is the very negation of the fundamental principle of forestry, namely, to make forests productive not only of a vegetative cover to clothe and protect our mountains, but also of the greatest possible amount of lumber, forage, and other forest products.

Forests cannot be productive under light-burning because:

- Light-burning destroys most of the seedling trees necessary to replace the old stand as it is removed for human use.
- Light-burning gradually reduces the vitality and productiveness of the forage.

---

7 Excerpted from Aldo Leopold, "'Piute Forestry' vs. Forest Fire Prevention," *Southwestern Magazine*, March 1920, 12–13.

- Light-burning destroys the humus in the soil necessary for rapid tree growth, (that is, rapid lumber production, and germination of the seed.)
- Light-burning, by inflicting scars, abnormally increases the rots which destroy the lumber, and increases the resin which depreciates lumber grades and intensifies subsequent fires.
- Light-burning, in most cases at least, increases the destructive effects of wood-boring insects.

... The Forest Service policy of absolutely preventing forest fires insofar as humanly possible is directly threatened by the light-burning propaganda. It is up to the public and especially the users of the forests to decide whether they wish that policy continued or whether they wish to try "Piute Forestry." If the public desires the continuance of forest fire prevention, now is the time to put the quietus on the agitation for light-burning.

It is, of course, absurd to assume that the Indians fired the forests with any idea of forest conservation in mind. As is well known to all old-timers, the Indian fired the forests with the deliberate intent of confusing and concentrating the game so as to make hunting easier. It appears to be a fact that when deer or other game animals smell a smoke they stand stupefied with their heads in the air until actually singed by the heat or flames. They then make a wild break in any direction and largely lose their usual caution and ability to escape their human enemies. A bunch of deer with their heads in the air waiting for a fire presented an easy mark, even to the Indian's bow and arrow, and it was this fact, and not any desire for fancied forest conservation, which caused the Indians to burn the forests.

The destructive effects of Piute Forestry can readily be seen in California and in many areas of the Southwest. It can be stated without hesitation that a large percentage of the chaparral or brush areas found in the Southwestern states were originally covered with valuable forests, but gradually reverted to brush after repeated light-burning had destroyed the reproduction. In fact, the remains of large old stumps and pitchy roots can be found in these brush areas in many places. It is probably a safe prediction to state that should light-burning continue for another fifty years, our existing forest areas would be further curtailed to a very considerable extent. It is also a known fact that the prevention of light-burning during the past ten years by National Forest administration has brought in growth on large areas where reproduction was hitherto largely lacking. Actual counts show that the 1919 seedling crop runs as high as 100,000 per acre, and in some cases 400,000 per acre. It does not require any very elaborate argument to show that these tiny trees, averaging only two inches high, would be completely destroyed by even a light ground fire.

It is an old saying that fire is a good servant but a poor master. It is the opinion of foresters generally that the light-burners who propose to make fire their servant will find that forest fires are not so easily subjugated. In fact, it would be in practice absolutely impossible to fire the forests without destroying the young growth, not to mention the constant risk of the fire breaking out of bounds and destroying buildings, fences, and mature timber. Most light-burning propagandists undoubtedly know this already, but do not care whether the young growth is destroyed or not. Their investments are in mature timber, and the less young growth there is left in the country the greater their chance for speculative profits. But the public does care, because wholesale destruction of young growth means timber famine at some time in the future. To actually control light-burning would cost more than the entire present system of forest administration (about three cents per acre per year, gross) of which fire prevention is but a fraction. Why pay such a price for the privilege of burning up our future timber supplies?

Charles E. Ogle, from "Light Burning" (1920)[8]

Although a great deal has been said on both sides of the question of the systematic burning of the forest floor each year or every other year as a means of protection against fires and pine beetles, too little has been done, as this subject deserves serious consideration. Many thousands of dollars are spent each year in forest protection and while the methods employed are successful to a large extent, thus far at least, in keeping the destructive fires from doing any material damage to the forests, each year the hazard is becoming greater. In past years timber was of little value and the early settlers gave no thought to the prevention of fires except when their homes were endangered and fires started by hunters, Indians, and lightning ran unchecked through the forests year after year, keeping the underbrush, windfalls, and needles burned out and preventing an accumulation of trash on the forest floor, which is yearly becoming a greater menace as a breeding place for destructive fires.

The fact that up until a few years ago the forests were continually swept by fire would disprove the theory that this method, if practiced today, would be fatal to the young growth and while it must be admitted that much of the young growth is destroyed by these fires, sufficient of it has thus far escaped to keep the forests up to normal, and the proper thinning out not only enables the remaining timber to get a better growth but makes it possible to remove the ripening timber without serious damage to the coming growth.

Another theory advanced is that the fires stunt the growth of the timber. This is easily disproved as many of the largest trees in our standing timber today show evidence of having been severely burned at an early stage of their development. While sections which support only stunted growths of timber are cited as evidence that light burning is detrimental it will be noted that there is none but stunted timber in these localities and it is improbable that the entire section of the country would be evenly burned as to cause a uniform stunting of the entire locality. The cause may be soil or altitude. Many bad fires are pointed out as being the result of these early fires which were allowed to go unchecked, and while it is true that many barren hills bear evidence of this statement, a survey of all of the bad fires which have left large areas without standing timber will show most of them to be in places where a fire, once started, could not keep from doing great damage before any natural conditions

---

8 Excerpted from Charles E. Ogle, "Light Burning," *Timberman*, July 1920, 106–108.

FIRE FIGHT, 1919–1924

arose to check it. On heavily timbered mountain sides crown fire could not be checked when aided by a high wind, until it spent itself at the top of the mountain. No doubt when the majority of these fires occurred the atmospheric conditions were ideal for their uninterrupted progress, and if a fire should start in a similar place and under like conditions at the present time the accumulation of trash and brush which is now so evident would undoubtedly cause a much more serious conflagration than any could have been in former years.

The northern part of Klamath county has been cited as an instance where destructive fires have stunted the timber but no mention has been made of the fact that a great deal of this territory is composed of volcanic ash or pumice stone from Mount Mazama[9] and that many thousands of acres support no growth whatever except a scrubby jack pine growth with only occasionally a small patch of yellow pine timber. On the other hand, there are some of the higher parts of northern Klamath and parts adjacent to fertile valleys which support a very good growth of yellow pine and some exceptionally good sugar pine, fir and cedar.

The desire for the preservation of second growth has probably been the greatest drawback to effectual fire protection. . . . Nature has always taken care of the proper production of new growth and as the fires ran unchecked through the forests a proper amount of thinning was affected and the remaining trees were thereby given a better chance to mature. Under the present system of fire control and the elimination of the thinning element the young growth is allowed to control the destiny of the mature timber, and if present misguided attempts to preserve a stunted forest for posterity are not corrected, a complete destruction of our standing timber of today and the elimination of possible second growth of practical value may be the result.

Another angle of light burning which is not to be overlooked is the value of fire as a pine beetle destroying agent and preventative. While very few are wont to give this subject serious consideration in the belief that there is no real danger to be feared from these destructive pests, a proper study of existing conditions proves this assumption to be erroneous. . . .

The Klamath and Lake Counties Forest Fire association in Oregon have done some systematic burning and the effect has been very gratifying. This burning has been done in conjunction with the pine beetle protection work and is easily done in the fall and spring of the year without damage to the standing timber.

In the early part of the months of May and November, the old logs and brush can easily be cleaned out, along with the accumulated beds of pine

---

9 Mount Mazama (elevation 8,157 feet) in the Cascade Range in Klamath County, Oregon.

needles, with practically no danger of damage to the standing timber if a little attention is given to the pitch butt trees in the locality of the area to be burned. A little soil thrown into the hollow of the pitch butt, or, in bad cases, a trench dug entirely around the tree in question, will prevent its destruction by the light fire necessary, while if a fire were to occur in the heat of Summer no such precautionary measures would be available and more than likely several thousands of feet of merchantable timber would be a total loss.

It is true that light burning would be very difficult to effect in many localities in which the forest floor has been so long neglected but each year this difficulty is increasing, and in time will come an accidental fire, which would gain considerable headway before it could be controlled and would do more damage than the controlled blaze at the time of the year when it could easily be handled.

If the forest floor were thoroughly burned once any fire could be easily handled if the entire forest area were kept burned off on every year or two and at the same time no fire could gain enough headway to do any material damage to the coming young growth and the danger from all sources would be reduced to minimum.

Paul G. Redington, *"Hic Jacet* (An Epitaph): Light Burning" (1923)[10]

The California Forestry Committee, at its meetings in San Francisco on January 5, unanimously voted that further investigation and work in cooperation with "light burning" was unnecessary, since the results of the last three years' work have demonstrated that such burning is impractical, both from a seasonal and financial point of view. This committee is made up of representatives of the Pine and Redwood Lumber Manufactures' Associations, the University [of California] Forest School, the State Board of Forestry, the Southern Pacific Railroad, and the Forest Service.

The conclusions of the committee coincide with those reached by the Forest Service investigators three years ago. The ghost of light burning is laid to rest.

---

10 Paul G. Redington, *"Hic Jacet* (An Epitaph): Light Burning," *California District News Letter,* January 1923, 5.

Donald Bruce, "Light Burning—Report of the California Forestry Committee" (1923)[11]

The following report, in most particulars self-explanatory, was unanimously adopted by the California Forestry Committee at its January meeting. This committee is composed the following members : P. G. Redington, District Forester, representing the U.S. Forest Service; M. B. Pratt, State Forester, representing the State Department of Forestry; R. F. Danaher, Manager of the Michigan-California Lumber Company, representing the California White and Sugar Pine Manufacturers' Association; C. R. Johnson, President of the Union Lumber Company, representing the California Redwood Manufacturers Association; B. A. McAllaster, Land Commissioner, representing the Southern Pacific Railway Company; Donald Bruce, Professor of Forest Engineering, representing the Division of Forestry of the University of California. The committee was organized in 1920 to study the question of light burning. This question, which has been the basis for a dispute lasting many years, was being heatedly discussed at that time, the light burning theory being supported by powerful and influential interests. Not only was cooperative fire protection between the Forest Service and lumbermen endangered, but the controversy threatened ill feeling along more general lines. The matter was brought to a head by three meetings of the California Section of the Society of American Foresters. The first of these was private and disclosed a wide divergence of opinion among Society members, not so much on questions of fact as on the adequacy of existing information and on the most advisable policy to be pursued. The two later meetings were open, with lumbermen and others interested in the forests specifically invited. At the first S. B. Show presented the views of the Forest Service, while at the second the arguments of the "light burners" were stated by Stewart Edward White, the well-known author, who also was a timber owner on a large scale. These meetings accomplished little directly save expose the actual and potential danger of the existing controversial situation, but it was largely as a result thereof that the California Forestry Committee was organized.

This committee is unusual in the simplicity of its organization and in its complete lack of clearly defined functions and responsibilities. It came into

---

11 Donald Bruce, "Light Burning—Report of the California Forestry Committee," *Journal of Forestry* 21, no. 2 (February 1923): 129–133.

FIRE FIGHT, 1919–1924

existence to meet a specific need, it meets only when occasion arises and were its usefulness to cease, it would die without the formality of disbanding. It is responsible to no one and has no authority. Its findings have weight only because of the nature of its membership and because it can act only by unanimous vote. All these peculiarities, which might seem weaknesses, have proved great sources of strength and vitality.

Its work and findings on the original issue are sufficiently described in the report itself. It may be of interest to add, however, that at a later date it was given a quasi-official standing through an action of the California State Board of Forestry. The board requested the committee to enlarge its personnel by adding a representative of the redwood lumbermen (the redwood region not having been involved in the light burning dispute) and to hold itself ready to act in an advisory capacity on matters of forest policy involving possible controversy. It has accordingly passed on numerous proposed legislative measures and has undertaken an investigation of the relative costs and advantages of "high lead" and "ground lead" yarding. According to many foresters the modern type of "high lead" yarding, claimed by the lumbermen to be decidedly cheaper, so completely destroys all seed trees and reproduction as to make subsequent fire protection the locking of an empty stable's door. The work of the committee on this question is barely commenced.

The theory of "light burning" is based on three postulates:

- That under favorable circumstances fire will run through the forest, consuming dead needles and branches, but with little or no damage to living trees;
- that the intensity of a given fire depends largely on the amount of inflammable debris which has accumulated on the ground since the preceding fire on the same area;
- that complete prevention of fire is impracticable. If these three statements are true it seems to follow that numerous light fires, particularly if they occur at chosen favorable times, will do less damage than will the occasional but inevitable fire under a system of fire prevention which will probably occur at the worst possible moment and which, fed by an accumulation of inflammable debris, will very probably become an unquenchable conflagration.

Opponents of the theory reply:

- that even light fires always do some damage both to mature timber and more especially to reproduction;

- that on the one hand the accumulation of true "debris" under a system of fire prevention ceases after five or six years, being from then on offset by decay, while on the other hand the accumulation of inflammable reproduction is an essential to timber production;
- that reasonably complete protection has been proven practicable by the experience of the United States Forest Service.

A lively discussion along these lines, which at times became quite controversial in its nature and which was prejudicing any harmonious action looking toward the betterment of forest conditions in this State, resulted in the formation of the California Forestry Committee. Its original purpose was to investigate amicably the merits of the aforementioned theory.

It would seem that the investigation of the three simple postulates above stated would involve few difficulties, since each is demonstrably either true or false. As a matter of fact, however, the work of the committee could not be thus simplified. The issue was a practical one which involved not so much the truth or fallacy of a theory as a practical and economical application of whatever truth there might be therein. The concrete problem, therefore, was not the correctness of certain theories but rather a determination of whether any modification in the existing system of fire protection could profitably be developed therefrom.

From its inception the committee found that the light-burning theory when translated into a concrete program of work was not a simple nor a single idea. Each of its adherents advocated a fairly definite procedure, but these procedures were diverse on such practical matters as the season of the year which should be selected for burning, and the like. While the existing system of the U.S. Forest Service was definite, standardized and well understood, the light-burning plans seemed to have in common only their opposition thereto and their reliance on the three postulates already stated.

It is true that the Indians are often referred to as the originators of light burning and this so-called "forestry" of theirs is regarded by some with an admiration which their agriculture and stock-raising methods (both equally suited to their simple needs) has failed to inspire. The fact remains, however, that no definite and complete information is available, either as to what they did or as to its results, and that economic conditions have since too radically altered to permit our adopting their methods with impunity.

During the first year of its activities the committee restricted its efforts to a critical analysis of existing evidence and to an observation of the efforts of a number of timberland owners to put the untried theory into practice. Without going into details, in each case observed valuable information was obtained as to how not to light burn, but in no instance was a practicable plan encountered.

The second year was spent in an attempt to apply the lessons of the first year on a large-scale experiment on Moffatt Creek, a few miles south of Yreka. After considerable effort the consent of the landowners involved, all of whom favored light burning, was obtained and several weeks during the late spring were spent in trying to find conditions neither too dry to be dangerous nor too wet to make the expense of the operation prohibitive. Such a condition was not found, and only a small area was burned. On this the results were unsatisfactory.

The third year, further work was done on the same drainage, but with a more limited objective. Specific information was sought on three points:

- On the relative desirability of controlled fires burning down hill and up hill;
- on the effect of a second burn on land already burned off two or three years before;
- on the effect of burning on reproduction during the fall after growth had stopped.

Work was done on several tracts, the general method of procedure being, first, to make a detailed examination, cruise, and record of each; second, to burn it over; and, third, to re-examine it to determine the results. The spring work was unsatisfactory in that although conditions were so damp that fire would only run on the drier slopes, there was material damage done to both mature timber and more particularly to reproduction. In the fall the most dangerous portion of the fire season was abruptly terminated by heavy rains, after which the debris never again became dry enough to burn.

The conclusions of this and previous seasons are as follows:

- Spring burning is dangerous because by the time the litter is sufficiently dry to burn satisfactorily the season is normally far advanced. No more rains can be counted on and smoldering logs and snags may hold fire well on into the fire season.
- Summer burning can be kept under control, but apparently only at an expense out of proportion to the benefits obtained.
- Fall burning is often impracticable, because while vegetation dries out slowly it may become saturated with water in a few hours. Not infrequently the most critical period of the fire season is terminated by heavy rains, after which the ground never again becomes dry enough for burning. This

condition may not be universal, but it seems sufficiently frequent to make fall burning impracticable as a generally applicable plan.

- At any season the cost of light burning appears considerably greater than the benefits resulting.
- Down-hill burning is decidedly preferable to up-hill burning, but it seems impracticable to avoid some up-hill burning on large experiments and even down-hill fires are not free from damage.
- No burn yet observed failed to damage seriously reproduction. This statement includes down-hill fires and second fires on lands burned off previously within two years.
- No burn yet studied critically failed to cause damage to mature timber which is considerably larger than would be apparent to a casual observer.
- Under conditions where light burning is at all practicable it is unnecessary, since under such conditions protection by the ordinary methods is easy and far less expensive.
- Under conditions where light burning seems most necessary it is too dangerous to be practicable.
- Light burning on large areas at one time is impossible because the moisture conditions on slopes of different directions vary widely.

After three years of work the committee has not been able to find or to devise a fire protective system based upon the light-burning theory which seems more practicable and economical than that already in effect on the National Forests. At a meeting held January 5, 1923, it was therefore unanimously voted to discontinue this experiment.

"Suggests Indians Manage National Forests" (1924)[12]

The President of the Mission Indian Federation, San Jacinto, California, recently wrote President Coolidge suggesting that the control of the National Forests be given into the hands of the Indians.

The Acting Secretary of Agriculture [Howard M. Gore], in replying to this communication, pointed out that the administration and protection of the National Forests presented a great many problems, which called for the services of men of wide experience and training, but stated that many of the Indians, if properly trained, could doubtless qualify for positions in the Forest Service, and that anyone so qualified would be given every consideration for appointment.

---

12 "Suggests Indians Manage National Forests," *California District News Letter*, November 14, 1924, 3.

Fig. 8. Beginning in the 1920s, Herbert Stoddard began to conduct some of the first experiments using what is now called prescribed fire to regenerate quail habitat and longleaf pine forests. For him, smoke was a sign of forest health. In 1958, he and several colleagues founded the Tall Timbers Research Station near Tallahassee, Florida. Since then, its Fire Ecology Program has analyzed the ability of controlled fire to sustain the open, parklike, and biodiverse character of longleaf pineries, once the dominant forest type in the lower South. Credit: Roy Komarek and Tall Timbers Archives.

Part 3

Bringing Fire Back

Fig. 9. The results of annual, controlled burns on the Tall Timbers Research Station. Credit: Tall Timbers Archives.

Southern Backfires

The first sustained, non-Indigenous challenge to the fire-suppression paradigm emerged in the US South in the late nineteenth century, years before the Forest Service tried to stamp out fire via policy and action. This resistance would evolve in relationship to the federal agency's commitment to suppression across the twentieth century as scientists and researchers tested the assumptions embedded in its conviction that all fires were bad: that they were bad because they incinerated the very economic asset locked in trees' board feet and because they destroyed soil fertility.

The counter-narrative in the South arose because of a keystone species: the longleaf pine. Although Scottish geologist Charles Lyell was not the first to learn of the relationship between this species and Indigenous fire-management practices, his 1849 comment about the connection is one of many nineteenth-century observations that set the stage for a more complex understanding of fire's ecological place in the southern pineries. Forty years later, Ellen Call Long, the only woman to speak at the 1888 American Forestry Congress, delivered a detailed and ecologically precise talk on why fire was critical to the regeneration of longleaf-pine forests. Her observations gained scientific credence through the experiments of H. H. Chapman of the Yale Forest School, whose research, like that of Roland Harper in Alabama, challenged the Forest Service's fire-suppression convictions even as these were being developed, as did botanist Eliza Frances Andrews's experimental work in Georgia. Some of the findings in this earlier work culminated in S. W. Greene's 1931 sharp critique of the enduring effort to dismiss fire's generative influence. His criticism made the editor of *American Forests* so uncomfortable that he felt compelled to insert a prefatory rebuttal! He conceded that there was an ecological need for fire in longleaf and other pine forests, but he subordinated that knowledge to economic demands and political realities.

That subordination would become harder to maintain in the post–World War II era, when southern fire researchers accelerated their investigations and presented them at the Tall Timbers Fire Ecology Conference, established in the early 1960s in Tallahassee, Florida. Many of these presentations, writes historian Hal K. Rothman, "directly contradicted the Forest Service model," and they did so deliberately. The "most innovative and even heretical ideas usually could get a hearing" at the conference. Among those whose ideas were once deemed heretical was Herbert Stoddard, a co-founder of the annual confab, whose pathbreaking analyses of the benefits of controlled burning in southern longleaf pine forests dated back to the mid-1920s. Over time, some of the participants, as in the case of H. H. Biswell, migrated west for professional opportunities and carried their insights with them.[1] Even California, the fire-hardened stronghold of suppression, began to accept, however reluctantly, the application of prescribed fire to its forests.[2]

---

1 Hal K. Rothman, *Blazing Heritage: A History of Wildland Fire in the National Parks* (New York: Oxford University Press, 2007), 92.
2 Stephen J. Pyne, *California: A Fire Survey* (Tucson: University of Arizona Press, 2016), 147–149, 168–169.

Charles Lyell, from *Second Visit to the United States of North America* (1849)[3]

There is a flourishing college at Tuscaloosa [Alabama], standing upon a hill 450 feet above sea level. Here, I was welcomed by the professor of chemistry, Mr. Brumby, who had the kindness to set out immediately . . . to examine the coal-fields with me immediately north of this place. Starting in a northeasterly direction, we first entered the hilly country formed of sandstone, grit, and shale of the coal formation, precisely like the strata in which it occurs in England. These hills were covered with long-leaved pines, and the large proportion they bear to the hardwood is said to have been increased by the Indian practice of burning the grass; the bark of the oak and other kinds of hardwood being more combustible, and more easily injured by fire, than that of the fir tribe. Everywhere the seedlings of the long-leaved pine were coming up in such numbers that one might have supposed the ground to have been sown with them; and I was reminded how rarely we see similar self-sown firs in English plantations . . .

---

3 Excerpted from Sir Charles Lyell, *Second Visit to the United States of North America* (New York: Harper and Brothers, 1849), 2:69.

Ellen Call Long, from "Notes on Some of the Forest Features of Florida" (1888)[4]

So much of the State of Florida as lies north and west of a line extending from the head of Charlotte Harbor northwest to the Atlantic coast, about the 29th parallel of north latitude, is embraced in and forms the southeastern limit of what is known as the "Southern Maritime Pine Belt" in the subdivision of the Atlantic region of North American forest area.

This Maritime Pine Belt of the Southern States, extending southward from the 36th parallel of north latitude along the Atlantic from 100 to 150 miles in width to the points above indicated in Florida, and thence westwardly along the Mexican Gulf coast to the valley of the Mississippi, embraces within its limits no finer body of merchantable timber than is to be found in the State of Florida. The species giving identity to this division of American forest is *Pinus palustris*, or Southern long-leafed pine ... no other one kind of American tree has a more exalted value, not alone for lumbering purposes, but in the vast supply of tar, pitch, turpentine, and resin derived therefrom ...

The U.S. census returns for 1880 report 1,853,582,000 feet of sawed lumber (board measure) manufactured during that year from the Southern belt.

Of this output, which would lay a close floor one inch thick over an area of more than 66 square miles, Florida is said to have furnished about 200,000,000 feet, or something over the one-ninth part...

Much incorrect information has been furnished the public on the subject of Florida's forest areas and the supply of different timbers, a striking example of which occurs in a beautifully colored map of the State in the census report of 1880, wherein the four great counties of Jefferson, Leon, Gadsden, and Jackson are excluded from the timber-growing district.

It is, however, of some of the peculiarities of Florida's climate and soil, as related to forest reproduction, that the writer feels authorized to speak rather than of the economic and commercial values of her present forest supply.

There is, perhaps, no section of the United States so well suited to the rapid growth of forest trees as the whole State of Florida, and such parts of Alabama, Mississippi, and Louisiana as lie adjacent to the seaboard. The long

---

4 Excerpted from Ellen Call Long, "Notes on Some of the Forest Features of Florida, with Items of Tree Growth in That State," *Proceedings of the American Forestry Congress* 7, no. 1 (1888): 38–41.

growing seasons, the regularity of annual rain-fall, the average humidity of the atmosphere, high summer temperatures, absence of rocky sterility in the soils, and the very general distribution throughout the section indicated of the tertiary limestone formation, accompanied by widely diffused marine shell deposits and outcropping of phosphatic matter, give to this region conditions peculiarly fitted to vigorous tree growth.

The three agencies which militate appreciably against tree growth in this section are, in the order of their destructiveness, forest fires, cyclones, and lightning. The latter of these destroying causes, while far less conspicuous to the casual observer than either of the other two, is nevertheless a very potent factor in big-tree destruction along the gulf seaboard during the late summer months, when severe electric storms are of daily occurrence.

The writer, in the month of September 1886, counted eighty-six large pines, that had been recently struck by lightning, that could be seen from the carriage road along forty miles of travel through the pine woods southwest of Tallahassee.

The aggregation of such destruction, if equally distributed throughout the coast country, amounts annually to a great many hundreds of thousands of feet of first-class lumber destroyed by this means; for it is generally the tallest and largest trees that the fiery bolts light upon.

About the time of the autumnal equinox severe gales are apt to prevail in western Florida and along the coast to Texas. While these storms frequently assume cyclonic characteristics, they never acquire the velocity and severity that attaches to them in the Northwest, owing, we presume, to the fact that the Gulf coast region is so much nearer the breeding place or center of the disturbance.

While these equinoctial gales do destroy considerable quantities of timber in the southwestern regions of the Southern Maritime Pine Belt, they accomplish far less destruction than would be the case were this belt located further away from the storm centers.

"Forest fires" is a term of very different signification throughout the Southern pine belt from the meaning attached to it in the North and West. There, they are destroyers of forests, pure and simple, without any economic advantages attending their occurrence.

But there is sound reason for believing that the annual burning of the wooded regions of the South is the prime cause and preserver of the grand forests of *P. palustris* [Longleaf pine] to be found there; that, but for the effect of these burnings, the pine forests would never have been, and but for the continued annual wood firing that prevails so generally throughout the South the Maritime Pine Belt would soon disappear and give place to a jungle of hardwood and deciduous trees.

In the persistent application of the law of the survival of the fittest *Pinus palustris* alone has been able to contend with the condition of fire as it annually occurs over the grassy surface of the Southern forest.

In their earlier stages of growth all other species of Southern trees are not only slow in their growth, but their dying foliage is combustible, their stems and young shoots are bare and unprotected, and their buds and growing eyes are on the outside, exposed to the flame of the burning grass and fallen leaves as the fire creeps over the surface of the land, so that with each recurring annual burning all plants which have sprung up in the woodlands since the preceding spring, are overtaken and readily destroyed when the dry grass and leaves take fire in the fall, and are thus perpetually prevented from gaining a foothold and arriving at so advanced a stage of growth as to lift their buds above the reach of flames.

On the other hand, the long-leafed pine shoots up from the spring-sown seed with astonishing vigor, attaining an average altitude of about 16 inches by the time of the occurrence of the winter fires. Its young stem is without buds and eyes on the outer surface, and this surface throughout its length is protected by a dense growth of peculiarly non-combustible green foliage that will not blaze except when subjected to much more intense heat than generally results from the slowly burning wire-grass covering the pine forest. The growing bud of *P. palustris* is also at the very top of its stem, closely encased in a thick pellicle of protecting green. Thus, this tree is enabled to survive, to become proud master of the situation, and by annually reproducing its species to perpetuate the grand forest of the Southern Maritime Pine Belt.

The truth of this theory of the predominance of *P. palustris* in the Southern pine belt has thousands of practical illustrations in the experience and observation of persons throughout the region in question whose residence has been long enough to enable them to note the results where intervening roadways, farm clearings, and other obstructions have interrupted the annual march of fire in the pine woods. Localities protected for a short time from fire rapidly become covered with oak, hickory, magnolia, dog wood, &c, and become in time "Hammock" lands. The presence of hard wood underbrush is prohibitory of the growth of *P. palustris.*

The statute-books of almost every Southern State contain enactments prohibitory of setting fire to the woods, and severe penalties are attached to violations of the law. There may be sound reason for such legislation, since great loss of property often results from burning fences and buildings. But viewed from a forestry standpoint we believe the total abolition of forest fires in the South would mean the annihilation of her grand lumbering pineries....

Herman H. Chapman, from "Forest Fires and Forestry in the Southern States" (1912)[5]

The future timber supply of the Eastern States must come from one of two sources, either from the Pacific Coast by rail or water, or from home-grown timber. Pine or soft woods will continue to occupy the relatively important place they now hold, in the demand for lumber. It cannot be expected that the far West can ever supply lumber to the East even by the Panama Canal in sufficient quantities to wholly keep pace with the demand or at prices as low as the present rates on Southern yellow pine lumber. The problem of providing large future crops of pine in the East is an urgent one, and it is already certain that before such crops could grow to commercial size, practically all of the present stand of pine, both North and South, will be exhausted. The situation in the northern States is well known—the cut in the eastern portion is now largely spruce and hardwoods, while in the Lake States, hemlock and hardwoods are being cut that were worthless as long as pine remained. In Minnesota, a fifteen-to-twenty years cut of pine remains for some mills, but the total output is rapidly shrinking.

The alarming fact here is that throughout the northern pine region forest or brush, fires have practically eliminated the prospects for a second crop, and completely destroyed all young pine timber. Efforts at reforestation so far have not assumed proportions that promise a future supply of commercial proportions—in fact, planting must in most cases be resorted to and there are not funds available to plant the millions of acres of devastated lands in need of restocking.

This disastrous condition arises from two causes—the susceptibility of northern pines, especially white pine, to destruction by fire, and the enormous fire hazard resulting from logging operations. It is not too late to solve this problem in a small way, for small areas, by brush piling, planting, and forest reserves, but in these Northern States the big opportunity to secure natural reproduction over wide areas is forever lost.

This is not so in the South. Here we have an area originally pine land, much greater in extent than that occupied by northern pines. The soil varies from fertile clay loam through silt to grades of fine or coarse sand, sometimes underlaid by hard clay, elsewhere apparently very deep and holding little moisture.

---

5 Excerpted from Herman H. Chapman, "Forest Fires and Forestry in the Southern States," *American Forests*, August 1912, 510–517.

Over this great area the logging and manufacture of southern yellow pine is almost at its height, although already the States on the eastern seaboard have been practically cut over for virgin pine.

The future of these pine lands of the South is the most urgent problem of eastern forestry today. Shall they be opened up for settlements or retained to grow more pine timber? These lands are practically all in private hands, and largely belong to firms whose business it is to run one or more large modern sawmills, and to earn, if possible, a fair rate of interest on the millions of capital invested in mills, equipment, lands, and timber. Once cut over, these lands are seldom regarded as having any possible value as sources of another cut of lumber. Hence, they must be sold as farmlands. There are and will be for a long period millions of acres of lands of this character in every Southern State—lands which have been until recently regarded by the natives as of little agricultural value. The old settlers farm the better classes of soil lying along the bottoms of the smaller streams not overflowed [flooded]. In many districts more land has been abandoned after being farmed for varying periods than is now under cultivation.

It is true that these pine soils are the poorest soils of the South, and that under the old systems of farming, with cotton as the principal crop, their fertility was rapidly lost. But with the development of agricultural experiment stations in the South and the increasing use of leguminous crops, better crop rotations, and truck and fruit farming, poorer soils are being used profitably and prosperous communities are springing up here and there dependent wholly on the agricultural use of these pine lands. Thus, the whole question of the future growth of timber crops on southern pine lands is challenged at the outset on apparently valid grounds, and by the overwhelming interest of practically all elements of the communities affected.

It will be difficult for a long time to strike a proper balance between agricultural use and forest use of these southern lands. But one thing is certain; every agricultural community no matter how fertile the soil, is better off if a certain percent of the land is growing trees. Every farm is more valuable if it possesses a woodlot, and the poorer the soil the greater the percent of the total area which can be devoted to tree growing, to the best interests of agriculture and of the community . . .

There is a striking difference between southern and northern pine in their resistance to fire. White pine is killed easily by fires even when mature. But the three southern pines are all remarkably fire resistant and the longleaf pine has adapted its whole structure and growth as a seedling to the primary object of surviving ground fires. Probably not a single pine in the South has ever grown to maturity without having survived repeated fires. Conditions in these States make fires almost inevitable. In spite of the abundant rainfall, the late spring and summer months are usually dry, and fires burn readily. These fires are set carelessly or purposely to improve grazing, which in most sections is getting steadily poorer in the woods.

The effect of these fires upon the forest has been deplored by foresters, and the tendency seems to be to try to pass laws modeled after those of Northern States, which seek to absolutely prevent fire in the forests and establish a system of fire wardens for this purpose. But it is more than probable that such a policy in the South would defeat its own ends and should never be attempted. It is the right policy for Northern States, where fires can and should be absolutely prevented. But there is abundant evidence that the attempt to keep fire entirely out of southern pine lands might finally result in complete destruction of the forests.

On longleaf soils, the pine needles form a very inflammable layer, which is supplemented by the growth of grass in open stands. In many districts, fire runs over these lands every year. In two-or-three years' time, if no fire occurs, there will be enough of an accumulation to make a very hot blaze, fatal to young seedlings in most cases. The risk gets worse as the period extends till at the end of ten to fifteen years, if fire is set in a dry time, the mature longleaf timber may be killed. This has actually occurred, though it is so seldom that fires have been kept out of such lands for more than a year or two, that such destruction is very rare.

In Shortleaf pine forests, fire is much less of a problem. The needles are small and accumulate slowly. There is more shade, less grass, and plenty of hardwood growth whose leaves do not burn with the heat and flame which distinguishes a grass or pine needle fire. Evidence from stumps of trees which have been burned into shows that fires occur in shortleaf at intervals of five to eight years, instead of every year or two, as in longleaf. Shortleaf seedlings are very easily destroyed by fire. But the young tree soon develops a thick bark and will resist small ground fires. In a region studied this spring in Southern Arkansas it was found that it took the average seedling only five years to reach a diameter of over an inch, and become fairly fire resistant, when growing in open places. Seedlings growing in the forest under partial shade grow more slowly and may be killed by fire at 8 or 10 years of age.

But the young trees which spring up on cut over areas would have plenty of sun and room and five years would be enough to bring them to a fire-resistant size.

On longleaf lands, the fires are at present so frequent that seedlings do not have time to get by the first two years when they are small and ill protected. If it were possible to keep fires out of an area for five years, these longleaf seedlings while still very short—probably not over a foot high—would be an inch or more thick. None but a hot fire in dry weather could possibly kill them all at this stage. This frequency of fires is not a natural condition. Fires in the past, while evidently recurring every few years, did not necessarily burn every year. The conclusions are that both longleaf and shortleaf pine forests are capable of resisting small fires with little injury, but are destroyed by large fires at long intervals; that every acre of pine timber in the South has grown to maturity in spite of fire and accompanied by fire; and that the proper use of fire and not complete fire prevention is the only solution of the problem of future forestry in the South. Even the seedbed of these species is soil which has been barred of vegetable accumulations, chiefly by fire; and seedlings do not start on litter or pine needles.

But between proper use of fire and promiscuous burning there is all the difference between success and failure. A lumber company, conducting a logging operation, may desire to return for a second cut over the same lands before retiring from the business. In this case, in either longleaf or shortleaf pine, the most intelligent plan is to leave the small fast-growing trees, not on a diameter limit, but by selection and marking. Two things may then be accomplished— the remaining stand can be protected from fire injury and cut with profit in 20 years, and a crop of seedling pine may be secured on the ground that will be well along towards making lumber and will have a prospective value by the time the older trees are cut. The great risk to the trees left standing comes immediately after logging, when they may blow down, or be destroyed by fire when the tops are burned. The wind danger is overcome by selecting windfirm trees to leave. These can be distinguished with a little training. The fire danger is lessened by burning the ground before logging ...

Once this fire risk is eliminated, these young trees are practically safe from small fires. They will produce seed abundantly, and a so-called third crop of seedlings will be almost sure to spring up on the land so well prepared as a seedbed by logging and burning. . . .

In the light of these facts it would be very questionable policy for Southern States by legislation to prohibit the burning of woods or attempt to prevent the use of fire. It would be far wiser for those States to establish State forestry departments with a technically trained man in charge, who can devote his entire time to educating and encouraging landowners to practice forestry by keeping their natural forest land in timber. An owner who desires to establish a protected area of the kind above described should receive the support of the State in his efforts to keep out fire and protect reproduction of pine, which under proper conditions he is almost certain to get. But a promiscuous enforcement of forest fire laws, borrowed whole from Northern States, and utterly unsuited to the South, will never result in anything but dissatisfaction and contempt on the part of practical men for forestry. A study of actual conditions and laws designed to meet these conditions is the only route by which the South will ever improve her wonderful opportunity to preserve her lumber industry for future generations.

Roland M. Harper, from "The Forest Resources of Alabama" (1913)[6]

... It has been known that the longleaf pine, the most useful and originally the most abundant tree in Alabama and some adjoining States, withstands fire better than almost any other tree, but very few persons seem to have realized that fire is well-nigh essential to its existence. In the dense coniferous forests of the northernmost States and Canada, the destruction of a large amount of timber and often of other property as well, and it is therefore looked upon as a calamity, to be averted by all possible means. In the Middle States forest fires are not very destructive to standing timber, but they burn up the humus and thus impoverish the soil, which is another reason why writers on forestry regard fire as one of the greatest enemies of the forest.

Different forests vary in their relation to fire, however, and some can stand much more frequent fires than others. In the northern coniferous fire perhaps does not visit any one spot more than once in the lifetime of a tree, on average, while most of the longleaf pine forests, even the scattered bodies of this pine in the mountains, are now burned over nearly every year. A fire in a longleaf pine forest is practically always a ground fire, feeding upon the pine needles and dense herbage, and doing little or no damage to mature and sound trees, for their bark is thick and almost fire-proof, and their branches are all high up and out of reach of the flames. Such fires, do, of course, burn the humus, which the pine seems to have little use for, but at the same time, they return immediately to the soil the mineral plant food stored up in the dead leaves. The amount of available plant food in the soil of the pine forests is usually rather limited, and these frequent fires thus enable the pine to do business on a small amount of capital, as it were.

If the herbage was never burned off, most of the pine seeds, which are very light, would lodge in the grass and fail to germinate, and at the same time, oaks and other hardwoods would take advantage of the enriched soil and invade the pine forests, ultimately making enough shade to prevent the reproduction of pine, which eminently an intolerant or light-demanding tree. Proof of this can be seen in many places in the longleaf pine regions, where bluffs too steep for fire to descend readily, or peninsulas between two streams, with soil originally

---

6 Excerpted from Roland M. Harper, "The Forest Resources of Alabama," *American Forestry*, October 1913, 657–670.

SOUTHERN BACKFIRES

the same as in the pine forests, are now covered with shady hardwoods, commonly known as hummocks.

Fire must have been started in the pines by lightning or other natural cause in prehistoric times, otherwise the longleaf pine could not have maintained itself against the encroachments of the hardwoods. At present, of course, most of the fires are started by human agency, purposively or accidentally. Stockmen burn off dead grass to facilitate grazing, and turpentine operators for another reason. In the regions where the longleaf pine is the most abundant tree most of the trees are tapped for turpentine, each presenting several square feet of very flammable within very easy reach of ground fires. When fire comes into contact with such a tree it not only destroys several weeks' accumulation of gum, but also seriously injures the tree, sometimes killing it. To guard against the turpentine men every winter chop away the grass for a few feet around each tree that is being worked, and then set fire to the woods; the idea being that the oftener the grass is burned the less combustible material there will be each time, and therefore the less danger there will be to setting fire to the trees. If the burning is done in winter, and the ground is damp, the danger is reduced to a minimum.

Probably no tree, not even the longleaf pine, can reproduce itself where fire sweeps over the ground every year; but this pine at the age of four or five years, if not earlier, becomes practically immune to fire, so that any suitable spot that escapes burning for a few years is likely to be covered with a thicket of young pines, which thin themselves naturally as they grow older. And even if the opportunity for seedlings to grow should come but once in fifty years on any particular piece of ground, that would be sufficient to perpetuate the forests. This noble tree is holdings its own remarkably well, too, in spite of too frequent fires and other inroads of civilization.

In view of the above facts, while it might be well for the conservationists in their efforts to discourage the willful burning of the pine woods, the accidental fires need not cause any apprehension, for they probably come just about often enough to protect the pine from the encroachments of the hardwoods, most of which are much less valuable for timber. Although the increase in population tends to increase the number of forest fires, it also restricts the area over which each conflagration can spread, by providing more roads, railroads, clearings, and other barriers. The prevalence of fires in the western prairies has been greatly diminished by the extension of settlements, and the same thing will doubtless come about in the longleaf pine regions, independently of any conservation campaign.

Eliza Frances Andrews, from "Agency of Fire in Propagation of Longleaf Pines" (1917)[7]

The important part played by forest fires in the life history of the longleaf pine has been recognized by a number of recent writers, and Harper even goes so far as to say "that if it were possible to prevent forest fires absolutely the longleaf pine . . . would soon become extinct." The connection between the periodic recurrence of these catastrophes and the success of the pine seedlings in competing for possession of the soil was pointed out by Mrs. Ellen Call Long, of Tallahassee, more than 25 years ago, but the suggestion appears on the face of it so at variance with universal experience as to give little occasion for surprise that it should have been received with incredulity, or at best with indifference, by those unacquainted with the adaptive provisions of the species and the conditions prevailing in its habitat.

The writer has recently been favored with exceptional opportunities for investigating this subject by means of an experiment carried out by nature herself, in the native home of the longleafs, with all the exactness of detail that could be expected in a well ordered laboratory. Even that refined test of scientific accuracy, a control experiment, was provided by a neighboring group of the same species that was not exposed to fire on the occasion referred to. The scene of this spontaneous demonstration lies on the northern slope of Lavender Mountain, in Floyd County, Georgia, a ridge of the Southern Appalachians which is certainly very near, if not actually itself, the extreme inland and upland limit of the longleaf pines as they occur at present. The crest of the ridge, according to the United States Geological Survey, attains a maximum height of 1695 ft. above sea level, and extends for 12 miles or more in an approximately east and west direction. It is divided transversely by three deep depressions carried on, and the intervals between the gaps are subdivided by numerous ravines into more or less widely separated spurs and knobs. The southern slopes are covered with the remains of great forests of this valuable timber, interspersed with various hardwood trees and with shortleaf pines (*P. virginiana and P. echinata*).

They have repeatedly been cut for lumber and burned over by "ground fires" started in spring by farmers to provide a free range for their cattle, but

---

7 Excerpted from Eliza Frances Andrews, "Agency of Fire in Propagation of Longleaf Pines," *Botanical Gazette*, December 1917, 497–508.

the longleafs continue to reproduce themselves with a pertinacity which, if not too diligently thwarted by the blundering incompetence of county officials and the shortsighted greed of ignorant timber cutters, will in the course of a generation or two repopulate the southern mountain slopes with a new forest growth sprung from the old stock.

While there are traditions of the former presence of this species on the northern side of the mountain, the only traces of them that I have been able to find there consist of two small, isolated groups which furnished the apparatus for nature's instructive experiment alluded to. They are situated on opposite sides of a deep ravine which starts near the top of the mountain, at Fouche Gap (the westernmost of the three passes), and descends in a gradually widening rift to the bottom. The larger and more important of these groups occupies a portion of a steep incline between the crest of the ridge and a now abandoned road that winds along the eastern edge of the ravine. It numbered only five individuals, so far as could be seen when I first took note of them, in the summer of 1913. Of these, the rugged patriarch, together with two smaller specimens in the background, one of them a mere sapling, were the only members of the colony conspicuous enough to attract the attention of any but a particularly interested observer. The other two were seedlings not over 4–5 dm. in height, and at this stage of development, when the needles are the only part above ground, so like the coarse grasses around them that even an expert, unless keenly on the lookout, would be liable to pass them by unnoticed.

This group of five individuals was scattered over an area of half an acre, more or less, on the edge of an open copsewood which has repeatedly been cut for timber and cleared of undergrowth by minor forest fires. The rest of the declivity, from the gap to the crest of the ridge, had been cleared several years before for cotton planting, but after a short trial was abandoned as too rugged for cultivation. It was at this time (July 1913) neck deep in weeds, mixed with a scrub growth of brush and brambles; and not being in quest of the zoological specimens likely to abound in such places, I did not explore this jungle until two years later, after one of the periodical spring fires had cleared the ground.

The second group, which served as the "control," is situated on the farther side of a low spur or knoll, separated from the neighboring colony by the intervening ravine and the wooded crown of the knoll. It included, when first observed, four individuals, three of which were adults of full cone-bearing age, the largest one measuring 2 m. in girth. The offspring of these was limited to one solitary seedling, a disproportion the significance of which will be apparent later, when compared with the progeny of the "patriarch" on the other side of the gorge. The soil in both situations is the same, a hard, dry, rocky clay, with a characteristic ground cover of *Pteris aquiline, Tephrosia virginica*, and a number of coarse grasses that have a strikingly familiar aspect to one acquainted with the vegetation of the great pine region of the South Atlantic coastal plain. The typical wire grass (*Aristida stricta*) of the southern forests is here replaced by a correspondingly arid growth of "old field broom" (principally *Andropogonfurcatus, A. virginicus,* and *A. scoparius*), with a few sedges (*Scleria triglomerata, Cyperus retrofractus,* etc.) intermixed. In fact, the only difference in the environment of the two groups is the isolated position of the knoll, the top of which is protected by an encircling turnpike road and by the wooded slopes of two deep ravines, watered by mountain springs and clothed with a heavy growth of broad-leaved trees, conditions which oppose an effective barrier against the spread of fire.

It was not until April 1915 that I made another visit to these straggling longleaf outposts, which had interested me at first merely as landmarks of what seemed to be the Ultima Thule of their advance in this direction. But a great surprise awaited me. The region around the gap had recently been burned over, and amid the wreckage of skeleton limbs and blackened stubs to which the weedy jungle in the old clearing was now reduced, there appeared a thriving colony of 33 young longleafs, ranging from a few decimeters to a meter or more in height. This new growth was confined mainly to the old clearing, although the "patriarch," whose progeny it presumably is, stands squarely on the border line between the old cotton field and the copsewood, and had no doubt distributed his favors impartially to both. But the absence of trees in the clearing would naturally facilitate the scattering of seeds in that direction, and during the first year or two, before the weeds and brush began to crowd them out, they would germinate freely in the open ground. I had simply overlooked them on my former visit, for the reason that they were hidden in the jungle, where, after making a successful start in life during the palmy days before their little Belgium was overrun by the horde of weedy invaders, they were at last overpowered by numbers and buried out of sight.

Deprived of the sunshine so necessary to this sun-loving race, all save the oldest and strongest among them must have perished but for the timely intervention of their powerful ally, the fire, which swept away all rivals and left the young longleafs in undisputed possession of the soil. That such was the case, we have their own direct testimony, for every one of them bore unmistakable marks of fire. Some were so scorched and blackened that anyone unacquainted with the habit of the species would unhesitatingly have pronounced them dead. An examination, however, of a number of the worst injured plants showed that in not a single instance had the growing point been killed, or even seriously damaged.

On the other side of the ravine conditions were unchanged except that a new road had been cut around the knoll since my former visit, almost completely encircling it, and one of the adult pines that stood in their way had been felled by the road builders. The fire had not spread in this direction, and I had some difficulty in finding again, among the coarse grasses which these nurslings so closely resemble, the solitary seedling upon which the future hopes of the colony depend. A careful search among the under-growth failed to bring to light any further additions to this decadent family, and as matters now stand, it looks as though the last remnants of the longleaf forest that once clothed the knoll were doomed to early extinction.[8]

It would, of course, be rash to attribute this result solely to the absence of fires. Various other factors may intervene, among which must be reckoned the infrequency of seeding that characterizes this species, a full crop being produced only at intervals of four or five years. If a forest fire should occur during one of these "lean" periods, it would have comparatively little effect, since there would be few seedlings to take advantage of the opportunity offered, while one closely preceding a season of abundance would prepare the way for a proportionate increase in the longleaf population.

Another fact to be considered is that the early growth of the longleaf seedling is very slow. The main energy of the plant during the first year or two is expended in developing the long taproot which enables it to cope successfully with the poverty of its habitat by making the most of the meager resources of the soil, and later provides a safe anchorage for the towering shaft of the adult tree ... But while giving due weight to these considerations, I think that after we have studied the effects of fire a little more closely in those cases where its agency is too obvious to be doubted, we cannot deny that it is, and has been in the past, an important factor in the propagation and distribution of the longleaf pines.

In July and August of the same year (1915) I made a longer stay on the mountain, during which time I was able to continue my observations on the pines to better advantage. In the lower group, on the knoll, there was little of interest to record, everything remaining very much as when I last saw it. On the upper slope, however, matters were very different, and a more exact count brought the census of the new generation up to 40. Of this number, all of those within the old clearing must have germinated during the 7 or 8 years since the cultivation of this part of the land was abandoned, for they

---

8 Later observations (September 1917) show a flourishing group of 66 saplings and seedlings in the first colony; while the lower one on the knoll has been reduced to 2 individuals by the loss of the seedling and one of the adult trees. [Note from original.]

would assuredly have been weeded out had any of them dared to show their heads above ground where "cotton was king." To estimate the ages of different individuals with accuracy, however, is not easy, on account of the great irregularity in the rate of growth. While very slow during the first 2 or 3 years, as already pointed out, it becomes proportionately rapid after the critical period of "infant mortality" is past. The growth for the year 1915, up to the first of August, on two saplings of 2.75 and 2 m. in height respectively, was found by measurement, while seedlings 12–18 cm. high showed a gain of only 2–4 cm. for the same period.

These figures show that the young longleaf, after attaining adolescence, is fully capable of holding its own in the competitive strife of the plant world. The chief danger to the species in this unceasing contest is in the risk that the seedling, during its long period of infancy, may be starved and crowded to death by the rapidly advancing host of weeds and bushes that outstrip it in the battle for food and sunlight. Their only safeguard against these enemies is, as we have seen, the forest fire.

This naturally brings up the question, how does it happen that the young pines themselves are not killed by the heat which destroys their hardier competitors? The answer is before our eyes. The great rosettes of bristling needles, which give to the longleaf pine its venerable aspect, are not the mere decorative emblems of ancient descent that they seem. They are fulfilling the important function of a defensive armor against the most destructive enemy (after man) that the plant population of the world is exposed to. The young of most species quickly succumb at the first onset of even an ordinary ground fire; but the longleaf pine seedling has its growing point closely enveloped in a crown of spear-like needles... before the stem begins to rise above the ground. These may be anywhere from 20 to 40 cm. long, including the sheaths, which average about 3–4 cm. When fresh they ignite so slowly as to be practically incombustible.

Strictly speaking, they can hardly be said to ignite at all, but are bitten off and consumed where the fire comes in contact with them. Moreover, the application of heat causes a violent sizzling and contortion of the parts affected, accompanied by a series of small explosions which are sometimes capable of extinguishing a match; and I have even known them, on one occasion, to put out the flame of a candle. At another time, I was trying to ignite a fresh "pinetop" (as these tufts are called in our Georgia vernacular) by the flame of a kerosene lamp, when it fumed and sputtered and caused such a commotion in the burning wick that I cut short the experiment for fear of exploding the lamp and transferred my operations to the kitchen. There was a slow wood fire in the stove, into which I thrust the pinetop, and awaited results, watch in hand.

SOUTHERN BACKFIRES

When I removed the stub at the end of 4 minutes, the needles had all been consumed, but the sheaths, especially those of the vigorous young fascicles crowded around the growing point, remained for the most part intact. The bud itself, though considerably scorched and blackened externally, appeared, like the stem, not to have suffered beyond the possibility of recovery, though this point, as the final result will show, was open to doubt.

It may be explained here that in excursions through the mountains it is desirable to avoid all unnecessary encumbrances in the way of luggage, and, as the conditions of life are very primitive in the regions of greatest interest to the botanist, one often has to resort to homely makeshifts when supplementing observation by experiment. It is surprising, however, what interesting results may sometimes be obtained by very simple means when one is determined to get to the bottom of a thing. To complete the experiment, I next placed a couple of fresh pinetops in an upright position over a brisk blaze of chips and twigs out of doors, so as to approximate, as closely as possible, the normal conditions of an ordinary brush fire. After 8.5 minutes, when the flame had subsided and the needles were all burned away, down to their sheathed bases, I placed the stubs in water, together with the one that had been subjected to the ordeal of the kitchen stove on the day before. At the end of 12 days, when my stay on the mountain came to an end, the latter was found to have sustained internal injuries which left it in all probability beyond recovery.

The other two came out of the fiery ordeal, if not altogether unscathed, yet with an appearance of vitality sufficiently unimpaired to warrant the presumption that had they remained attached to the living stem, like their kindred in nature's outdoor experiment, they would, like them, quickly recover from the effects of the fire. The effectiveness of this provision for the safety of posterity is further assured by the tendency of the needles to persist on the stem of the young shoot for several years, until the more delicate parts are lifted beyond the reach of danger. As the growth of the sapling progresses, and the increasing thickness of the bark provides for the protection of the stem, the needles become massed around the growing axes at the end of the branches, where they form the tassel-like clusters or "pinetops," which are such a striking characteristic of the longleaf pines. Under the influence of light the lateral stems supporting these tassels tend to curve upward. This upright position has the advantage that the fire, which ordinarily makes its attack from below, has to cut its way through the entire phalanx of protecting needles before it can reach the growing point. If the rosettes were drooping as in the winter condition of the white pine, they would, instead of protecting the buds, act as refractors to converge the heat upon them.

With such efficient fire protection it can easily be seen why the longleaf seedling is able to withstand a degree of heat that would be fatal to older and in other respects hardier plants. The same facts also explain why, in a state of nature, these trees tend either to congregate in pure forests over large areas or to become extinct if exposed to unrestricted competition with hardwoods. In the latter case the older conifers may hold their own for a time, but as these die out from superannuation or other causes, the new generation that should replace them, unable to develop in the shade, and cut off from the sunlight by the broad leaves of the hardwoods, fails to reach maturity and the race in time becomes extinct. On the other hand, when forest fires, especially of the minor type known as "ground fires" and "brush fires," occur at not too frequent intervals, the immunity of the pines enables them to take the lead in the work of reforestation, and through the gradual elimination of their rivals to become finally the sole possessors of the soil.

S. W. Greene, from "The Forest that Fire Made" (1931)[9]

[Original Editor's Note] *In this article, the author raises questions that will be warmly controverted. His conclusions that the longleaf forests of the South are the result of long years of grass fires and that continued fires are essential to the perpetuation of the species as a type will come as a startling and revolutionary theory to readers schooled to the belief that fire in any form is the arch enemy of Forests and Forestry. Professional foresters accustomed to distinguishing sharply between indiscriminate woods burning and carefully controlled, intelligently directed and limited use of fire for specific silvicultural ends will be less startled, though they may dissent in varying degree from the particular views expounded.*

Mr. Greene, it should be pointed out, is not a forester. For the past fifteen years, he has represented the Bureau of Animal Industry at the Coastal Plains Experiment Station at McNeill, Mississippi, in the study of the effect of ground fires upon forage production in the South. For a number of years, his work has been in cooperation with the United States Forest Service in its study of the influence of fire upon forest growth. His conclusions, therefore, while not official expressions of the government, have been arrived at through study and observation at first hand.

In publishing the article, American Forests does not vouch for the accuracy of Mr. Greene's conclusions. It does, however, believe them worthy of consideration. It is unalterably opposed to the unrestrained and irresponsible burning of the woods that now characterizes the South. Controlled burning intelligently applied and practiced where proven beneficial is an altogether different thing. Regulated burning under certain conditions and limitations may have an important place in the management of the longleaf forests. The Forest Service has been studying fire and forestry in the South for the past ten years and in view of Mr. Greene's contentions, the facts so far as determined by it should be brought to light as quickly as possible.

In the meantime, the American people, so prone to be careless with fire in the woods, must distinguish between the meaning of controlled and uncontrolled forest fires. The difference is as great as that between the subdued fire in the hearth that warms the home and the devastating flames that reduce the home to ashes. Discussion of the subject must not lessen the public's regard for care with fire in the woods.—Editor.

---

9 Excerpted from S. W. Greene, "The Forest that Fire Made," *American Forests*, October 1931, 584–584, 618.

The use of fires has been adopted, nursed and cultured as the greatest tool of mankind in the industries and professions, but in the field of forestry it has been branded with a curse to be dreaded and feared at every turn.

The importance of fire to the mechanical industries is apparent. Fire is a force of nature and not the invention of man, who has learned only to control and use it. Without its use, man's greatest invention, the wheel, would have remained only a wooden wheel of little use as a cog in the kind of machinery the world has known for centuries....

All fires in the woods are by no means forest fires that destroy useful timber, even though they are uncontrolled, and not all foresters are fanatics on the subject of fires. There are many foresters and landowners "aged in the wood," who can stand calmly by and study the effects of fires of different sorts without shouting "forest fire." Thoughtful men of the southern piney woods have stood calmly by and made such a study for generations without knowledge that the study of the relation between trees and their environment had such a scientific classification as ecology. Their conclusions were not set down as scientific treatises but were passed along under the common name of woodcraft and the lore of the woods told them when, why and how to use fire. As early as 1855 a trained ecologist [Eugene Hilgard], working in the longleaf pine area of southern Mississippi, discovered that ground fires in the forest were understood by the natives and were applied for a useful purpose which he mentioned in one short sentence. Secrets of nature were so commonplace that they were considered hardly worth mentioning and so the story of "The Forest That Fire Made" is just coming to general notice although "The Fire-Made Forest" itself was the most amazing physical characteristic of the South when traversed by DeSoto and his men from 1539–42 and has remained such for centuries.

Longleaf pine (*Pinus palustris*) stretched in unbroken, almost pure stands from Virginia into eastern Texas, a distance of more than 1,200 miles and DeSoto and his men traveled the length and breadth of it, for here was a highway free from underbrush, where deer could be seen through the timber as far as the eye could reach. An army of mounted men accompanied by 300 head of hogs needed an open country to prevent ambush by the Indians and to keep the band together. When swampy, brushy, or rough country was encountered the narratives of DeSoto's men made particular mention of the fact. Historians seem to have traced DeSoto's travel route mainly by the descriptions of the country set down. He tried travel north of the longleaf belt and was turned back; then he spent a year trying to penetrate the hardwood brush west of the Mississippi, only to turn back to the east where the going had been found easier.

No forest of such extent in pure stands and of such commercial value has been found on the face of the earth. Here was a poser, indeed, for the ecologist to ferret out the force of nature responsible for so favoring a single species of tree or the peculiarities of the species itself which enabled it to dominate over so vast an area. It was readily apparent that the northern extent of longleaf might be limited by temperature but farther south, in a region of heavy rainfall and mild temperature, one would expect a forest growth of greater variety with a jungle undergrowth of vines and shrubs. Why did we get such a pleasant place to live and travel instead of a jungle?

There was no lack of a variety of seed trees of other species to promote their spread, for in the stream bottoms occurred slash, loblolly, and various other species of pines, in addition to numerous hardwoods; but none of these could gain a foothold away from the wet land. The prevalent idea that hill soils were particularly favorable to longleaf and the bottoms to other pines will not hold, for, since the removal of the virgin longleaf forest, slash and loblolly pines in numerous instances have spread rapidly and have grown much faster at early stages than longleaf, even to the extent of crowding it out under longleaf seed trees.

It was noticeable that other species crowded out longleaf only in the absence of annual grass fires and since the southern region has a long growing season and a heavy rainfall, there is always a heavy grass growth and a carpet of resinous pine needles that burn readily until the edge of the swamp is reached. There fire stops. Fire, then, was a good clue and when approached from every angle the scent of fire became constantly stronger. But how could fire stop everything else yet encourage longleaf?

A peculiar habit of growth of longleaf possessed by no other pine gave the clue of the final solution to the tangle. We expect all woody plants as soon as they germinate to send up a stem in search of light but longleaf does no such thing. It forms a bundle of leaves in the grass and for a period of five, ten, and no one knows how many years it merely calls on reserve food supply in the roots to form a new set and goes on growing. No one knows what determines the start of its upward growth but when it is ready it sends up a husky shoot and makes a rapid growth, often three feet or more a year. Other pines spend their energy of the first year in building a stem and top which are easily destroyed by fire and the seedlings are killed.

The longleaf pine has two serious enemies—the hog and the brown spot needle disease. Hogs root the seedlings up and can live on the stored food material in the roots. However, hogs had no effect on the virgin stand for there were no hogs until the Spaniards introduced them. The needle disease is caused by a fungus, which is often a very serious enemy of the young seedlings underneath a "rough" of dead grass. Burning the dead grass in winter is an effective means of control.

The picture now clears up. Where seed trees are available all that is necessary to get a pure stand of longleaf without a hardwood undergrowth is to have frequent grass fires. Indians and lightning could and did set fire to the dead grass and strawfall and the material was ready to burn over expanses of hundreds of miles in extent any time after frost and in the summer if it had not burned the previous year. Fire offered no threat to the life and property of the Indian for they were not forest fires but merely grass fires that cleared the undergrowth of grass and hardwoods, making travel as easy as it does today. No roads or fields were in the way and fire could go across or around the head of small streams until it reached large river courses or was rained out. In the year 1773 William Bartram traveled with the Indians over much the same trail as DeSoto from South Carolina to the Mississippi River and gave detailed descriptions of the longleaf pine country. He speaks repeatedly of the open pine forests, describes Indians chasing deer on horseback through the woods and says of Indians setting fires:

> which happens almost every day throughout the year, in some part or other, by the Indians, for the purpose of rousing game, as also by the lightning. The very upper surface of the earth being mixed with the ashes of burnt vegetables, renders it of sufficient strength or fertility to clothe itself perfectly with a great variety of grasses. The cattle were as large and fat as those of the great grazing pastures of Moyomensing and the chief ordered some of the best steers to be slaughtered as a general feast in compliment of our arrival.[10]

If, at rare intervals, fire gave slash and other pines a chance to start on the hills, they found longleaf already in possession of the ground. This confined hardwoods and pines other than longleaf to the bay heads and swamps where hot fires could not reach them. Longleaf could rarely establish itself in the wet places because in the five years or more necessary for it to start height growth, the other species had already topped it and shaded it out.

Thus, we have "The Forest that Fire Made" and "The Forest That Fire Protects," for where fire is kept out for a number of years and a heavy rough of grass and pine straw accumulates, a summer fire during a dry time gives a real forest fire that actually kills saplings of good size. Winter grass fires in the southern longleaf pine areas appear to be highly desirable as a means of

---

10 Bartram, Travels, 1791, 151–152. [Note from original.]

checking undesirable species of hardwood, preventing the formation of a jungle, and encouraging growth of grasses and legumes to enrich the soil and as a range for cattle and quail. Without annual grass fires the grasses are smothered out and neither cattle nor quail can long exist in such a forest.

The field of study for the use of fire under other species of pine after they are once established, is a broad one. The strawfall from pines gives annual fuel that, if burned during the winter while the trees are dormant, causes little if any damage and prevents the piling up of a fire hazard that may later cause a real forest fire. Forest owners may yet turn to the use of fire to fight fire and get fire insurance for the cost of a match by knowing how and when to use a match as the natives of the southern piney woods have known for generations. To these people fire was not a master but a servant.

H. H. Biswell, from "Prescribed Burning in Georgia and California Compared" (1958)[11]

Prescribed burning is the use of fire in forestry for certain definite reasons where the conditions for firing are carefully planned in advance. Such burning may be done to improve grazing for livestock, to improve habitat conditions for game, to reduce wildfire hazard, to reduce hardwoods, to control disease, and to prepare seedbeds. In most cases a single burn will serve more than one purpose.

The author prescribed burned in the pine forests of Georgia from 1942 to 1947 and in second-growth ponderosa pine in California from 1951 to 1958. The purpose of this article is to compare experiences in the two places with the thought that they might be helpful in better understanding prescribed burning, particularly in California where it is hardly used at all. At present about one-half million acres are burned each year in the South and southeastern states, all the way from North Carolina to Texas.

In Georgia, the experiences were gained on the Alapaha Experimental Range, near Tifton. At that time the idea of burning was fairly new to me, and I looked upon fire as the arch enemy of forests and forestry. But the work proved to be enlightening. Here burning was used under control as a most helpful tool in land management. It was back in the twenties that S. W. Greene, Animal Husbandman with the U.S. Department of Agriculture, had discovered the benefits of prescribed burning in range improvement; he also observed that fire might have values in forestry. As a result of this pioneer work, Greene wrote a most interesting article, "The Forest that Fire Made." In this he pointed out clearly the role of continued light grass fires in developing and maintaining a vast pine forest. Among other early investigators were H. L. Stoddard, who advocated prescribed burning in upland game management and H. H. Chapman, who studied its use in longleaf pine silviculture.

Since 1940 a large amount of burning has been done in the South and Southeastern states, where the use of fire wisely planned and supervised, under many and variable conditions of overstory and understory vegetation, has become an important phase of forest-land management. During the early years this was pretty much confined to the longleaf-slash pine forests. But now

---

11 Excerpted from H. H. Biswell, "Prescribed Burning in Georgia and California Compared," *Journal of Range Management* 11, no. 6 (November 1958): 293–297.

it is widely used in the loblolly and shortleaf types; for example, about one-half of the 225,000 to 250,000 acres burned annually by the U.S. Forest Service in the past 8 years has been in these types.

Prescribed burning seems to more useful and essential in the South as forestry increases in intensity. It is given much credit at present, but the using of it beneficially in management have by no means been exhausted. Heretofore, the thinking has been largely that of fitting fire into forest-land management, but those experienced in fire use are beginning to see that certain forestry practices might be altered to fit into prescribed burning, thus making better use of this tool than is possible under present management.

In California prescribed burning in second-growth ponderosa pine has been studied in two places: on the Teaford Forest in the Central Sierra Nevada, near North Fork, and at Hobergs in the North Coastal Range. Very few other studies of prescribed burning have been made in California. About the only one report was that by the Forestry Committee, published by Donald Bruce in the February 1923, issue of the *Journal of Forestry*. At that time "light burning" was not found useful for numerous reasons. But great changes have taken place since then and some of the reasons advanced at that time for not burning are no longer valid, especially in the light of the information gained in the past seven years.

The studies in California were started specifically to determine whether or not prescribed burning can serve as a means of manipulating brush covers to improve conditions for game, and if it will reduce the danger of wildfires in summer. The thinking was this: if it is used successfully over such wide areas and under such variable conditions as those found in the South and the Southeastern states, why could it not also be used in California? This idea was also developed from the fact that frequent light fires had probably been the most important force in molding the virgin forests of California. During the past few years several articles covering various aspects of prescribed burning in California have been published. . . .

This article compares the various aspects of prescribed burning in southern pine forests with those in second-growth ponderosa pine in California. It is based on several years of actual experience in each place. Prescribed burning is widely employed as a tool in forest-land management from North Carolina to Texas; on the other hand, it was scarcely tested in California before 1951. A principal reason for its use in California would be to reduce wildfire hazard and risk.

It must be remembered that California has a Mediterranean-type climate characterized by long, hot, dry summers. The fuels for wildfire during this time become extremely dry and tinderlike. In recent years some of the wildfires have been large and destructive; for example, in 1955, 141,222 acres of timbered land burned in an 18-day period from August 27 to September 10 killing nearly all of the trees over vast areas. Fires of these proportions not only cost millions of dollars but also do untold damage in accelerating floods and erosion, and in producing other ill effects. If prescribed burning will reduce the hazard and risk of wildfires, and lessen the damage on areas burned, it may be a highly worthwhile tool in forest-land management in California...

E. V. Komarek, from "The Use of Fire: An Historical Background" (1962)[12]

Fire in Nature and its use by man has been the subject of much controversy throughout the world for many years. I, however, cannot help but be impressed, after a perusal of world literature on fire, by the great number of excellent scientific studies that have verified the "folk-wisdom" of pioneer peoples and primitive tribes who had to take their sustenance directly from the land. These peoples, generation upon generation, developed a knowledge of the use of fire that was akin to "art." This art of the use of fire was not only used for very definite purposes that were valuable to them but was virtually necessary for their existence. . . .

Man throughout his long history has had little use for forest except for fuel and wood for shelter. On continent after continent he fought the forest with fire and other means to increase grassland and field land for pasture and farming. It was only in the early nineteenth century along with man's early technological development that forest products began to loom large in his economy, and it was only then that he began to protect and replace the forests he formerly tried so hard to destroy. This awareness of the future importance to him of forests first became apparent in central Europe, then it spread to northeastern United States and to southeastern India. Curiously enough, these are the only large areas of hardwood deciduous species (beech and maple) in the world where fire can be said to be the most damaging and perhaps of the least possible use in forest management.

I am not the first to notice this transfer of "culture" and forest management thinking for in 1926, E. A. Greswell, Forester of the Indian Forest Service in India, wrote in the *Indian Forester Journal*:

> . . . [S]tatements . . . by writers on the Himalayan conifers, with which I have mainly had to deal, have forced me to the conclusion that our management has hitherto been based on pussyfoot principles. Excessive indulgence in alcohol is no argument for total prohibition. The same applies to fire and grazing and perhaps other natural phenomena to which our forests have been subjected for centuries. We talk glibly

---

12 E. V. Komarek, "The Use of Fire: An Historical Background," *Proceedings: Tall Timbers Fire Ecology Conference* 1 (1962): 7–10.

about following nature and forget that the nature we are visualizing may be an European nature inherited from our training and not an Indian nature. We, therefore, intuitively welcome the proof provided by the few cases in which they are so and by inductive reasoning arrive at general conclusions which may be incorrect if not dangerous.

This inherited European training has undoubtedly been at the root of many of our differences of opinion here in the South as well as elsewhere. This European philosophy of forest economy and the conservation of natural resources has had the effect of confusing our opinions. Early in the 20th century the need for the protection of our natural resources in this country became so apparent that efforts were made toward the establishment of such conservation agencies as the U.S. Forest Service. However, in this "fight" to save our forests, grasslands, and wildlife there were strong economic counterforces. The "timber barons" as they were called then, and powerful grazing interests all fought the initial establishment of conservation agencies. To me, it is not surprising, that with such strong opposing viewpoints, both very strong politically, that fire should have become the scapegoat and have been singled out as the greatest single destructive force to our forests, our grasslands, our soils, and our wildlife. Fire had only a courageous few to represent it and to point out that it was a tool, a most valuable one, but like many of man's tools it could be very destructive if improperly or accidentally used. The consequences were that fire was blamed for all the destruction—not the wasteful and improper lumbering practices that preceded it—not the excessive overgrazing—not wasteful and even dangerous farm practices. Money and manpower were literally poured into the fight, to fight the common enemy demon-fire.

Is it any wonder that the differences on the use of fire became heated and controversial? Is it strange that the literature is filled with statements, evidence, and even scientific experiments that are conflicting? The process of education against the use of fire as well as its place in nature, has been long and so complete that even today many find it difficult to believe that fire may be useful, in spite of the fact that fire is an accepted tool by many agencies in the Southeast and other regions. State Forest Services now announce on TV when conditions are proper for burning as well as give assistance to those landowners wishing to use fire. Experiment Stations and Extension Services recommend its use on native as well as improved pasture grasses or cattle range, and its use in the production of such wildlife as the Bobwhite Quail is standard practice on many lands.

In the Southwest, fire is used in the management of grasslands on an increasing scale in the suppression of undesirable growths such as sage, mesquite, and others. Let me cite a few other examples. In India its use is standard practice in the management of Chir Pine forests and even in the hardwood forests of sal and teak. In Australia fire is used increasingly in the management of Eucalyptus forests as well as grasslands. In South Africa burning and rotation grazing have become a regular management feature in the production of meat. And yet, as recently as 1959, the late Dr. John T. Curtis, Plant Ecology Laboratory of the University of Wisconsin, wrote that the prairies and savannas of that state . . . have become victims of the bureaucratic dictum, that since most forest fires are the source of economic loss, therefore all fires are bad and must be prevented at any cost. This dogma has been supported by such an intensive propaganda campaign that there is danger of its being accepted as truth. Many additional citations could be made where fire may be a useful and sometimes necessary tool in land management. In some fields the "dogma" referred to by Dr. Curtis still prevails, but continued research and experimentation have so broadened our knowledge of the effects of fire on the environment that much interest is now evident in the development of techniques to make fire a safer tool in the management of forest, grassland, and wildlife.

Herbert L. Stoddard, from "Use of Fire in Pine Forests and Game Lands" (1962)[13]

. . . I will attempt to sketch a brief history of one of the most bitterly fought battles of the forestry-wildlife conservation movement, and explain why after fifty years of misunderstanding and bickering, we are gradually getting closer together in thought and practice.

I will start with some discussion of conditions in the Florida pinelands before 1900 and bring the matter up to 1962, as I see it. I am aware that some of my statements and conclusions may be questioned by others who hold contrary views. It would be strange indeed were this not the case when dealing with such a controversial subject, and in the absence of adequate and unbiased longtime experimentation and research. In addition to my own observations of over sixty years, I have been influenced by the discussions and the writings of several foresters, botanists, and students of ecology with long field experience in the region. Among these men I want especially to acknowledge my indebtedness to Professor H. H. Chapman, Dr. Roland Harper, and Messrs. Frank Heyward and S. W. Greene, all of whom did yeoman's service in publishing on the use of fire and its effects from the forestry, botanical, grazing, and soil-fertility standpoints.

In my opinion the much maligned pioneer cattlemen of the Florida "flatwoods" and elsewhere in the piney woods of the southeastern coastal plain, had many valid reasons for burning off the dead grasses, pine needles, and other forest debris in the vast forests that covered much of the terrain surrounding them. I will discuss a few of their reasons as I heard them firsthand well before the day of the wild claims and counterclaims that characterized a later period of bitterness and confusion. . . .

Some with no firsthand knowledge of these hardy and capable pioneers, would have us believe that they set fires just to see them burn, and some propagandists schooled in the west European forestry traditions, referred to them as morons, imbeciles, etc. These people had to do a multitude of things correctly to live isolated lives in the "pine barrens." They produced or built almost everything they needed or used, and they lived rich and interesting lives.

---

13 Excerpted from Herbert L. Stoddard, "Use of Fire in Pine Forests and Game Lands," *Proceedings: Tall Timbers Fire Ecology Conference* 1 (1962): 31–42.

SOUTHERN BACKFIRES

The objectives of the cattlemen were probably almost identical with those of the red men that had used fire from time immemorial, for land clearing, hunting, etc. So it is safe to state that the magnificent Longleaf Pine forest that covered the high terrain, had grown to its centuries-old maturity under the programs of man, white and red, who got much the same results as had Mother Nature for thousands of years before man with her lightning-set fires. The speaker was most fortunate to have lived in these forests that so thrilled William Bartram in the late 1700s: forests that grew because of, not in spite of, the handling given the land by sparse populations. But not owning the ranges they used contributed to the downfall of most of the pioneer cattlemen.

The forefathers of these cattlemen had come in from the North Carolina mountains long before the nineties. They spent much of their daylight hours on horseback, thus having an advantage over the earlier Indians. As they rode the ranges, they set fires at intervals when conditions were right for light burning, from early fall to late spring. They knew from the way the cattle gravitated to the fresh burns that the tender grass would make them grow and fatten. It put them in shape to market, or survive the hardships of the coming "dry season," and occasional severe cold. Curiously, some swivel-chair foresters of the north that had little or no field experience in the deep Southeast, at a somewhat later date claimed that "rough" range nourished cattle better in their weird anti-fire propaganda. Finally after some eleven years of careful research by the U.S. Bureau of Animal Industry under S. W. Greene and associates in coastal plain Mississippi; the cattlemen were proved right and their critics completely wrong; the cattle showed some 40 percent higher gain on annually burned wiregrass range than on the "rough"! The propagandists had been mistaken by wishful thinking.

This and many other things showed that these early cattlemen could not properly be called "ignorant" or "vicious," nor did they "need their heads examined," as one not too bright sociologist, hired to analyze their behavior by the anti-fire propagandists, reported several years later at the height of the anti-fire battle.[14] Our little family had taken up residence in the Florida backwoods in 1893, and we left the state in 1900, the year turpentining of the virgin Longleaf and Slash started in our region. Three or four years later the virgin pine started through the sawmills, so we saw the very last of its glory. Now, I "ran with the cattlemen" seven months of the year from 1896 to 1900. At that time the cattlemen did not use severe sweeping fires on their ranges. It was in the early 1920s that some in desperation started using such fires in an endeavor to save a remnant of their herds. It was then that the propagandists so blackened their

---

14 John Shea, "Our Pappies Burned the Woods," *American Forests*, April 1940, 159–162.

name. I had an opportunity to see the great abundance of quail that frequented the virgin pine lands, and how small fields that were opened up and planted attracted them as a magnet. Such observations were to be of great value to me over twenty years later when starting studies of the Bobwhite Quail. . . .[15]

A few foresters and ecologists began to see the true picture soon after 1910, as previously mentioned. It remained for me, as a result of my several-year study of the Bobwhite Quail, to point out the values of using controlled fire for the benefit of quail and other upland game and wildlife. If our minority group of less than a dozen "outlanders" who wrote on the subject were right, and the use of fire was necessary and desirable to perpetuate the flora and fauna of the region, the big questions to answer were when to burn, under what conditions to burn, how to burn, and with what frequency to burn, for best results with both pine forestry and wildlife. While progress is being made, it will take many more years, and a vast amount of dedicated research and experimentation, to provide all the right answers and to work out refinements. Until then, it seems likely that well-meaning but uninformed people will continue with the hoopla— "Keep Florida Green," "Keep Georgia Green" - and publicly deplore "setting fires in the woods," just as if no such legitimate thing as controlled burning existed and would at times, under certain conditions, do the job much better from every viewpoint than would fire exclusion! True, fire-tender seedlings of Loblolly and Slash Pine do require fire exclusion for several years, when controlled burning can be safely started and used to great advantage for the remainder of their life span, to reduce fuel, keep out broadleaved "brush," etc. Longleaf and Shortleaf are true "fire types," however, and should be handled accordingly.

The present-day U.S. Forest Service can be complimented on making rapid progress during recent years in working out useful techniques for controlled burning. Several of the State Forest Services are "coming around," also, and have even published bulletins informing landowners how to control burn where it is advantageous all around for them to do so. I refer especially to Georgia, Florida, and South Carolina.

This is a far cry from what I ran into in the '20's and early '30's. The U.S. Biological Survey (now the U.S. Fish and Wildlife Service) was one of the smallest bureaus of the U.S. Department of Agriculture, while the Forest Service was one of the largest and most powerful. Some of the leaders of the "old school" were opinionated and unreasonable from our standpoint to say the least, when the time came to publish "The Bobwhite Quail." I had first outlined the fire

---

15 Herbert L. Stoddard, The *Bobwhite Quail: Its Habits, Preservation, and Increase* (New York: Charles Scribners' Sons, *1931*).

chapter in 1928 and 1929, for I anticipated we were going to run into publication difficulties of a serious nature. Manuscript originating in one bureau had to "go through channels" and be approved by others concerned before publication. To make a long story short, I rewrote the fire chapter five times in the attempt to get it cleared. Finally, seeing no other course to pursue, I passed the word where I knew it would spread to the effect that the fire chapter, already sadly "watered down," would have to be cleared for publication or else I would resign and write a book on the subject that would not be a compromise.

The sportsmen who had financed our study to the tune of over fifty thousand dollars included several of the most powerful men in the country, politically and financially; I knew they would back me to a man. If those in the saddle at the Forest Service preferred a fight to "okaying" the chapter as rewritten, they could have it, for we had compromised as far as we would. It was soon reluctantly cleared in the form it appeared in "The Bobwhite Quail" in 1931.

I am happy to state that there was no opposition to our fire findings or their publication in the Biological Survey; just the contrary. We had the full backing of the late W. L. McAtee, head of the Division of Food Habits Research under which the quail investigations were organized. And this support continued after 1931, when the new Cooperative Quail Study Association was organized, financed, and started operations under private auspices. Our backers were practically the same group that had instigated and financed the earlier investigation, and were represented by Mr. H. L. Beadel as Secretary and Treasurer. Mr. Beadel had ably pointed out that the original investigation had but opened up several important lines of inquiry, among which the use and control of fire on game lands was probably the most important. This was to be pushed by the new association through research and experimentation, as its importance warranted. It was clear by this time that the income from thriving pine forests could be made to help pay the costs of developments for upland game, especially the quail and wild turkey. We believed the production of forest products, as well as such agricultural products as corn, could be dovetailed with the game developments. Hence we intended to find out all that we could about the effects of controlled burning on the pine forests as well as on the game. This was disturbing news to our previous antagonists, and the battle flared up again. But now we were in an independent position, and in any case. Tome it was, however, quite regrettable that we had never had the opportunity to set up a large series of fire ecology, genetic, and other plots; continuity has to be assured when the results of many of the tests and experiments do not give maximum results for over a hundred years!

This problem was solved in a most satisfactory way when Mr. H. L. Beadel decided to leave his Tall Timbers Plantation of 2,800 acres of ideal land, buildings, machinery, and a substantial sum of money for biological research, with special emphasis on long-time studies on the ecology of fire. The place, however, is ideally adapted to a variety of lines of both terrestrial and aquatic research, including bird banding and life-history studies of a wide variety of birds, mammals, reptiles, fishes, insects, and other creatures too numerous to mention here.

There are also fine possibilities for education in natural history. With plenty of land, opportunities are almost unlimited for ecological research on the effects of fire use on forests and all the living creatures and vegetation that are affected for better or worse by its use. Mr. Beadel has long been interested in this.

Formation of the Tall Timbers Research Station and preliminary plans have been continuing for the past three years. In February and March of 1959, we set up 84 half-acre plots (see Tall Timbers Research Station Bulletin No.2, 1962), well distributed over highlands and lowlands, and including samples of the four species of pines common on the place. Some will be burned in summer, some in winter, and at intervals varying from annually to once in over 100 years. Some forestry, botanical, and insect studies have been carried on, while the controlled burning of the shortest-period plots has been conducted according to plans. This series will soon be followed by another of forest genetics plots of an acre in size, in which burning will also have a part.

Mr. Beadel's desires for the future of the station, so far as fire studies are concerned, have been incorporated both in his will and the Charter of Tall Timbers Research Station, and every precaution known to man has been taken to see that his desires are followed perpetually. Prospects seem bright that we will finally get our "adequate and unbiased experimentation and research" in at least the forest type of the Tallahassee-Thomasville region. We hope that others will conduct similar studies in other forest types of the deep Southeast.

I did not read this paper to stir up a rumpus or kick a sleeping dog or anything like that. I did want it on record that the early pioneer cattlemen of central Florida had neither horns nor spiked tails. Since nobody had come to their defense in the last half century, I felt an obligation to do so.

Tall Timbers Audience Comment (1962)[16]

If you will permit a comment from an outsider, it seems to me that I detect a note of a good bit of self-questioning, but I don't think we should have it. You are so far ahead of the rest of the country that you shouldn't have it. My forestry experience has been in northern New England and in the Northwest. For various reasons—fuel type and topography and past history—we have been not only timid with fire; we have been scared to death. We have tried for many purposes to use fire in small experiments where we are concerned about moose management and woodcock management and in many other ways, and we know a little bit maybe about Ponderosa Pine control burning, but it's just a scratch on the surface compared to your knowledge. Mr. [Herbert] Stoddard mentioned perhaps we didn't have any woodsmen among our professional men. I won't necessarily admit to that, but we might be in the same position as Daniel Boone. We never admit to being lost but we have been confused.

---

16 Audience comment in *Proceedings: Tall Timbers Fire Ecology Conference* 1 (1962): 178.

Fig. 10. On June 10, 1937, President Franklin Roosevelt accepted James Montgomery Flagg's fire prevention poster, which would be distributed nationwide. Standing behind the president, from left to right, are Flagg, Secretary of Agriculture Henry Wallace, and Forest Service chief Earl Clapp. Credit: Library of Congress.

Fig. 11. Smokey Bear was the mascot of the Forest Service's fire suppression campaign. This photograph reflects how deeply this symbol penetrated into American culture, as Big Smokey and two progeny march in a May 1965 parade in Washington State. In this instance, Forest Service employees from the Mount Baker National Forest donned these bulky costumes. Credit: NARA 7106718.

National Reassessment, 1923–1959

At the same time that the Mission Indian Federation raised questions about the Forest Service's clamorous defense of fire suppression, non-Indigenous researchers began to examine the implications of this fire-exclusion policy in a variety of ecosystems. Often these reevaluations were couched in deference to the insights of "old timers." R. L. Hensel, a Kansas agronomist, had listened to stockmen in Arizona and his home state who believed that fire suppression had led to the spread of mesquite in the Grand Canyon State, while their peers further east practiced controlled burns to stimulate the regeneration of grassland, much as the Indigenous people of the Great Plains had done. Hensel, in response, conducted some of the first scientific analyses of fire's influence on the timing and intensity of grassland reproduction. His 1923 data revealed that those plots he burned grew back more quickly and fully than those left untouched, and with fewer weeds. His speculation that similar results might pertain in Arizona are intriguing, not least because forester Aldo Leopold asked similar questions about what he called that state's brushlands. Given that he worked for the Forest Service, and had earlier affirmed its now-deep commitment to fire suppression, his theoretical analysis seems a qualified reversal: under certain conditions and places, fire might restore grasslands in the southern portion of the state that mesquite, juniper, and pine were overrunning; if reburned, as the Indigenous people had done, there would also be less erosion.

Amid the Great Depression of the 1930s and early 1940s, two foresters who had spent their entire careers in the Northern Rockies weighed in on the problematic character of the Forest Service's fire-exclusion strategy, which had been ramped up by the so-called "10 a.m. Rule." Announced in 1935, the policy decreed that every fire on the national forests and grasslands must be extinguished by 10:00 a.m. the day after it had been reported. In a controversial article published that same year, forester Elers Koch suggested that fire-suppression in remote wildlands was too costly, inefficient, and counterproductive. The furious professional pushback Koch received gives ample reason why Allen Calbick, a ranger on the Flathead National Forest, would only admit that fire was a cleansing, beneficial force in private correspondence with former chief Gifford Pinchot.

That silence began to break, slowly and partially. California, which had proved critical to the establishment of the fire-suppression paradigm, by the mid-twentieth century became the site of revived debate. In the 1940s, when the National Park Service collaborated with the Forest Service's firefighting policy in the central Sierra Nevada, notably in Yosemite National Park, it sparked an internal rebuttal. The park's forester, Emil Ernst, laid out the historical and ecological case for returning fire to the Yosemite Valley; so touchy was the subject that the publication's editor warned readers Ernst's perspectives were not official policy. Harold Biswell, who as a Forest Service researcher had studied the ecological benefits of controlled burning in the US South, replicated his research agenda in California. The results, which he published in academic journals and in popular venues like *National Parks Magazine*, proved highly controversial among traditional foresters in the state; but these investigations are also credited with shifting opinions about the value of light burning. So, too, is the 1963 Leopold Report that the National Park Service commissioned. Among other managerial strategies, the document argued that henceforth the federal agency should utilize prescribed burns for forest regeneration because this was "the most 'natural' and much the easiest and cheapest to apply." Even so, forester Rita P. Thompson mused in 1976, fire ecology—as idea and discipline—had not been fully integrated into Forest Service land management, a consequence in part of "administrative inertia" which itself was a reflection of the light-burning controversy's enduring power.

R. L. Hensel, from "Recent Studies on the Effect of Burning on Grassland Vegetation" (1923)[1]

The forester whose work throws him into contact with stockmen, and especially with the older class of stockmen, very often finds himself at a loss to explain satisfactorily some of the questions put to him. While in Arizona a few years ago I was discussing the Santa Rita Range Reserve with an "old timer" who was pointing out how mesquite had spread on areas under protection. The fact that mesquite was actually spreading had been vouched for by competent authorities. This man was making the point that regular burning at the right time of year would hold mesquite in check and not injure the grass. He discussed certain areas in Texas with which I was acquainted, saying that thirty years ago these were all open grassland, whereas they are now densely covered with shrubbery. Were this an isolated instance not much weight could be attached to it, but similar statements have been repeated so often that some credence must be given to them.

Practically everyone who has ridden through forests in the spring has come upon areas which had been burned during the preceding winter or early spring and has noticed the striking difference in vegetation of the burned portions. Especially noticeable is the difference in the time at which growth begins, as in all cases the vegetation turns green earlier on the burned portions. In explaining the difference between the fresh green color on the burned, and lack of green growth on the unburned, parts we always used the same explanation: the difference was only imaginary, for if we examined the un-burned parts closely, we would find as many green shoots as on the burned parts. In my own case I offered this explanation so often that I really believed I could prove it without even stopping to examine such areas. In recent years this belief has been shattered by experiments which have been conducted at the Kansas Experiment Station. These will be discussed in the following pages, because it is believed that they will be of interest to those foresters whose work leads them along grazing lines.

In Kansas, as well as in adjoining states, the custom of burning pastures in the spring is still practiced to a considerable extent. Some of the settlers farther west who will argue that burning is desirable are very often men who

---

1 Excerpted from R. L. Hensel, "Recent Studies on the Effect of Burning on Grassland Vegetation," *Ecology* 4, no. 2 (April 1923): 183–188.

emigrated from this section. The actual practice has its beginning perhaps in the Indian custom of burning to make available fresh feed early in the spring for use of game animals which it was desired to hunt. There were two purposes in view, one to provide desirable feed in the spring, and the other to burn off all winter feed excepting that in certain localities so chosen as to make hunting more easy. It is within the realm of possibility to suppose that the white man copied this ancient custom on his farm pastures, using it for what he believed to be an advantage.

Opinion among stockmen on the burning question is divided. Some favor it strongly, while others are decidedly opposed to it. Among scientific men the belief has always been held that it is injurious. This belief is founded on the fact that fire is always injurious to existing plant life both in the seed and herbage stages, and second that burning consumes some of the organic matter that should go into the soil.

Among Kansas farmers the objects of burning are, first, to get rid of areas so lightly grazed during previous seasons that there is danger of uneven grazing during the coming season. Stock prefer the fresh green feed in closely grazed areas to the green feed that is mixed with last year's residue. Second, by burning they feel that feed is made available sooner than on unburned areas, and third the belief is held that burning keeps down weeds and brush. The experiments were conducted with these objects in view. From the scientific standpoint the work was approached as follows:

1. The effect of burning on the life and growth of the principal forage plants.
2. The effect of burning on soil temperatures at one- and three-inch depths under the surface.
3. The effect of burning on the yields of hay.

The area upon which the work was done is typical Kansas prairie lying between the elevations of 1,200 and 1,400 feet. The soil is a dark brown loam with an underlying subsoil consisting of clays and shales. The average annual precipitation is 31.5 inches, the principal part falling in April, May, and June.

The important grasses are big blue stem (*Andropogon furcatus Muhl.*), little blue stem (*A. scoparius Michx.*), side oats grama (*Bouteloua curti- pendula Michx.*), and Kentucky blue grass (*Poa pratensis L.*). Grasses of lesser importance are hairy grama (*Bouteloua hirsuta Lag.*), blue grama (*Bouteloua gracilis H. B. K.*), sand drop seed (*Sporobolus cryptandrus Torr.*), switch grass (*Panicum virgatum L.*), and Indian grass (*Sorghastrum nutans L.*). Two sedges, *Carex pennsylvanica Lamarck* and *C. Meadii Dewey*, are common in the region.

The experimental area consists of two adjoining plats, each 70 feet square. One, called section A, was burned between March 23 and April 13 each year. The other section, D, was never burned. Stock were kept off both areas throughout the year, as they might have seriously injured the thermographs and the quadrats. To imitate grazing in some degree both sections were cut with a scythe about September 15 each year. The cut material was raked off the plats. It would have been better had we been able to graze the experimental area, but this was impossible because we felt that the quadrats, being so small, should not be disturbed in the least. In future work we will try to check our work with similar plats located where stock will have access to them at all times. It is not probable, though, that such checks will influence present findings to a marked extent.

In the vegetation studies, seven quadrats, each 10 x 12 inches in size, were constructed of 1-inch x 2-inch material. Tacks were driven at one-half-inch intervals all around the frame, and from these, string was woven across the frame, dividing the interior into one-half-inch squares. These frames were carefully placed in the sod and firmly staked down. In use the vegetation in each square was recorded on a chart. Thus, one quadrat might contain 70 squares of big blue stem, 50 of little blue stem, and 100 of Kentucky blue grass. For grasses and sedges, the compilation was made on the basis of squares of each grass contained in the quadrat. In the case of weeds the specimens in each square were counted and the compilation was made on the basis of specimens instead of squares. These quadrats were charted three times each spring. The first was made about three weeks after burning and the remaining two at intervals of two weeks. This schedule could not always be maintained, however, on account of inclement weather.

... [T]here was always decidedly more vegetation on the burned quadrats in the early charting. An examination of the April 9, 1918, and April 17, 1919, chartings, which were the earliest made, shows a decided preponderance on the burned section. The table shows further that there was always more grass on the burned plat. The point should be made that the original chartings showed that there was slightly more vegetation on the burned section from the outset, but the vital feature is, however, that this advantage was maintained throughout the four years. To prove this, we can take the June 3, 1918, chartings and compare them with the July 1, 1921, chartings. It will be found that there was 21 percent more grass on the burned section at the later date, while there was only 7.5 percent more on the unburned.

In view of these facts it seems plausible to conclude that so far burning has not injured the grass stand as far as amount is concerned. The stand is 21 percent heavier than it was when the experiment was started. The un-burned section has held its own.

The question now arises: What effect did burning have on the different grasses in the stand? When the experiments were first started, little blue stem was the most abundant grass on both plats, and big blue stem was next in order. In 1921 things had changed considerably in that little blue stem showed a decided increase (48 percent) on the burned area and a decrease (6i percent) on the unburned. Big blue stem decreased approximately 20 percent in the burned section and increased 75 percent in the unburned. Side oats grama decreased in both plats, and Kentucky blue grass spread 250 percent on the burned, while on the unburned it increased from no specimens to 135. It is taking the entire unburned area rapidly.

From these data it appears reasonably well established that burning actually starts vegetation earlier than on similar areas not burned; that it does not decrease the total number of plants, but it does have an influence on composition. As far as Kansas grasses are concerned, the change in composition has, if anything, been in favor of burning, because little blue stem is slightly more desirable than big blue stem.

The data with respect to weeds also show the unexpected. If burning were injurious to the grasses, we could expect one or both of two things—either a decrease in density of the stand or an increase in weeds. It is well known that an injury to the sod is reflected in an increase in weeds. If we were committed to the belief that burning was injurious to the grasses, we would expect an increase in weeds on the burned area and at least a stationary condition on the unburned. Up until May 31, 1919, there were slightly more weeds on the burned section than on the unburned. Since that date the tide has turned, so that there are now more weeds on the unburned area. By chartings, the differences have shown 25, 10, 55, 50, and 50 percent, respectively, more weeds on the unburned section. These figures are large enough to prove that in the first four years burning has not caused weeds to spread.

To determine what influence burning has on soil temperatures, two thermographs were used on each of the plats. The bulbs were placed at one and three inches under the surface and the clocks started immediately after burning in the spring. From the records thus secured the mean maximum and minimum temperatures at one- and three-inch depths on the burned and unburned plats were obtained. The data show that on the burned portion at one inch under the surface mean maximum temperatures are on the average 12° F. higher than on the unburned area. On the burned plat at the same depth mean minimum temperatures were 1.8° higher, and at three inches under the surface the mean maxima were 5.2^0 higher; mean minimum temperatures were also higher by 4^0.

These differences, and especially those at one inch, are great enough to influence growth early in the season. That growth starts earlier was shown in the vegetation studies. It is felt that the temperature data explain in a satisfactory manner why this takes place. The removal of the surface covering by burning exposes the soil to the sun's rays, permitting it to absorb more heat than the soil on unburned areas, which is shaded to a considerable extent by surface litter.

. . . It is still too early to make any definite recommendations based on these findings. More work must be done before the results can be accepted as final. Plans for a more extensive study are being made, and it is hoped that contributions to the literature on the subject can be made from time to time. The plans at the Kansas Station also include a detailed study of the effect of burning on brush. This will be a major study and of wide appeal, because the question of brush on pastures as well as on many forest ranges is serious. If, by burning, shrubbery can be held in check on areas of value chiefly for the grass which they produce, such a practice will be worthwhile, providing, of course, that the danger of losing control of the fire is overcome. Indeed, the whole problem of the application of the burning practice to National Forests is to provide methods that will overcome the danger to commercial timber on or near areas to be fired. Before this can be considered, however, adequate conclusive data on the benefits of burning must be forthcoming.

Elers Koch, from "The Passing of the Lolo Trail" (1935)[2]

The Lolo Trail is no more.

The bulldozer blade has ripped out the hoof tracks of Chief Joseph's ponies. The trail was worn deep by centuries of Nez Perce and Blackfeet Indians, by Lewis and Clark, by companies of Northwest fur traders, by General Howard's cavalry horses, by Captain Mullan, the engineer, and by the early-day forest ranger. It is gone, and in its place there is only the print of the automobile tire in the dust.

What of the camps of fragrant memory—Camp Martin, Rocky Ridge, Noseeum Meadows, Bald Mountain, Indian Grave, Howard Camp, Indian Post Office, Spring Mountain, Cayuse Junction, Packer Meadows? No more will the traveler unsaddle his ponies to roll and graze on the bunch grass of the mountaintops. No more "the mule train coughing in the dust." The trucks roll by on the new Forest Service road, and the old camps are no more than a place to store spare barrels of gasoline.

No more will the mountain man ride the high ridges between the Kooskooskee and the Chopunnish, "smoking his pipe in the mountains, sniffing the morning cool."

It is now but three hours' drive from the streets of Missoula to the peak where Captain Lewis smoked his pipe and wrote in his journal: "From this elevated spot we have a commanding view of the surrounding mountains, which so completely enclose us that though we have once passed them, we almost despair of ever escaping from them without the assistance of the Indians." Only ten years ago it was just as Lewis and Clark saw it.

So it is everywhere.

The hammer rings in the CCC camp on the remotest waters of the Selway. The bulldozer snorts on Running Creek, that once limit of the back of beyond. The moose at Elk Summit lift their heads from the lilypads to gaze at the passing motor truck. Major Penn's beloved Coolwater Divide has become a motor road.

---

2 Excerpted from Elers Koch, "The Passing of the Lolo Trail," *Journal of Forestry* 33, no. 2 (February 1935): 98–104.

NATIONAL REASSESSMENT, 1923–1959

171

No more can one slip up to the big lick at Powell on a frosty October morning and see the elk in droves. The hunters swarm in motorcars in the public campgrounds.

And all to what end? Only a few years ago the great Clearwater wilderness stretched from the Bitterroot to Kooskia, from the Cedar Creek mines to the Salmon River and beyond. No road and no permanent human habitation marred its primitive nature. There it lay—the last frontier—an appeal to the mind of a few adventurous souls who might wish to penetrate its fastness and plunge for weeks beyond human communication.

The Forest Service sounded the note of progress. It opened up the wilderness with roads and telephone lines and airplane landing fields. It capped the mountain peaks with white-painted lookout houses, laced the ridges and streams with a network of trails and telephone lines, and poured in thousands of firefighters year after year in a vain attempt to control forest fires.

Has all this effort and expenditure of millions of dollars added anything to human good? Is it possible that it was all a ghastly mistake, like plowing up the good buffalo grass sod of the dry prairies? Has the country as it stands now as much human value as it had in the nineties when Major Penn's forest rangers first rode into it?

To answer the questions let us first examine what manner of country this is and what it is good for. I have before me a map of north Idaho made up on the basis of the combined judgment of the best qualified forest officers, which shows in green Zone 1, the area of unquestioned value for timber production; in white Zone 2, areas which may possibly have some future timber productive value; and in yellow Zone 3 areas which owing to altitude, rugged topography, permanent inaccessibility, or inferior timber growth, will never, so far as best present judgment indicates, come into the picture as timber producing land.

The three northern national forests in the state are considerably cut up as to zones, but with green and white greatly predominating on the map. Farther south the picture changes. The upper reaches of the North Fork of the Clearwater, the Lochsa, Selway, and Salmon Rivers form a great solid block of yellow Zone 3 on the map, covering 3,000 square miles, or two million acres in round numbers. This is a different geological formation. Departing from the Precambrian shales of the north end of the state, this is part of the great granite batholith of central Idaho. It is a country of deep canyons, rushing, boulder-strewn rivers, mountain lakes, and high peaks. The decomposed granite soil is thin, coarse-grained, and shallow. Prior to the intervention of the Forest Service, the tide of civilization surged round it, and few men entered it. Elk, moose, mountain goats, deer, and fur bearers maintained a natural existence, protected by the country itself.

It seems obvious that whatever value the area may have, it is not for timber production. Rather its value lies in whatever pleasure man may get out of its recreational resources in the way of isolation, scenery, fish, and game.

. . . Would that I could turn the clock back and make a plea for preserving the area as it was twenty-five or even five years ago. Alas, it is too late. Roads are such final and irretrievable facts.

The Forest Service built these hundreds of miles of road and these thousands of miles of trail and telephone line for one purpose only—to facilitate the suppression of forest fires.

The whole history of the Forest Service's attempt to control fire in the backcountry of the Selway and Clearwater is one of the saddest chapters in the history of a high-minded and efficient public service. In the face of the most heroic effort and the expenditure of millions of dollars and several lives, this country has been swept again and again by most-uncontrollable conflagrations. The Lochsa Canyon is burned and reburned from Pete King to Jerry Johnson, and the Selway from the Forks to Moose Creek.

Many fires have been controlled, but when the time is ripe for a conflagration, man's efforts have been puny in the face of nature's forces. I am not criticizing the efforts of others. I have personally taken part in four major fire campaigns on the Lochsa River, in 1910, 1919, 1929, and 1934. Each year we made a greater effort and threw larger forces of men into the battle, but so far as results were concerned there is little difference between 1919, when crews of thirty or forty men, in a vain but courageous gesture, were trailing the leeward end of each of five or six gigantic fires, and 1934, when firefighters were counted in thousands, and the fires swept 180,000 acres.

When fire gets a good start in the dry fire-killed cedar and white fir of the Selway and burning conditions are just right, the whole United States Army, if it was on the ground, could do nothing but keep out of the way. After years of experience I have come to the considered conclusion that control of fire in the backcountry of the Selway and Lochsa drainages is a practical impossibility. I firmly believe that if the Forest Service had never expended a dollar in this country since 1900 there would have been no appreciable difference in the area burned over. It is even possible that, by extinguishing fires in favorable seasons which would have run over a few hundred or a few thousand acres, the stage was only set for the greater conflagrations which went completely beyond fire-line control. After all, this country existed and maintained a general timber cover before man was born and for millions of years before the Forest Service came into being. Surely its existence as wild land capable of sheltering its game and holding the watershed together cannot now be altogether dependent on the efforts of the Forest Service. No important new element has been introduced. Not a single one of the greater fires which have swept the country since 1910 has been man-caused. And even 130 years ago we have Lewis and Clark's testimony that the Indians habitually set fire for such a trivial purpose as to insure fair weather for a journey.

. . . What is the future line of action which should be taken by the Forest Service in this country? There seem to be three alternatives:

1. Continue on about the present basis with some gradual extension of roads, trails, landing fields, and other facilities and about the present force of protection men.
2. If Congress can be induced to appropriate necessary funds, greatly intensify the protection setup, open all the remaining inaccessible country with roads, and greatly increase the protection forces.
3. Set up a carefully defined unit of about two million acres as a low-value area which does not justify the cost of fire control. Maintain only existing roads and the major trails. Withdraw the entire fire-control organization and retain only a police force of two or three rangers to protect the game and direct recreational use.

The first alternative has been found by twenty years' experience to be practically useless. It has resulted in greatly modifying and to a large extent destroying the special values of a unique and distinctive wilderness area. The results in fire control have been almost negligible. Every really bad fire season has seen great conflagrations sweep completely beyond control, nullifying the results of every fire extinguished in the more favorable seasons. If I could show in color a map of this region with the areas burned over since the beginning of national forest administration, the country would be shocked at the lack of results for the millions expended.

The second alternative, a greatly increased intensification of protection, appears at least more logical than the first. We are now making vast expenditures with little or no results. To double or treble these expenditures and get the desired results would at least give the taxpayers something for their money. It would mean abandoning the wilderness area completely and opening the whole country with roads, but that has already progressed so far that there is really no wilderness left, and perhaps we might as well make up our minds to an automobile recreational use of this area rather than a primitive packhorse use, provided we are going to tackle the protection job.

. . . Even assuming the practicability of a fair degree of fire control through greatly increased expenditures, is the game worth the candle? The Forest Service men are a tough outfit, and it takes a lot to make them admit they are licked, but the amount of taxpayers' money involved is so great that no false pride or saving of face should prevent a scrutiny of the justification of maintaining such expenditures when weighed against the values obtained, even though it involves an admission of defeat.

Almost any forester or lumberman would agree that the character of tree growth, soil, and topography on the area in question is such that there is little likelihood of its being developed commercially in the future, even under a period of considerable timber scarcity; and even though a few of the best areas should sometime in the future be logged, the return would at best be far below the annual expenditures, to say nothing of interest on past investment.

Recreational use and watershed protection are the only other values to be considered. It is conceded that these values would be enhanced by control of fires. However, the country in question in its natural state before the intervention of the Forest Service supported a fair forest cover and did not show any serious indications of watershed injury. Its special recreational values were probably greater than they are after thirty years of Forest Service management.

This leads up then to the third alternative of withdrawing all fire control forces, stopping further expenditure for that purpose, and leaving the country pretty much to the forces of nature. It is a radical proposal and could far better have been adopted ten years ago before the period of road construction started. Be that as it may, if a mistake has been made it is better to recognize it and change the mistaken policy than to plunge blindly ahead because a certain line of action has been started.

Much has been said and written about the abandonment of submarginal agricultural land.[3]

Should it not also be recognized that there is such a thing as submarginal forest land? Proper land classification and planning should lead us to radically different treatment of the wide range in classes of forest land. The good land will merit intensive treatment, the less-good land less cultivation, and the least-good lands something entirely different.

... Suppose the Forest Service should go to the proper committee in Congress and say, "We can save $300,000 a year by withdrawing from attempted protection of two million acres of low-grade land in Idaho. Permit us to use this amount for the acquisition, management, protection, and planting of two million acres of the best Idaho land." Wouldn't that sound like a reasonable thing to do?

---

3 This was a policy directive related to the Franklin Roosevelt administration's attempt to resettle farm families from non-productive land, most famously during the Dust Bowl. The Resettlement Administration, established in 1935, spearheaded this initiative and two years later was renamed the Farm Security Administration.

The objection may be made that public opinion would not permit withdrawal of fire control from this area. Some day public opinion may rend the Forest Service for having accomplished so little protection for so much money. Public opinion can be molded, and it is the job of foresters to lead public opinion in the right direction in forestry matters. Both as citizens and public officials it is the duty of responsible men in the Forest Service to use the public funds wisely, and not to advocate expenditures that do not yield reasonable returns . . .

Forest Service Chief's Circular Letter Announcing the Ten a.m. Rule (1935)[4]

The approved protection policy on the National Forests calls for fast, energetic and thorough suppression of all fires in all locations, during possibly dangerous fire weather.

When immediate control is not thus attained, the policy then calls for prompt calculating of the problems of the existing situation and probabilities of spread, and organizing to control every such fire within the first work period. Failing in this effort the attack each succeeding day will be planned and executed with the aim, without reservation, of obtaining control before ten o'clock of the next morning. . . .

I am confident that the sum total of costs plus losses of all classes [of fires] will be lower in the long run under this policy than they have been under comparable conditions heretofore. To this end, I am adding the following notes for consideration in placing it into effect:

It may not be clear from the wording of the policy, but it is obvious nevertheless, that the objective sought also projects that policy into pre-suppression, since only by strengthening the pre-suppression forces in some quarters can the action contemplated be realized. This may call for increasing the standard of detection; plugging holes with additional fireman where so-called fireman or smoke chaser travel time is known to be longer than limits of safety; advanced placement of trained fire suppression crews to be held at carefully selected travel time limit centers. After full use of CCC, PWA, improvement and similar available manpower, these additional pre-suppression sources likely can be provided in the main only by drawing upon FF. To the extent that carefully thought out plans make this necessary, you are authorized to draw upon funds from that source to enable the building up of the pre-suppression forces to required strength.

Subject to the action required to meet the above quoted policy, expenditures for preparedness and suppression will be held to the absolute minimum, and will vary with the total of the tangible and intangible values endangered; being higher, if necessary, where values are high than in areas where values are low. In lower value country this may call for dropping back to more easily held lines no great distance from the firefront, and from these lines taking definite

---

4 Excerpted from its republication in *Journal of Forestry* 42, no. 8 (August 1944): 552–553.

and prompt action to extinguish the fire. In such country, lower expenditures will also be expected for fire breaks and other types of improvements than would be justified were higher values involved.

No fixed rule can be given to meet every situation; the spirit implied in the policy itself will determine the action to be taken in doubtful situations.

F. A. Silcox,
Forester

Allen Calbick to Gifford Pinchot (1940)[5]

... [I]n connection with fires, I have often wondered if this isn't nature's way of cleaning up her backyard, instead of letting timber die of old age, become bug-infested, full of blister rust or choked with brush and wind fells, she sent a fire along and cleaned up the rubbish and gave a new stand good clean ground on which to grow.

Of course, I know a fellow probably would be shot if he advocated this, but you know, Nature is a pretty wise old girl, and when man tries to improve on it, we generally get things unbalanced.

---

5 Excerpted from Allen Calbick to Gifford Pinchot, January 20, 1940, National Museum of Forest Service History, https://forestservicemuseum.pastperfectonline.com/archive/2AD41A37-C1CA-4C77-9C9F-536672491051.

Emil F. Ernst, from "Vanishing Meadows in Yosemite Valley" (1949)[6]

Today's visitor to Yosemite National Park, and to Yosemite Valley in particular, unconsciously accepts conditions as he sees them, little realizing that profound vegetal changes have occurred since the white man came to Yosemite. Whether these changes have been for the better or for worse the reader can decide for himself. However, that these changes have occurred, and how and why they have occurred, makes an interesting story.

Discovery by the White Man

The Yosemite Valley first became known to white men in March 1851 when members of the Mariposa Battalion, led by Major James Savage, beheld it from Old Inspiration Point. The name then decided upon and still in use is a corruption of the local Indian word "usumati" meaning "terrible" or "grizzly bear." The Indian inhabitants, themselves, called the valley "Ahwahnee," meaning "deep grassy place."

The Indian Mode of Life

Until March 1851, the Indians of Yosemite had managed the Valley in a primitive but, to them, effective way. They utilized the game and fish therein and over a hundred kinds of plants. Their dwellings and sweat houses were fashioned from products of the trees. Their utensils were made from reeds and willow bands. Their bows and arrow-shafts were made of selected woods. Their arrow tips were of obsidian from east of the range. It is of record that this primitive people practiced various forms of agriculture, including a form of silvicultural treatment of the oaks which supplied their principal vegetative food staple—acorns.

The management of the lands of the Valley, in addition to the agricultural practices already mentioned, involved processes of plant control for several objectives including

1. Clearing for the hunting of game

---

6 Excerpted from Emil F. Ernst, "Vanishing Meadows in Yosemite Valley, *Yosemite Nature Notes*, May 1949, 34–40.

2. Clearings to aid the procurement of roots, rhizomes and tubers at the end of the growing season
3. Clearings to eliminate lurking places for their enemies.

These clearings were accomplished mainly through the use of fire and through imposed clearing activities of children in the vicinities of their camping places which are now called "rancherias."

The Old Order Changeth

With the coming of the white man, also came dramatic change in the management of the lands of Yosemite Valley. The Indian wished to maintain the open, meadow-like character of the Valley while the white man wished to protect his investment and to utilize the natural resources in a far different manner from the original inhabitant. As a result of the white man's protective endeavors, he has brought about profound changes in the vegetative ground cover of the Valley.[7]

Except for old time observers and students interested in the problems wrought through the activities of well-intentioned but ill-advised conservationists, no recognition has been taken of the fact that the meadows and meadow-like areas of Yosemite Valley are far less in size than they were many years ago. As one keen observer and student remarked in 1882 in a report to the Governor of California, "protection has worked destruction."[8]

By 1937, when the last estimate was made, the aggregate area of meadows in the Yosemite Valley had declined to a total of 327 acres. In 1866, or 15 years after the coming of the white man, the total area of meadow land in the Valley was computed by State Geologist J. D. Whitney to be 750 acres. In the intervening years—1866 to 1937—the forests had encroached upon and taken over more than 56 percent of the meadow area in existence at the time of Whitney's survey. And in the same years, the open, park-like, land commented

---

7 "Protective endeavors" refers to the creation of the National Park and its mission to preserve the valley, which meant the agency would not clear away encroaching trees, bushes, and shrubs. Ernst is critiquing his employers' inaction, hence the disclaimer above.

8 M. C. Briggs, who was secretary to the Board of Commissioners and oversaw the management of Yosemite Valley while it was under state control—it was returned to the federal government in 1890—wrote in the 1882 biennial report to the governor: "In our brief report of 1880, we called attention to the rapidly increasing breadth of underbrush and second growth pines, and need not restate our convictions with respect to the importance of counter-working this spreading infestment [encroachment]. While the Indians held possession, the annual fires kept the whole floor of the valley free from underbrush, leaving only the majestic oaks and pines to adorn the most beautiful of parks. In this one respect protection has worked destruction." See M. C. Briggs, *Report of the Commissioners to Manage the Yosemite Valley and the Mariposa Big Tree Grove* (Sacramento: State Office, J. D. Young, Supt. State Printing, 1882), 10–11.

upon in many writings and reports has become more densely tenanted with trees, brush, and debris due to this white man's protection.

The loss in area of meadow land is, in itself, not serious when considered in the light of the basic principles and objectives of the National Park Service for no agricultural usages can be permitted. However, along with this loss has come the loss of numerous sublime views of the falls, the cliffs, and broad, open, park-like vistas stretching on through the Valley. Only through comparative photographs can one realize the extensive vegetative changes that have occurred in the Valley since the coming of the white man. . . .

The Written and Spoken Record

In 1866 a geological survey of the Yosemite region was made by a party headed by John D. Whitney. As part of the work a map was made of the floor of Yosemite Valley, which showed a total of 750 acres of meadow land. In 1937, only 327 acres could be so classified. Not so methodical and analytical are the numerous references, written and quoted, by other observers. However, the story remains the same, i.e., the Valley is not the same to successive returning visitors.

Dr. L. H. Bunnell, a member of the 1851 discovery party, many years later in an article apparently prepared for but not published by the *Century Magazine*, states:

> The Valley at the time of discovery presented the appearance of a well kept park. . . . there was little undergrowth in the park-like valley, and a half day's work in lopping off branches along the course enabled us to speed our horses uninterrupted through the groves.

Galen Clark was for many years the Guardian of the Valley during the period of trusteeship by the State of California. In 1894 he wrote to the Board of Commissioners of Yosemite Valley and the Mariposa Big Tree Grove:

> My first visit to the Yosemite was in the summer of 1855. At that time there was no undergrowth of young trees to obstruct clear, open views of any part of the Valley from one side of the Merced River across to the base of the opposite wall. The area of clear, open ground, with an abundance of luxuriant native grasses and flowering plants, was at least four times as large as at the present time.

William W. Stay, Rector of St. Paul's Episcopal Church at San Rafael, CA, has stated in a letter to the Secretary of the Interior dated December 10, 1890:

I visited the valley again . . . a lapse of twenty-four years since I had first seen it. The contrast between things then and now is something remarkable . . . [what] struck me forcibly with the contrast to 1866 was the immense increase of trees and small undergrowth everywhere visible in the valley . . . while the majestic Giant Trees of primeval growth seemed to be as numerous as in former days. The valley as I saw it in 1866, was more in the condition that the aborigines had left it. . . . In consequence, also, of the openness then existing, much better views existed of the waterfalls and cliffs, from the floor of the valley, in any direction.

H. J. Ostrander was a cattleman who, in his day, ran herds of cattle on lands now in the park. In one of the October 1897 issues of the San Francisco Call he is quoted as saying of the Yosemite which he had first seen a third of a century before:

And the windings of the beautifully clear Merced River could be traced for miles up the valley until lost sight if at the base of the "Cathedral Rocks." At that time in the graceful bends nestled beautiful meadows, noble pines, Douglas firs, and cedar dotted the valley. No underbrush, cottonwood nor second growth pines and firs to obstruct the marvelous walls of the valley.

Another of the well-known State Guardians, James M. Hutchings, as early as 1881 in a report to the State Commission complains:

A dense growth of underbrush, from one end of the valley to another, not only offends the eye and shuts out its magnificent views, but monopolizes and appropriates its best land, to the exclusion of valuable plants and wildflowers.

Hutchings was a confirmed nature lover and the unwarranted destruction of a tree or a flower was a disgraceful thing in his eyes. The situation must have been serious and its potentialities apparent to Hutchings who had settled in the valley as early as 1861.

Many of the Army-officer Acting Superintendents of the parklands surrounding Yosemite Valley repeatedly referred to the great areas of dense brush and the potential fire hazards existing in the forests. In their annual reports the majority blamed the thickets on suppression of fires What had happened on the floor of the Valley was also occurring on adjoining protected areas. Dense

NATIONAL REASSESSMENT, 1923–1959 / 183

thickets of brush and forest reproduction were coming in on areas where they formerly had been absent.

Indian Methods of Brush Control

At this point, the reader naturally will wonder what caused the pronounced decrease in the acreage of meadow in Yosemite Valley and also why it was possible for the trees to become so numerous and so tall that they obliterated many of the views and open vistas existing in the earlier days. The explanation may be found in the observations and the views of numerous responsible individuals who have visited and recorded their reactions an findings. . . .

Reference has been previously made that the Indians of Yosemite Valley practiced clearing of the meadows and the adjacent forests. The Indians did not have any labor-saving mechanical devices. It was natural for them to use fire. Carl O. Sauer[9], speaking of all or most tribes in America, states: "Fire and smoke became labor saving devices, for overpowering, trapping, and driving game . . . Fire aided the collection of fallen fruits . . . the earlier economies collectively may be called 'fire economies.'"[10] Later he says, "Recurrent fires sweeping across surfaces of low relief are competent to suppress woody vegetation. Suppression of fire results in gradual recolonization by woody species in every grassland known to me."

At least in one instance the Indian inhabitants of Yosemite Valley were observed to be using fire to clear the ground. H. Willis Baxley recorded this observation in the fall of 1861:

A live-glow in the distance, and then the wavy line of burning grass, gave notice that the Indians were in the Valley clearing ground, the more readily to obtain their winter supply of acorns and wild sweet potato root (hukhau).[11]

Speaking of the Miwoks, of which the Indians of Yosemite were a branch, Barrett and Gifford state: "The only other control of vegetation which they attempted was burning off of dry brush about August. This was said to have been done to get a better growth the following year. Underbrush was less

---

9 Carl O. Sauer (1889–1975) was a professor of geography at the University of California, Berkeley.
10 Carl O. Sauer, "Vegetation Climes, Fire and Man"(paper presented to the annual meeting of the Northern California Section, Society of American Foresters, December 4, 1948).
11 H. Willis Baxley, *What I Saw on the West and North Coast of North America and the Hawaiian Islands* (New York: D. Appleton, 1865).

184   BRINGING FIRE BACK

abundant anciently than now, so informants said, and perhaps was due to periodic burning."[12]

When in 1928 Carl P. Russell talked to Maria Lebrado, a member of the Yosemite band taken into custody by Captain Boling's party in 1851, she expressed a good deal of concern because the Valley is now "too bushy."

... Galen Clark in 1894 also wrote:

> The valley had been exclusively under the care and management of the Indians, probably for many centuries. Their policy of management for their own protection and self-interests, as told by some of the survivors who were boys when the Valley was first visited by Whites in 1851, was to annually start fires in the dry season of the year and to let them spread over the whole Valley to kill young trees just sprouted and keep the forest groves open and clear of all underbrush, so as to have no obscure thickets for a hiding place, or an ambush for any invading hostile foes, and to have clear grounds for hunting and gathering acorns. When the forest did not thoroughly burn over the moist meadows, all the young willows and cottonwoods were pulled up by hand . . .

The Record on the Ground

If the statements recorded here have any truth in them, then evidence supporting them should be available in the forests in the Valley and elsewhere. Study of those trees on the floor of the Yosemite Valley which are obviously over one hundred years old, reveals that large numbers of them have signs of severe and repeated fires. Those trees less than 100 years old are remarkably free of signs of fire. The evidence on the ground indicates that fires were, whether deliberately set or not, common enough to leave clear indications of trees existing before the coming of the white man. Although many more trees invaded the Valley since the coming of the white man, there is little to no evidence of fire on them.

On lands in the adjoining Stanislaus National Forest, E. I. Kotok, formerly of the California Region Forest and Range Experiment Station, made a study of fire scars on trees which showed fire had swept the 74 acres investigated 221 times between 1454 and 1912. This averaged one fire every two years. It is doubted that Nature could be so regular with fire for such a long period of time.

---

12 S. A. Barrett and E. W. Gifford, "Miwok Material Culture," *Bulletin of the Public Museum of the City of Milwaukee*, March 1933, 117–376.

The Immediate Future of the Valley

The past is the mirror of the future. As long as the Indians had control of the Valley, the evidence indicates that they kept it clear of brush and reproduction. This evidence also strongly points to the use of fire being the main instrument in clearing. Whatever they did ceased soon after the coming of the white man in 1851. In 1881, thirty years after the first white man, and twenty years after the first white settler, appear the complaints against brush and the reproduction.

Until the National Park Service assumed administration of the area in 1916, these complaints were numerous and came for the responsible officials in charge at the time. Clearing by fire was prohibited and the suppression of fire has been the rule since the white man became dominant in Yosemite Valley. The forests of the Valley continue to encroach on the meadows. Is Galen Clark's plaint of August 13, 1896, still valid today when, as he said: "All the open meadow ground in Yosemite is being covered with young cottonwoods and willows and drier portions of the Valley overrun by thickets of young pines and cedars. The great work of reclamation should be commenced as soon as possible and persecuted year to year until the whole Valley is again restored to its original, superior beauty."

H. H. Biswell, from "The Big Trees and Fire" (1961)[13]

The Big Trees, *Sequoia gigantea*, grow only on the western slope of California's Sierra Nevada. They are grouped in more than seventy groves, at elevations roughly between 4000 and 8500 feet, for about 250 miles from north to south, and are surrounded by vast forests of other conifers and brush fields. The climate is Mediterranean-like. Summers are long, hot and dry, with occasional thunderstorms and severe lightning. This landscape is so susceptible to fire that it must be considered a natural and characteristic feature of the environment. Before the Big Trees were discovered by the white man about 1850, fires in the Sierra Nevada were widespread and frequent, many being set by lightning, others by Indians. Fires are of great biological importance in a forest. John Muir, dean of the Sierra and its forests, referred to fire as the master controller of the distribution of trees. The frequent fires of aboriginal times kept the forests clean, open, and park-like, with the mature trees rather far apart. After intensive studies of fire history in the Sierra Nevada, Richard Reynolds, a student of geography, concluded that the forests in which the Indians lived were in dynamic relation to the periodic fires which ran through them.

Frequent fires permitted little opportunity for undergrowth of trees, brush, litter, or dry grass to accumulate before another fire would consume them. As a result, the fires were light and "friendly," and the trees' green canopy above was seldom burned. Very few statements can be found describing the actual behavior of fires in early times. However, John Muir saw a fire enter a forest of Big Trees from a brush field, and wrote a detailed account. The fire was in the forest between the middle and east forks of the Kaweah River, in early September, the driest season of the year:

> The fire came racing up the steep chaparral-covered slopes of the East Fork canyon with passionate enthusiasm in a broad cataract of flames ... But as soon as the deep forest was reached the ungovernable flood became calm like a torrent entering a lake, creeping and spreading beneath the trees ... There was no danger of being chased and hemmed in, for in the main forest belt of the Sierra, even when swift winds are blowing, fires seldom or never sweep over the trees in broad all-embracing

13 Excerpted from H. H. Biswell, "The Big Trees and Fire," *National Parks Magazine*, April 1961, 11–14.

sheets as they do in the dense Rocky Mountain woods and in those of the Cascade Mountains of Oregon and Washington. Here they creep from tree to tree with tranquil deliberation, allowing close observation ... A grand and interesting sight are the fires on the tops of the largest living trees flaming above the green branches at a height of perhaps two hundred feet, entirely cut off from the ground-fires, and looking like signal beacons on watch towers. From one standpoint I sometimes saw a dozen or more, those in the distance looking like great stars above the forest roof. At first, I could not imagine how these Sequoia lamps were lighted, but the very first night, strolling about waiting, I saw the thing done again and again. The thick, fibrous bark of old trees is divided by deep, nearly continuous furrows, the sides of which are bearded with the bristling ends of fibers broken by the growth swelling of the trunk, and when the fire comes creeping around the feet of the trees, it runs up these bristly furrows in lovely pale blue quivering, bickering rills of flame with a low, earnest whispering sound to the lightning-shattered top of the trunk, which, in the dry Indian summer, with perhaps leaves and twigs' and squirrel-gnawed cone-scales and seed-wings lodged in it, is readily ignited. These lamp-lighting rills, the most beautiful fire streams I ever saw, last only a minute or two, but the big lamps burn with varying brightness for days and weeks, throwing off sparks like the spray of a fountain, while ever and anon a shower of red coals comes sifting down through the branches, followed at times with startling effect by a big burned-off chunk weighing perhaps half a ton.

Bark Is Fire-Resistant

The Big Trees, with their asbestos-like bark, are very resistant to fire; nevertheless, nearly all of the older ones show fire scars. Some of the stumps of trees sawed down years ago show scars that have been healed over 2000 years or more. By studying fire scars, plant ecologists have been able to tell a great deal about the fires that burned hundreds of years ago. In the process of healing, the edges of fire wounds become covered with a layer of woody growth which serves as a permanent record of a fire that once covered an area. . . .

A Big Tree which towers above the forest canopy in the Sierra Nevada for thousands of years must eventually be struck by lightning; probably no mature Big Tree has escaped. It is logical to conclude, therefore, that many of the fires in aboriginal times were started by nature's lightning strikes. . . . In addition to fires started by lightning, others were set by Indians during aboriginal times. This is borne out by various explorers and naturalists who observed the results at first hand. Among them was Galen Clark, for many years the guardian of the Yosemite Valley. In 1894 he wrote to the Board of Commissioners of Yosemite Valley and the Mariposa Big Tree Grove:

> My first visit to Yosemite was in the summer of 1855. At that time there was no undergrowth of young trees to obstruct clear, open views in any part of the valley from one side of the Merced River across to the base of the opposite wall. The area of clear open ground, with abundance of luxuriant native grasses and flowering plants, was at least four times as large as at the present time. Probably for many centuries the valley had been exclusively under the care and the management of the Indians. Their policy of management for their own protection and self-interest, as told by some of the survivors who were boys when the Valley was first visited by whites in 1851, was to annually start fires in the dry season of the year and let them spread over the whole Valley to kill young trees just sprouted and keep the forest groves open and clear of all underbrush, so as to have no obscure thickets for a hiding place, or an ambush for any invading hostile foes, and to have clear grounds for hunting and gathering acorns.

Indians True Foresters

Others who noted the Indians' use of fire were M. C. Briggs, in a report to the State Commission of Yosemite Valley and Mariposa Big Trees Grove (1882); Dr. L. H. Bunnell, a member of the 1851 Yosemite discovery party; and Joaquin Miller . . . In the past sixty years the custom has been to suppress forest fires as quickly as possible. All good conservationists know that this is essential. Without protection against wildfires the Sierra Nevada with its Big Trees could not very well be managed for landscape and recreation, water production, timber growing, and other uses. But as a result of protection, fire hazards have become enormous in many places, and wildfires are now the greatest "enemy" destroying California's forests.

In the past few years they have destroyed a wealth of vital resources. For example, in the early fall of 1959, in one thirty-six-hour period, 50,000 acres were charred in the Sierra Nevada, with final estimates of damage running as high as $66,000,000 in timber and watershed alone. Wildfires of this sort are a major disaster. But as the population and wealth of California increase, the costs and damage from wildfires will become even greater, unless improved methods of hazard reduction are developed. The contrast of affairs at present with those in aboriginal times points up the dilemma facing those concerned

Two Changes Noted

Two great changes have taken place as a result of fire protection, leading to the extreme and difficult fire hazard conditions. First, the more shade-tolerant white fir and incense cedar have developed in dense thickets in the understory of many Big Trees and pines. They greatly add to the fire hazard. Many people view this change as natural, undisturbed succession leading toward climax vegetation. In this reasoning, however, they fail to recognize that fire, too, was a natural and characteristic feature of the environment in earlier times.

Some people are quite concerned about the increase in white fir in the Big Tree groves of our national parks. It has been pointed out that the parks were in a natural condition when the stands of trees were discovered. But because of the suppression of nature's fires the whole forest prospect is gradually being altered. White firs are crowding in among the Big Trees, and are closing out the views. Furthermore, they are competing with the Big Trees for soil moisture and nutrients. No one knows what the final result will be. But one thing is sure, this is something to be concerned about and is a problem that needs immediate as well as the most careful attention.

The second change of great importance in the Sierra Nevada forests is the large increase in debris on the forest floor. Many forests that were relatively clean, open, and park-like in earlier times, and could be easily traveled through, are now so full of dead material and young trees and brush as to be nearly impassable; thus great fire hazards have developed in many places. The primeval forest so frequently burned by the "friendly" fires of nature consisted of two fuel layers—the green canopy above, and the herbs, needles, and leaves on the ground. But exclusion of fire has encouraged the development of a solid fuel layer in many places from the tops of the tallest trees to the young saplings and brush and litter on the ground. Is it any wonder that the wildfires in such situations are so devastating and difficult to control?

... After studying the contemporary wildfire situation, it became obvious that new ways must be sought to avert the mounting danger of great fires and the destruction of our vital resources. Accordingly, in the spring of 1951 some burning experiments were started in two places to determine if light fires could be used to reduce wildfire hazards and maintain low fire-hazard conditions. These particular studies are in ponderosa pine, and are being carried out in two steps: broadcast burning, followed by cleanup burning. Broadcast burning is being done by raking a trail and lighting the pine needles on the edge.

This operation is being carried out only in the wet season after enough rain has fallen to wet the duff to the mineral soil. Such burning is stopped in the spring when the soil becomes dry. After rain, the top needles dry in a day or two and burn readily, but the lower ones dry slowly. This allows for many days when broadcast burning is possible. Such fire removes much of the flash fuel, old logs, and stumps on the ground, and greatly reduces the fire hazard.

The cleanup burning consists of piling and burning dead brush, slash, dead fallen trees, and of prunings after an area has had a broadcast burn. A fire is started, and dead material is gradually piled up as it burns. After an area has been both broadcast burned and cleaned, the falling pine needles can then drop on the ground rather than drape themselves over the dead brush; consequently the fire hazard builds back slowly.

Research in both experimental areas shows clearly that deliberate burning under selected conditions reduces the danger of wildfires in summer. Furthermore, when summer fires break out they can be more quickly controlled, and will do much less damage. These results are similar to those reported by Harold Weaver, working in Arizona and in the State of Washington, who found fuels to be reduced fifty percent by a single broadcast burn, and the damage done by wildfires to be reduced by ninety percent. From this research, it may be concluded that prescribed burning is simulating the most important element that had functioned in aboriginal times to develop a stable "fire type" climax forest in the Sierra Nevada-frequent light fires . . .

Would it not be worthwhile to select at least two groves of Big Trees—a dozen would be better—with their surrounding forests for some distance back, and manage them with light fires as a part of the environment, somewhat as they were managed by nature and the aborigines through thousands of years in the past? To begin with, the fires would have to be handled with great care, because of the extreme fire hazards that now exist. But the fire hazards can be quickly reduced, after which the danger will not be great. Soon it will become evident that a forest fire can be a "friend," as it was in aboriginal times, and not our worst "enemy" as it is today.

From "Wildlife Management in the National Parks: The Leopold Report" (1963)[14]

The Concepts of Park Management

2. Few of the world's parks are large enough to be in fact self-regulatory ecological units; rather, most are ecological islands subject to direct or indirect modification by activities and conditions in the surrounding areas. These influences may involve such factors as immigration and/or emigration of animal and plant life, changes in the fire regime, and alterations in the surface or subsurface water...

4. However, most biotic communities are in a constant state of change due to natural or man-caused processes of ecological succession. In these "successional" communities it is necessary to manage the habitat to achieve or stabilize it at a desired stage. For example, fire is an essential management tool to maintain East African open savanna or American prairie.

The Goal of Park Management in the United States

... When the forty-niners poured over the Sierra Nevada into California, those that kept diaries spoke almost to a man of the wide-spaced columns of mature trees that grew on the lower western slope in gigantic magnificence. The ground was a grass parkland, in springtime carpeted with wildflowers. Deer and bears were abundant. Today much of the west slope is a dog-hair thicket of young pines, white fir, incense cedar, and mature brush—a direct function of overprotection from natural ground fires. Within the four national parks [in California]—Lassen, Yosemite, Sequoia, and Kings Canyon—the thickets are even more impenetrable than elsewhere. Not only is this accumulation of fuel dangerous to the giant sequoias and other mature trees but the animal life is meager, wildflowers are sparse, and to some at least the vegetative tangle is depressing, not uplifting. Is it possible that the primitive open forest could be restored, at least on a local scale? And if so, how? We cannot offer an answer.

---

14 Excerpted from "Wildlife Management in the National Parks: The Leopold Report," March 4, 1963, https://www.nps.gov/parkhistory/online_books/leopold/leopold.htm.

But we are posing a question to which there should be an answer of immense concern to the National Park Service.

Methods of Habitat Management

... Of the various methods of manipulating vegetation, the controlled use of fire is the most "natural" and much the cheapest and easiest to apply. Unfortunately, however, forest and chaparral areas that have been completely protected from fire for long periods may require careful advance treatment before even the first experimental blaze is set. Trees and mature brush may have to be cut, piled, and burned before a creeping ground fire can be risked. Once fuel is reduced, periodic burning can be conducted safely and at low expense. On the other hand, some situations may call for a hot burn. ...

Rita P. Thompson, from "Are Land Managers Applying Our Current Knowledge of Fire Ecology?" (1976)[15]

In a technological age it becomes increasingly more difficult—and increasingly less meaningful—to give a "yes" or "no" answer to anything. If my experience were limited to the Bitterroot National Forest, where certain Forest personnel, along with individuals from the Northern Forest Fire Laboratory, Forestry Sciences Laboratory, and Forest Research have been innovative and dedicated to applying the principles of fire ecology to land management, I might have a distorted view. However, there are many instances where this is not the case. The following comments focus on some of the reasons and/or legitimate excuses for the ecological role of fire being neglected in land management planning and implementation.

1. Administrative Inertia

It is administratively "comfortable" to operate within the realm of the tried, true, tested, manualized method of doing business. Pathetically, too many agency employees prefer being comfortable to being correct. The use of fire to achieve certain land management objectives is still "new" and still requires a certain amount of intestinal fortitude on the part of the manager. It is true that the life systems with which we deal are complex, and we don't have all the answers—nor all the questions—but these should not be excuses for inertia and procrastination. Policy is written by mere mortals and can be changed. The natural laws governing the operation of systems come from a higher authority. We cannot continue to short-change natural processes—including, but not exclusively fire—and expect to have quality land management. I am not proposing rebellion and manual burning. I am encouraging objectivity. If a method or procedure is biologically sound—good for the land, compatible with the inherent functioning of the system—it should not be rejected solely because it is not a part of formal policy. It's not the idea that needs changing or rejection, it's the policy.

---

15 Excerpted from Rita P. Thompson, "Are Land Mangers Applying Our Current Knowledge of Fire Ecology? A Panel Discussion," *Proceedings: Tall Timbers Fire Ecology Conference* 14 (1976), 433–435.

2. Fear of Negative Public Reaction

Our agency has a program called "Inform and Involve." It is based on a sound philosophy, but I personally feel that it has gotten out of balance. In my opinion, we have involved our external publics about land management decisions far beyond the degree to which we have informed them of our management rationale. We have neither informed nor involved our internal public to the extent that we have our external publics. The public is not informed by one-shot public meetings, multicolored maps and multitudinous overlays, and two-page newspaper spreads. The public is informed by observing, talking with, and hearing from agency employees on the job. Informing the public starts with informing the people doing the work, and it is a continuing process. The land manager must regard all employees under his authority as his public. The understanding of and commitment to land management practices start with them. Do all employees know why they are doing what they are doing? In implementing land management decisions, we have to be way beyond giving orders—we need to be giving explanations and developing understanding. The more innovative the management direction, the more necessary the internal commitment and understanding. The urgency of this need applies at all levels of organization.

3. Fire Ecology is a Specialty

We might get very basic and question to what extent basic principles of plain old ecology are being applied in land management? To what extent is a lack of ecological understanding responsible for lack of initiative and fear of trying something different? How well equipped are we to explain the rationale of a land management decision, should one of our employees or one of our external publics question it? As land managers we have some vague understanding that the functioning, behavior, and ultimate destiny of the systems we manage are governed by natural laws that affect the living and non-living components of those systems. We hopefully realize that as land managers we cannot control systems, but we can direct the change that is inherent to them. We must realize that the direction we give systems results in quality land management only if that direction is compatible with natural laws and processes. If fire is a natural process in a system, but for some reason or another we cannot use it, do we know enough about the operation of that system to determine an ecological equivalent of fire? Solutions to problems such as these do not lie in creating a workforce of "90-day wonder" fire ecologists. They lie in a continuing effort of getting our entire work force thinking in terms of natural systems and the way they function—rather than in terms of functions and the ways in which man-made policy can be systematically applied to them. We have been embarrassingly remiss in seeing to the educational needs of our field personnel. As regards the concepts of ecology and how they apply to "everyday" land management, there are essentially no programs intermediate between nothing and a program of master's degrees caliber. In summary, fire ecology is a specialty—a superstructure that belongs on a foundation of a working knowledge of basic ecological concepts and principles. Some of us aren't ready for fire ecology. A knowledge gap is nothing to be ashamed of provided it is not used as an excuse for a cookbook approach to land management. Individuals at all levels engaged in the management of natural systems must themselves be as dynamic as those systems—and at times as resilient in compensating for deficiencies.

Fig. 12. An annual, rotating two-acre burn on Junco Meadow on the Cleveland National Forest conducted in collaboration with the California Indian Basketweavers' Association, early 2000s. Credit: Scott Grasmick, Forest Service.

Part 4

Return Cycle

Fig. 13. At Junco Meadow, firefighters only use diesel-fuel drip torches on the extreme edges of a prescribed fire. Doing so protects tribal basket weavers, who place the post-fire new growth stems in their mouths while weaving, from absorbing the toxic residue. Credit: Scott Grasmick, US Forest Service.

Return Cycle

Fire never really left the land. For Indigenous Californians, that claim is at the heart of their oral histories, cultural memory, and contemporary practice. Often the most direct references are genealogical: Dawn Blake, a Hupa tribal member, remembered that as a child she watched her "grandmother maintain her basketry material by burning her gathering patches."[1] As director of the Yurok Tribal Council and a member of the State Board of Forestry and Fire Protection of California, Blake has been "working to uphold my grandmother's and my mother's tribes' sacred practices of cultural burns." Bill Tripp's great-grandmother was similarly influential. Now the director of the Karuk tribe's Department of Natural Resources and Environmental Policy and a member of the Biden administration's Wildland Fire Mitigation and Management Commission, Tripp credits his great-grandmother Bessie Tripp with teaching him, at four years old, how to use fire as a land-management tool.[2] Yurok tribal member Elizabeth Azzuz also started young: "I've been burning since I was four—my grandfather and my father taught me," she told the *Guardian* in 2019. "For us, when little kids start playing with matches is when they need to learn about the importance of how we use fire and why we use fire."[3]

Reclaiming the familial past also has been part of a larger, collective assertion of tribal sovereignty. In this case, control over the use of fire to cultivate cultural and ritual resources and food sources, to restore ecosystems

---

1 Dawn Blake, "Cultural Burns Critical for Tribal Land Management," *Times-Standard* (Eureka, CA), February 3, 2023. Her memory is confirmed in Pliny Earle Goddard, *Life and Culture of the Hupa* (Berkeley: University of California Press, 1903), 39: "For basket making the woman needs slim round twigs for upright ribs, pliable material for twining around horizontally, and dyeing material to make her basket more beautiful. For ribs she goes to a place where a fire has burned over a hazel patch. She finds there shoots all of a size. For the larger baskets she takes the shoots the second or third year after a fire. These shoots are from *Corylus rostrata var. californica*, called mûkaikitloi, 'on it one makes a basket.'"
2 Malcolm Terence, "Unleashing the TREX," *North Coast Journal of Politics, People & Art*, November 3, 2016, https://www.northcoastjournal.com/humboldt/unleashing-the-trex/Content?oid=4132514. TREX refers to Prescribed Fire Training Exchanges.
3 Susie Cagle, "'Fire is Medicine': the Tribes Burning California Forests to Save Them," *Guardian*, November 21, 2019.

and watersheds and the flora and fauna that once thrived within them, and to minimize the threat of catastrophic wildfires that since the early twenty-first century have burned the very mountainous landscapes in California and the West from which fire has long been excluded. This latter concern is especially troublesome. According to a 2021 study in the *International Journal of Environmental Research and Public Health*, Indigenous Californians are three times more concentrated in census tracts that have burned with greater frequency and the largest amount of acreage scorched. In August 2023, the McKinney Fire torched the Karuk tribal archives and was responsible for a significant salmon die-off along the Klamath River; three years earlier, the Karuk lost homes in the Slater Fire. When the 2023 Oak Fire burned in and around Yosemite National Park, members of the Southern Sierra Miwuk Nation lost their homes. It was not lost on tribal member Irene Velasquez that had her people's cultural burning strategies not been suppressed her home and property might not have burned: "If we were able to impart that wisdom and knowledge to European settlers, to the agencies, to not stop our burning, we would be in a way different place."[4]

To (re)gain that place requires the dismantling of the paradigmatic politics that has framed wildfire suppression protocols for more than a century. Some initial signals of this undoing are legislative and reflect decades-long work by Indigenous polities and their allies, at the congressional level, to secure greater protection for tribal forest management and even the return of federal land to Native nations. In California, state legislation protects tribes' right to burn and protects cultural fire practitioners from certain liabilities. Another sign is the emergence of such advocacy groups as the Indigenous Peoples Burning Network. And a third is the proliferation of academic and agency research that integrates Indigenous knowledge and western scientific analyses that, as Forest Service researchers Frank Lake (Karuk) and his frequent, non-indigenous collaborator Jonathan Long observe, "facilitate placed-based understanding of how fire and various management practices affect tribal cultural resources and values."[5] This site-specific approach frames

---

4 Alexander Wigglesworth, "This Tribe was Barred from Cultural Burning for Decades—Then a Fire Hit Their Community," *Los Angeles Times*, May 7, 2023; Shahir Masri, Erica Scaduto, Yu-fang Jin, and Jun Wu, "Disproportionate Impacts of Wildfires among Elderly and Low-Income Communities in California from 2000–2020," *International Journal of Environmental Research and Public Health* 18, no. 8 (2021): 3921.

5 Frank K. Lake and Jonathan Long, "Fire and Tribal Cultural Resources," in *Science Synthesis to Support Socioecological Resilience in the Sierra Nevada and Southern Cascade Range*, edited by Jonathan W. Long, Lenya Quinn-Davidson, and Carl N. Skinner (Albany, CA: U.S. Department of Agriculture, Forest Service, Pacific Southwest Research Station, 2014), 173.

the concluding section's essays by Bill Tripp, Julie Cordero-Lamb (Chumash), Jared Dahl Aldern, and Teresa Romero (Chumash), and Dawn Blake. Like Michael Connolly Miskwish's essay that opens *Burn Scars*, each of these speaks to the pressing need for more cultural fires, more good fires: Good in that they are controlled, good in that they produce essential resources, good in that they help restore compromised ecosystems. They are good, too, because these flames are active signals of tribal legitimacy, a reassertion of a self-sustaining communal vision and authority that settler-colonial nations deliberately sought to extinguish.

"Tribal Forest Protection Act in Brief" (2004)[6]

The Tribal Forest Protection Act basically authorizes the Secretaries of Agriculture and Interior to give special consideration to tribally-proposed Stewardship Contracting or other projects on Forest Service or BLM land bordering or adjacent to Indian trust land to protect the Indian trust resources from fire, disease, or other threat coming off of that Forest Service or BLM land.

We want to encourage the development of contracts or agreements to reduce threats in areas mutually agreed to by both Tribes and Forests. The following provides key elements of this critical legislation.

- To qualify, the Indian land (either tribal or allotted) must be in trust or restricted status and must be forested or have a grass, brush, or other vegetative cover. Burned-over land capable of regenerating vegetative cover also qualifies.
- Tribal projects can be under Stewardship Contracting or "such other authority as appropriate."
- Within 120 days of a Tribe submitting a request to enter into an agreement or contract, the Secretary may issue a public notice of either initiation of any necessary environmental review or of the potential of entering into an agreement or contract with the Tribe.
- If the Forest Service or BLM deny a tribal request to enter into an agreement or contract, the agency may issue a notice of denial to the Tribe that: identifies specific factors in, and reasons for the denial, -identifies corrective courses of action, and -proposes consultation with the Tribe on how to protect the Indian trust land and tribal interests on the Forest Service or BLM land.
- The Tribe must propose its project to take place on National Forest System or BLM land which borders or is adjacent to Indian trust land and: poses a fire, disease, or other threat to the Indian trust land or community, or needs restoration -is not subject to some other conflicting agreement or contract, and involves a feature or circumstance unique to the proposing Tribe (i.e., legal, cultural, archaeological, historic, or biological).

---

6 "Tribal Forest Protection Act in Brief," https://www.fs.usda.gov/detail/r5/workingtogether/tribalrelations?cid=stelprdb5351850.

- To formally initiate a project request, a Tribe formally submits a request to enter into an agreement or contract with the Forest Service or BLM.
- When the Forest Service or BLM evaluate and consider entering into tribal agreements or contracts, the agencies may: use a best value basis (special consideration for local jobs and business), and give specific consideration to tribal factors.

Bill Tripp, "Our Land was Taken. But We Still Hold the Knowledge of How to Stop Mega-Fires" (2020)[7]

The solution to the devastating west coast wildfires is to burn like our Indigenous ancestors have for millennia. As wildfires rage across California, it saddens me that Indigenous peoples' millennia-long practice of cultural burning has been ignored in favor of fire suppression.

But it breaks my heart, that regardless of our attempts to retain our cultural heritage and manage our homelands in a manner consistent with our Indigenous customs, the Slater fire is burning down the homes of our tribal members, our tribal staff, and our community.

Prescribed fire and cultural burns are fires that are intentionally set during favorable conditions, sometimes at regular intervals to achieve a variety of socio-ecological benefits. They reduce the density of small trees, brush, grass, and leaves that otherwise fuel severe wildfires. Clearing undergrowth allows for a greater variety of trees and a healthier forest that is more fire-resistant, and it provides more room for wildlife to roam with beneficial effects such as enhancing the success of our hunting. Fire suppression, meanwhile, involves extinguishing fires using teams of people, bulldozers, fire engines, helicopters, and airplanes by land management agencies assigned that duty by federal, state and local governments.

Our land was taken from us long ago and our Indigenous stewardship responsibility was taken from us too. The land is still sacred, and it will forever be part of us. We hold the knowledge of fire, forests, water, plants, and animals that is needed to revitalize our human connection and responsibility to this land. If enabled, we can overcome our current situation and teach others how to get it done across the western United States.

In 1850, the California legislature passed a law that essentially forced many Indigenous people into servitude and criminalized Indigenous burning. This was followed by the creation of the National Forest System and the focused suppression of our cultural burning practices in northern California. Karuk people were shot for burning even as late as the 1930s. Federal laws were created that were interpreted to call for fire suppression but were not to have an impact on hunting and fishing.

---

7 Bill Tripp, "Our Land Was Taken. But We Still Hold the Knowledge of How to Stop Mega-Fires," *Guardian*, September 16, 2020.

RETURN CYCLE

The Karuk tribal constitution defines Karuk tribal lands as consisting of our Aboriginal Territory, service areas and all lands subsequently acquired by and for the tribe, whether within or outside of the tribe's Aboriginal Territory. On these lands, we have the right to use fire in the perpetuation of our culture.

In fact, the courts have deemed that Karuk people are not Indians of a reservation. We remain a sovereign, independent nation occupying our original homelands. That is supposed to mean something. Yet our hunting and fishing areas are diminishing, while forests burn at larger scales and more sediment is added to our streams.

Fire itself is sacred. It renews life. It shades rivers and cools the water's temperature. It clears brush and makes for sufficient food for large animals. It changes the molecular structure of traditional food and fiber resources making them nutrient dense and more pliable. Fire does so much more than western science currently understands.

The Red Salmon Complex fire is currently burning on an area sacred to the Karuk people. Our sacred values are negatively impacted when state and federal land agencies dig fire lines with bulldozers and send hundreds of people into places where only a few at a time should go. Rare endemic plants get trampled, archaeological evidence gets rearranged and chemicals get dumped into the watersheds we drink from and salmon inhabit. Indigenous peoples have to respond to protect these things.

The space we traditionally visit for solitude, prayer and carrying out cultural burning has become a space of turmoil, sorrow, and trauma. That's why many Indigenous people have been fighting to use fire in the right way all our lives.

In recent decades, our area has been plagued by large fires, including the Big Bar Complex fire in 1999, the Backbone Complex fire in 2009, and the Butler fire in 2013. Time and time again we find ourselves dropping everything to respond to fire suppression activities while trying to keep up the fight to revitalize our Indigenous responsibility as we witness our culture being destroyed. The federal and state governments spend billions of dollars each year fighting wildfires in California while putting very little toward prescribed burning or understanding that cultural burning can and should be practiced.

We know the solution is to burn like our Indigenous ancestors have done for millennia. But too often we are told we can't burn. Simply put, it's either because we don't have the proper environmental clearance for burning under the National Environmental Policy Act, because of liability or because there aren't enough personnel available to supervise the burn. This year it is because smoke will be bad for Covid-19 patients.

These are excuses, not solutions. We carry the same qualifications as the federal and state agencies when it comes to prescribed burning or otherwise managing fire, and we hold the Indigenous knowledge that is needed to get the job done right. We have the knowledge to conduct cultural burning that is perfectly safe, and in many cases, we do not even need fire lines. Yet the federal agencies still do not allow us to lead prescribed burns on lands administered by the National Forest System.

We will not let these things stop us. We will just burn for another year on the 2% of the landscape that is held as private land and not considered part of the national forest. We will continue to build our own funding sources like the Endowment for Eco-Cultural Revitalization Fund. We will continue to fight for our Indigenous rights and tribal sovereignty to be taken seriously. Overcoming the structural racism at the root of this problem has been a multigenerational task. It shouldn't have to be.

Frequent prescribed fire and support for cultural burns conducted by individuals and families is the solution proposed by the Karuk Tribe and Western Klamath Restoration Partnership. We can do this, and we can do it together, but we need to permanently fund tribal programs that are engaged in shared stewardship activities and allow Indigenous people to lead the way.

Julie Cordero-Lamb, Jared Dahl Aldern, and Teresa Romero, "Bring Back the Good Fires" (2020)[8]

In Santa Barbara County, just below Romero Canyon, lies an old family cemetery in Montecito. The old cemetery is today unmarked, without headstones, and it carries the remains of ancestors for generations. It holds both Chumash and Californio ancestors carrying a distinct cultural history and landscape that is familiar among Tribal communities in Southern California. The old Romero trail is in actuality an old Chumash trail that led to villages through the Coastal ranges along with many other trails. Stories of these trails have been passed on orally through families for generations. It is a place where families gathered traditional foods and medicines, including acorns.

Just before the massive Thomas Fire of December 2017, large manzanita, ceanothus, and other chaparral shrubs filled Romero Canyon from floor to rim. Within the canyon and nearby, these shrubs encroached on sacred sites and Chumash gathering areas that, prior to settlement and fire-suppression policies, had been kept clear of shrubs by periodic Chumash cultural burns. The ferocious Thomas Fire had no problem clearing the closely packed shrubs, burning out even their large, extensive root systems and leaving only loose ashes in the root holes, which extended, in some places, up to six feet underground. When the heavy rains of January 8–9, 2018, rolled off the topsoil that the fire had baked to a waterproof finish and then surged into the underground "pipes" formed by the now-vacant root holes, whole hillsides came loose and crashed with their mud, boulders, and trees onto houses, living people, plants, and animals, and the bones of ancestors. What the fires had not consumed, and the smoke had not choked, the floods, finally, engulfed.

In the face of these catastrophes, it is time for federal, state, and local agencies to ensure a place at the table for the knowledgeable, Indigenous experts on native plant species, fire, and hydrology, and to negotiate cost- and time-efficient agreements to reintroduce cultural fire, ecosystem by ecosystem, microclimate by microclimate, as the traditional, regenerative horticulturalists of Native California have always done. In Santa Barbara and Ventura counties,

---

8 Julie Cordero-Lamb, Jared Dahl Aldern, and Teresa Romero, "Bring Back the Good Fires," *News from Native California*, Spring 2018, and revised for publication on the Institute on California and the West blog, October 6, 2020, https://icwblog.wordpress.com/2020/10/06/bring-back-the-good-fires/.

site of the massive Thomas Fire and the deadly debris flows that followed, modern Chumash practitioners have worked to reclaim their heritage as tenders of the land. Since there are no current agreements regarding the use of cultural fire management between any Chumash tribal organizations and government agencies, traditional horticulturalists do the grueling work of "being the fire" by hand. They choose a tiny area, rich in culturally important plants, acquire permits and secure access, carefully observe plant species and plant-animal interactions, recognize and note interconnections, bloom times, seeding patterns, and soil quality. They say their names, all of them, in Šmuwič, English, and Latin. They sing. Then they do the backbreaking work of pruning, coppicing, hand-grinding, mulching, and weeding out the dead brush and grasses. They use few or no power tools.

The tiny patches tended by Indigenous Californians grow lush, open, species-diverse, and more water-efficient. Fire, when it comes to such managed areas, burns low to the ground and moves through quickly. The tree crowns remain green and healthy. Any structures in such areas are easily defended. After the flames have moved through, the seeds that follow fire germinate at the first rain, since they survived the low-temperature burn.

But when the fire reaches the vast, un-tended zones that surround the green patches of hand-tended gathering areas, the dense, bone-dry fuel loads explode into fires of historic proportions, destroying homes, lives, livelihoods, and ancient landscapes. Severe, extensive burns in thick chaparral, on or near steep slopes with unstable soils, bring a high risk of subsequent mudslides. Closely following, intense rains nearly guarantee those extremely destructive debris flows. Some ecologists and activists argue that this type of fire is "natural," but saying that chaparral naturally grows to be dense, impenetrable, and explosive is like saying elders and children naturally starve without the work and intervention of those who care for them. These results are only natural when we do not tend to or nurture chaparral, elders, or children. The sheer age of healthy oaks, sycamores, bay trees, and elderberry in Southern California point to a long history of more frequent, less intense burns. Burns like the Thomas Fire kill many of these trees. It is clear that fire is beneficial when it occurs at appropriate frequencies, scales, intensities, and severities. We know—from elders, from knowledge conveyed by songs, stories, and ceremonies, from scientific studies, and from personal, working experience—that the following burn frequencies, with the burns' acreages properly scaled, are appropriate for their respective plant communities:

- Annually under oaks and pines where the goals are to ensure good harvest and to control pests and diseases

- Three times in ten years in oak orchards or pine groves where the goals are to increase the diversity of plants growing under the trees and to encourage young tree seedlings to grow into maturity
- Annually around springs, maintaining shallow-rooted grasses and annuals (and perhaps one or two shade trees) where the goal is to sustain water level and flow
- Every three years in grasses and shrubs used for baskets, arrows, and bows, where the goal is to ensure the growth of straight shoots and sprouts in the plant materials
- Every ten to fifteen years in chaparral, where the goal is to maximize seed and fruit yield and to control pathogens
- Much longer intervals in sage (which is killed by higher-frequency fire) and in patches of denser vegetation (to maintain them as denning, nesting, or hiding habitat for various animals)

These burning frequencies will vary as the various plant communities intersect with each other, and fire-lighters always keep hydrology in mind: the idea is to balance the distribution of shallow-rooted grasses and annuals with shade trees and shrubs throughout the watershed so that surface water flow is maximized, groundwater is as high as possible, and plants stay as green and fire-resistant as possible. Also, as climates change, fire seasons shift, droughts lengthen, storms intensify, and invasive plants and animals show increasing potential to move into freshly burned areas, Indigenous horticulturalists may adjust the seasonal timing of their burns or follow them up with maintenance programs to hand-clear any undesirable plants that sprout. A current buzz phrase among land managers is adaptive management, by which they mean the systematic improvement of management by learning from the outcomes of past practices on the land. Indigenous horticulturalists have been adaptively interrelating with land since time immemorial, and the environmental dynamics of the twenty-first century are only the latest in a long history of sometimes tumultuous change to which these practitioners have responded. In that sense, they are the ultimate adaptive managers.

There will always be big fires in Southern California, especially during Santa Ana wind episodes, but when they burn, they do not have to be as destructive as was the Thomas Fire. The National Cohesive Wildland Fire Management Strategy—a framework for federal, state, local, and tribal fire agencies to collaborate – puts forward three key goals: 1) to respond effectively and efficiently to wildfires; 2) to develop fire-adapted communities, and 3) to restore and maintain landscapes. Much funding, training, and news stories have focused on the first goal (firefighting), even as wildfires appear to be increasing in frequency. Some journalists and columnists have recently focused more attention on the second goal (fire adaptation)—and it is absolutely necessary to better fire-proof our communities and homes with appropriate building materials, rooftop sprinkler systems, and adequate defensible space surrounding them. To extend the idea of defensible space to rural and remote landscapes would be to approach the third goal (fire restoration). When forests and shrublands are thinned and opened (with hand tools, with chainsaws and tractors, or with prescribed and cultural fire), and especially when they are thinned and opened in a targeted, strategic fashion that accounts for wind corridors, potential wildfire behavior, and good locations for cultivating important plants such as oaks and herbaceous foods, medicines, and materials, then not only will groundwater levels rise and will more of these cultural and natural resources survive big fires, but firefighters will have more fuel breaks and safety zones to aid in their defense of lives, homes, and homelands.

It is time for the era of deliberate suppression of cultural burning practices to end. Cultural fire suppression has culminated in a social, unnatural disaster. Chumash people have worked with tribes in Northern California on cultural burns, and they are ready to apply the knowledge gained to cultural burns in Southern California in the aftermath of the Thomas Fire and the Montecito mudslides. For federal, state, and local agencies to help bring the restoration of tribal fire to a broader scale in California, they must collaborate with tribal practitioners at every step in the process (after all, it's not cultural fire without the culture). And to successfully collaborate with Native people whose practices have so often been ignored or actively suppressed, non-Native fire scientists and managers will need to acknowledge Indigenous knowledge as valid, act in accordance with the diverse, local traditions of the tribes in their areas, and maintain a willingness to share decision-making power and an openness to learn from knowledge that is sometimes shared in unfamiliar formats. The required investment of funds, time, and effort into Indigenous fire will help to prevent a reoccurrence of recent tragedies and will return many other benefits to the people and land of our state.

California Senate Bill No. 332 (2021)[9]

Approved by Governor October 06, 2021. Filed with Secretary of State October 06, 2021.

... Civil liability: prescribed burning operations: gross negligence.

Existing law makes a person who negligently, or in violation of the law, sets a fire, allows a fire to be set, or allows a fire kindled or attended by the person to escape onto any public or private property liable for the fire suppression costs incurred in fighting the fire, the cost of providing rescue or emergency medical services, the cost of investigating and making any reports with respect to the fire, and the costs relating to accounting for the fire and the collection of specified funds.

Existing law authorizes the Director of Forestry and Fire Protection to enter into an agreement, including a grant agreement, for prescribed burning or other hazardous fuel reduction efforts with any person for specified purposes. Existing law requires the agreement to designate an officer of the Department of Forestry and Fire Protection or a certified burn boss as the burn boss with final authority regarding the prescribed burning operation and to specify the duties of, and the precautions taken by, the person contracting with the department and any personnel furnished by that person. Existing law prohibits a person from knowingly setting or permitting agricultural burning unless that person has a valid permit, as specified. Existing law prohibits, among other things, a person from setting fire or causing fire to be set to any forest, brush, or other flammable material that is on any land that is not the person's own, or under the person's legal control, without the permission of the owner, lessee, or agent of the owner or lessee of the land.

This bill would provide that no person shall be liable for any fire suppression or other costs otherwise recoverable for a prescribed burn if specified conditions are met, including, among others, that the burn be for the purpose of wildland fire hazard reduction, ecological maintenance and restoration, cultural burning, silviculture, or agriculture, and that, when required, a certified burn boss review and approve a written prescription for the burn. The bill would provide that any person whose conduct constitutes gross negligence

---

9 California Senate Bill 332, 2021, California Legislative Information, https://leginfo.legislature.ca.gov/faces/billTextClient.xhtml?bill_id=202120220SB332.

shall not be entitled to immunity from fire suppression or other costs otherwise recoverable, as specified. The bill would define terms for its purposes.

THE PEOPLE OF THE STATE OF CALIFORNIA DO ENACT AS FOLLOWS . . .

(a) The Legislature finds and declares that in order to meet fuel management goals, the state must rely on private entities to engage in prescribed burning for public benefit.

(b) Notwithstanding Sections 13009 and 13009.1 of the Health and Safety Code, no person shall be liable for any fire suppression or other costs otherwise recoverable pursuant to Section 13009 or 13009.1 of the Health and Safety Code resulting from a prescribed burn if all of the following conditions are met:

(1) The purpose of the burn is for wildland fire hazard reduction, ecological maintenance and restoration, cultural burning, silviculture, or agriculture.

(2) A person certified as a burn boss pursuant to Section 4477 of the Public Resources Code reviewed and approved a written prescription for the burn that includes adequate risk mitigation measures.

(3) The burn is conducted in compliance with the written prescription.

(4) The burn is authorized pursuant to Chapter 6 (commencing with Section 4411) or Chapter 7 (commencing with Section 4461) of Part 2 of Division 4 of the Public Resources Code.

(5) The burner has a landowner's written permission or the approval of the governing body of a Native American Tribe to burn.

(6) The burn is conducted in compliance with any air quality permit required pursuant to Article 3 (commencing with Section 41850) of Chapter 3 of Part 4 of Division 26 of the Health and Safety Code.

(7) Cultural burns conducted by a cultural fire practitioner are exempt from paragraphs (2) and (3).

(c) This section shall not be construed to grant immunity from fire suppression or other costs otherwise recoverable pursuant to Section 13009 or 13009.1 of the Health and Safety Code to any person whose conduct constitutes gross negligence.

(d) Nothing in this section affects the ability of a private or public entity plaintiff to bring a civil action against any defendant.

(e) "Cultural burn" means the intentional application of fire to land by Native American tribes, tribal organizations, or cultural fire practitioners to achieve cultural goals or objectives, including subsistence, ceremonial activities, biodiversity, or other benefits.

(f) "Cultural fire practitioner" means a person associated with a Native American tribe or tribal organization with experience in burning to meet cultural goals or objectives, including subsistence, ceremonial activities, biodiversity, or other benefits.

Katimiin and Ameekyaaraam Sacred Lands Act (2023)[10]

An Act to take certain Federal land located in Siskiyou County, California, and Humboldt County, California, into trust for the benefit of the Karuk Tribe, and for other purposes.

Be it enacted by the Senate and House of Representatives of the United States of America in Congress assembled...

SECTION 1. SHORT TITLE.
This Act may be cited as the "Katimiin and Ameekyaaraam Sacred Lands Act"

SEC. 2. LAND HELD IN TRUST FOR THE KARUK TRIBE.

(a) Findings—Congress finds that—
(1) the Katimiin and Ameekyaaraam land is located in the ancestral territory of the Karuk Tribe; and
(2) the Karuk Tribe has historically used, and has an ongoing relationship with, the Katimiin and Ameekyaaraam land.

(b) Definitions.—In this section:
(1) Katimiin and Ameekyaaraam land.—The term "Katimiin and Ameekyaaraam land" means the approximately 1,031 acres of Federal land, including improvements and appurtenances to the Federal land, located in Siskiyou County, California, and Humboldt County, California, and generally depicted as "Proposed Area" on the map of the Forest Service entitled "Katimiin Area Boundary Proposal" and dated August 9, 2021.
(2) Secretary.—The term ``Secretary" means the Secretary of the Interior.

(c) Administrative Transfer.—Administrative jurisdiction of the Katimiin and Ameekyaaraam land is hereby transferred from the Secretary of Agriculture to the Secretary, subject to the condition that the Chief of the Forest Service shall continue to manage the component of the National Wild and Scenic Rivers System that flows through the Katimiin and Ameekyaaraam land.

---

10 "Katimiin and Ameekyaaraam Sacred Lands," Act Public Law No. 117-353, January 5, 2023, https://www.congress.gov/bill/117th-congress/senate-bill/4439/text.

RETURN CYCLE 215

(d) Land Held in Trust.—The Katimiin and Ameekyaaraam land is hereby taken into trust by the Secretary for the benefit of the Karuk Tribe, subject to—

(1) valid existing rights, contracts, and management agreements relating to easements and rights-of-way; and

(2) continued access by the Chief of the Forest Service for the purpose of managing the component of the National Wild and Scenic Rivers System that flows through the Katimiin and Ameekyaaraam land.

. . .

(e) <<NOTE: Deadline.>> Survey.—Not later than 180 days after the date of enactment of this Act, the Secretary of Agriculture shall provide to the Secretary a complete survey of the land taken into trust under subsection (d).

(f) Use of Land.—

(1) In general.—Land taken into trust under subsection (d) may be used for traditional and customary uses for the benefit of the Karuk Tribe.

(2) Gaming.—Class II and class III gaming under the Indian Gaming Regulatory Act (25 U.S.C. 2701 et seq.) shall not be allowed on the land taken into trust under subsection (d).

(g) Wild and Scenic Rivers Management.—

(1) In general.—Nothing in this section affects the status or administration of any component of the National Wild and Scenic Rivers System, including any component that flows through the land taken into trust under subsection (d).

(2) Memorandum of understanding.—The Secretary of Agriculture shall enter into a memorandum of understanding with the Karuk Tribe, consistent with the obligations of the Secretary of Agriculture under subsection (c), to establish mutual goals for the protection and enhancement of the river values of any component of the National Wild and Scenic Rivers System that flows through the land taken into trust under subsection (d).

Approved January 5, 2023.

Dawn Blake, "Cultural Burns Critical for Tribal Land Management" (2023)[11]

As a child, I watched my grandmother maintain her basketry material by burning her gathering patches. She did this on an annual or even semi-annual basis. I am a Hupa Tribal member and a Yurok Tribal descendant, and by serving as forestry director for the Yurok Tribal Council, I am working to uphold my grandmother's and my mother's tribe's sacred practice of cultural burns.

Our use of cultural burns—a process by which we set small fires to prevent larger ones—is a form of land management that has been passed down through generations. It is called cultural burning because of the holistic changes that fire brings to the landscape, and it is important to us both spiritually and culturally.

Despite its numerous benefits, cultural burns have long been misunderstood and even outlawed—an egregious mistake that puts our forests and communities in grave danger. A century of European forestry management laws suppressing fires and banning Indigenous peoples from practicing cultural burns has made the landscape more susceptible to catastrophic wildfires over the last decade.

Cultural burns make the land healthier, more diverse, and better able to withstand catastrophic wildfires, like those occurring with increasing frequency in the Western United States. Indigenous cultural burns focus on what needs to be burned to revitalize the land, resources, and water, with the intent of returning to make use of the land again—to bring the ecosystem back to where it can reproduce on its own.

These burns grant us food sovereignty by allowing our traditional foods, like salmon, acorns, and berries, to flourish. In the space newly opened by a cultural burn, a variety of plants, bushes, and smaller trees can grow. Many of these species are dependent on fire and have been in decline for decades. Fire also opens up the forest to large animals, such as elk and deer.

Thanks to recently passed legislation, there are new resources to support this critical and sacred practice of burning the land to heal it. A California law has affirmed the right to cultural burns, reducing the layers of liability and permission needed to set "good fire" on the land. The law recognizes the value of our Indigenous knowledge and the experience of Native people with fire. It

---

11 Dawn Blake, "Cultural Burns Critical for Tribal Land Management," *Times-Standard* (Eureka, CA), February 23, 2023.

opens the door to us starting to take care of our land again with fire without fear of going to prison.

At the federal level, the Bipartisan Infrastructure Law provides grants to support cultural fire as it applies to ecosystem restoration. The Inflation Reduction Act provides $220 million in funding for tribes and tribal organizations for climate resilience and adaptation programs. This includes grants to support forest conservation and the development of fire-resilient forests. The principle of Tribal sovereignty supports flexibility in how Tribes spend those dollars in ways that make sense for our communities. For us, that includes the support and freedom to practice cultural fire.

We have been strongly advocating for years for our cultural right to use fire. Only now that there is consensus from the western scientific community are our voices finally being heard. Keeping fire out of the ecosystem is making our forests and communities far less resilient. We must re-learn how to live with fire and use it to protect the land and all who depend on it.

Index

"10 a.m. Rule," 163, 176–177
1910 wildfire season, 67–68, 86
2020 wildfire season, 1, 14

A

acorns, 8–9, 19, 207, 216
"Agency of Fire in Propagation of Longleaf Pines," 138–144
Alabama, 127, 136–137
Aldern, Jared Dahl, 207–210
American Forestry, 105, 136–137
American Forestry Congress, 60, 125, 128–130
American Forests, 12, 125, 131–135, 145–149
Anderson, M. Kat, 29
Andrews, Eliza Frances, 125, 138–144
Angeles National Forest, 94
Arizona, 163, 165
Arrillaga, José de, 6, 22, 30, 40–41
Azzuz, Elizabeth, 199

B

Backbone Complex Fire, 205
Barrett, Louis A., 16
Barrett, S. A., 183–184
Bartram, William, 148, 157
Baxley, H. Willis, 183
Beadel, H. L., 158
beavers, 21
beetles, 80, 98–101, 112–113
Bergoffen, W. W., 9
Big Bar Complex Fire, 205
"Big Trees and Fire, The," 186–190
Bipartisan Infrastructure Law (2021), 217
Biswell, H. H., 126, 150–152, 164, 186–190
Bitterroot National Forest, 171, 193
Black Hills (South Dakota), 70, 99
Blake, Dawn, 15, 199, 216–217

bobwhite quail, 12, 154, 158–159
Botanical Gazette, 138–144
Briggs, M. C., 179, 188
"Bring Back the Good Fires," 207–210
Bruce, Donald, 116–120, 151
Bunnell, L. H., 181, 188
Burcham, L. T., 8
Bureau of Indian Affairs (BIA), 23
Bureau of Land Management (BLM), 202–203
Butler Fire, 205

C

Cabrillo, Juan Rodríguez, 31
Calbick, Allen, 163, 178
California, laws and statutes of, 51–52, 211–213
California Board of Forestry, 66
California District News Letter, 115, 121
California Division of Forestry, 8
California Fish and Game Commission, 8
California Forestry Committee, 94, 115–116, 118, 151
California Indian Basketweavers' Association, 196, 198
California State Board of Forestry, 115, 117, 199
California State University, 14, 21
Casey, Jim, 8–9
Castañeda, Antonia I., 30
Catton, Theodore, 6
Century Magazine, 181
Channel Islands (California), 21
Chapman, Herman H., 125, 131–135, 150, 156
Chumash people, 207–210
Civilian Conservation Corps (CCC), 170, 176

220   INDEX

Clapp, Earl, 162
Clark, Galen, 181, 184–185, 188
Clarke-McNary Act (1924), 11
Cleveland National Forest, 196
climate change, 1, 209
Coastal Plains Experiment Station, 145–149
Colville Indian Reservation, 12
Coman, Warren, 7, 67–68, 87–88
Concepcíon Horra, Antonio de la, 42
Coolidge, Calvin, 24, 94, 121
Cordero-Lamb, Julie, 207–210
COVID-19, 205
Coville, Frederick V., 70
Crespí, Juan, 22, 29, 33–36
crown fires, 86, 89–91, 106, 113
"Cultural Burns Critical for Tribal Land
    Management," 216–217
Curtis, John T., 155

D
de Soto, Hernando, 146
"Did the Indian Protect the Forest?" 87–88
duBois, Coert, 10
Duflot de Mofras, Eugène, 45, 50

E
Ecology, 165–169
ecotones, 20, 23
"Effect of the Partial Suppression of
    Annual Forest Fires in the Sierra Nevada
    Mountains, The," 73–74
Eldredge, Inman, 13
e'Muht Mohay, 19
Endowment for Eco-Cultural Revitalization
    Fund, 206
Ernst, Emil F., 164, 179–185
European forestry, 90, 102, 104, 153–154,
    156, 216

F
Fages, Pedro, 22
Fairfax, Emily, 21
Ferrelo, Bartolomé, 31
Fillmore, Stephen, 18
"Fire and the Forest," 84–86
fire mosaics, 20, 24, 29
Flagg, James Montgomery, 162
Flathead National Forest, 163
Florida, 122–125, 128–130, 156–158, 160

Floyd County (Georgia), 138
"Forest Fires and Forestry in the Southern
    States," 131–135
"Forest Resources of Alabama, The,"
    136–137
"Forest that Fire Made, The," 145–149
Forestry and Irrigation, 75–78

G
General Allotment Act (1887), 6
Georgia, 138, 150–151
ghost trees, 3–6
Gifford, E. W., 183–184
Goddard, Pliny Earle, 199
Goode, Ron, 14
Gore, Howard M., 121
Grasmick, Scott, 196, 198
grasses, 20–22, 35, 37, 148–149, 165–169,
    208–209
Graves, Henry, 93, 95–97
"Graves Terms Light Burning 'Piute
    Forestry,'" 95–97
Greeley, William B., 93, 104–108
Greene, S. W., 12, 125, 145–150, 156–157
Greswell, E. A., 153–154
ground fires, 89–90, 95–96, 105–107, 111,
    136–138, 144–146
Guardian, 199, 204–206

H
Hankins, Don, 14
Harper, Roland M., 125, 136–144, 156
Headley, Roy, 93
Hensel, R. L., 163, 165–169
Heyward, Frank, 156
"*Hic Jacet* (An Epitaph)," 115
Hilgard, Eugene, 146
Hough, Franklin, 45–46, 55–59
"How Fire Helps Forestry," 79–83
Hoxie, George, 67, 79–83
Humboldt County (California), 214–215
humus, 77, 89–90, 110, 136
Hupa people, 199, 216–217
Hutchings, James Mason, 44, 61, 182

I
Idaho, 64, 68, 170–175
Indian Forester Journal, 153–154

INDEX

Indigenous peoples
    activism of, 14–15, 94, 121, 204–210,
        216–217
    condescension and dismissal of fire
        management practices, 6–9, 24,
        53–54, 57–59, 68, 76–77, 84–88, 105,
        110, 118, 121
    genocide of, 4–6, 29–30
    See also specific people, peoples, and tribes
Indigenous Peoples Burning Network, 200
Inflation Reduction Act (2022), 217
*International Journal of Environmental
    Research and Public Health*, 200

J

Jardine, J. T., 3
Journal of Forestry, 10, 116–120, 151, 170–177
Journal of Range Management, 150–152
Junco Meadow, 196, 198

K

Kansas, 165–169
Karuk tribe, 14, 16, 199–200, 204–206,
    214–215
Katimiin and Ameekyaaraam Sacred Lands
    Act (2023), 214–215
Kaufman, Herbert, 13–14
Keter, Tom, 4
Kitts, Joseph A., 67–68, 89–91
Klamath County (Oregon), 113
Klamath Reservation, 12
Klamath River Jack, 8–9
Koch, Elers, 12–13, 163, 170–175
Komarek, E. V., 153–155
Komarek, Roy, 122
Kotok, E. I., 10, 184
Kumeyaay people, 19–24
Kumeyaay Reservation, 18

L

Lake, Frank, 200
Lake County (Oregon), 113
Lasuén, Fermín de, 28, 43
Lavender Mountain (Georgia), 138
Lebrado, Maria, 184
Leopold, Aldo, 11, 93, 109–111, 163, 191–192
Leopold Report, 191–192
Lewis, James G., 11
Lewis, Meriwether, 170, 173

Life in California (1831), 49
"Light Burning" (1920), 112–114
"Light Burning" (1923), 116–120
Lolo Trail, 170–175
Long, Ellen Call, 125, 128–130, 138–144
Long, Jonathan, 200
Longino Martínez, José, 22, 39
longleaf pine, 12, 122, 125, 129–134,
    136–150, 157–158
Lyell, Charles, 125, 127

M

MacCleery, Douglas, 3–6
Manson, Marsden, 73–74
Manzanita Reservation, 18
Mariposa Grove, 61, 181, 188
McAtee, W. L., 158
McKinney Fire, 200
McSweeney-McNary Act (1928), 11
Mexico, 5
Miller, Joaquin, 46, 60, 188
Mills, William H., 46, 61–63
Miskwich, Michael Connolly, 17, 19–25, 201
Mission Indian Federation, 24, 94, 121
Miwok people, 14, 183
Moncado, Fernando, 29
Montecito, California, 207–210
Monterey, California, 50
Mount Baker National Forest, 162
Mount Mazama, 113
Muir, John, 69, 71, 186–187

N

National Cohesive Wildland Fire Manage-
    ment Strategy, 209
National Environmental Policy Act, 205
National Geographic, 67, 69–72
National Park Service, 11, 14, 164, 179–185,
    191–192
National Parks Magazine, 164, 186–190
New York State College of Forestry, 9
News from Native California, 207–210
Norgaard, Kari Marie, 7
North Fork Mono, 14
Northern Cheyenne Indian Reservation, 99
"Notes on Some of the Forest Features of
    Florida," 128–130

O

Oak Fire, 200
Ogle, Charles E., 112–114
Olmsted, F. E., 84–86
"On the Origin of Prairies," 47–48
Ostrander, H. J., 182
"Our Land was Taken," 204–206

P

Pacific Monthly, 87–88
"Passing of the Lolo Trail, The," 170–175
Pinchot, Gifford, 2, 6, 67, 69–72, 163, 178
Pine and Redwood Lumber Manufactures' Associations, 115
"Piute forestry" (derogatory term), 9–10, 16, 68, 76–77, 93, 95–97, 104–111
"'Piute Forestry' or the Fallacy of Light Burning," 104–108
"'Piute Forestry' vs. Forest Fire Prevention," 109–111
Plains Miwok, 14
Plumas National Forest, 10
Powell, John Wesley, 45, 53–54
Powers, Stephen, 15–17
prairies, 47–48, 59, 69–70, 137, 155, 166
"Prescribed Burning in Georgia and California Compared," 150–152
"Preventing Forest Fires by Burning Litter," 89–91

R

"Recent Studies on the Effect of Burning on Grassland Vegetation," 165–169
Red Salmon Complex Fire, 205
Redington, Paul, 10–11, 93–94, 115–116
"Relation of Forests and Forest Fires, The," 69–72
Report of the Arid Lands of the United States, 53–54
Report on Forestry (1882), 55–59
Reynolds, Richard, 186
Rivera y Moncada, Fernando, 37–38
Robinson, Alfred, 45, 49
Romero, Teresa, 207–210
Roosevelt, Franklin D., 162, 174
Roosevelt, Theodore, 6
Rothman, Hal K., 11, 14, 126
Russell, Carl P., 184

S

San Bernardino Mountains, 24
San Bernardino National Forest, 94
San Diego, 23, 32
San Francisco, 22, 93
San Francisco Call, 182
San Gabriel Mountains, 24
San Jacinto, 24, 121
San Joaquin Valley, 61, 75
Santa Barbara, 41
Santa Barbara Channel, 38–39
Santa Barbara County (California), 207–208
Santa Clara, 50
Santa Cruz, 22
Santa Cruz Mountains, 50
Santa Monica Bay, 31
Santa Rita Range Reserve, 165
Sauer, Carl O., 183
Savage, James, 179
Scenes of Wonder and Curiosity in California, 44
Second Visit to the United States of North America, 127
seeds, 19–22, 35, 37–39, 43, 71, 91, 130, 136, 140, 208
sequoias, 61, 73–74, 186–190
Serra, Junipero, 19, 22, 30
Shasta-Trinity National Forest, 3–4
Shinn, Charles Howard, 75–78
shortleaf pine, 132–134, 138, 151, 158
Show, S. B., 10, 116
Sierra Club Bulletin, 73–74, 84–86
Sierra Nevada Mountains, 73–74, 164, 186
Silcox, Ferdinand A., 176–177
Siskiyou County (California), 214–215
Six Rivers National Forest, 4
Slater Fire, 200, 204
Smokey Bear, 162
Society of American Foresters, 13, 116
South Dakota, 70, 99
Southern Pacific Railroad, 105, 109, 115–116
Southern Sierra Miwuk Nation, 200
Southwestern Magazine, 109–111
Spanish Empire, 5–8, 19, 29–46, 50, 94
Spokane Indian Reservation, 12
Stanislaus National Forest, 184
Stay, William W., 181–182

INDEX

Stoddard, Herbert L., 12, 122, 126, 150, 156–161
sugar pine, 73–75, 79–80, 82, 113
"Suggests Indians Manage National Forests," 121
Sunset Magazine, 79–83, 93, 98–103
surface fires, 67, 70, 89–91, 102, 106, 109

T

Tall Timbers Fire Ecology Conference, 12, 125–126, 153–161, 193–195
Tall Timbers Research Station, 122, 124, 160
Tallahassee, 122, 125, 138, 160
Tending the Wild, 29
Texas, 129, 165
Thomas Fire, 207–210
Thompson, Rita P., 164, 193–195
Timberman, 89–91, 95–97, 104–108, 112–114
Times-Standard, 216–217
Travels on the Pacific Coast (1841), 50
Tribal Forest Protection Act (2004), 202–203
Tripp, Bessie, 15, 199
Tripp, Bill, 14–15, 199, 204–206

U

United States Department of Agriculture, 70, 94, 158
United States Department of the Interior, 15, 71
United States Division of Forestry, 45, 55–59, 67, 69
United States Fish and Wildlife Service, 158–159
United States Forest Service
  "10 a.m. Rule" and, 163, 176–177
  criticisms of, 101–103, 125–126, 163–164, 170–175, 193–195
  fire suppression and, 2, 6–12, 67–68, 92–97, 176–177
  Indigenous peoples and, 6–9, 12–14, 67–68, 121, 200, 202–203
  Smokey Bear, 158
  Tribal Forest Protection Act and, 202–203
  use of fire, 84, 86, 97, 151, 158
United States Geological Survey, 45, 138
University of California, 115–116
University of Wisconsin, 155

"Use of Fire in Pine Forests and Game Lands," 156–160
"Use of Fire, The," 153–155

V

"Vanishing Meadows in Yosemite Valley," 179–185
Velasquez, Irene, 200
Ventura, California, 45, 49
Ventura County (California), 207–208
Vizcaíno, Sebastián, 32

W

Wallace, Henry, 162
Wallace, Idaho, 64
Wallowa National Forest, 3
Weeks Act (1911), 11
Wells, R. W., 45, 47–48
Western Klamath Restoration Partnership, 206
wetlands, 21, 23
White, Stewart Edward, 93, 98–103, 116
white pine (eastern), 131–132
white pine (western), 80–82
Whitney, John. D., 180–181
Wildland Fire Mitigation and Management Commission, 199
"Woodsmen, Spare Those Trees!" 98–103
"Work in the National Forests," 75–78

Y

Yale Forest School, 125
Yokut people, 16
Yosemite Valley and Yosemite National Park, 44, 61–63, 73, 164, 179–185, 200
Yosemite Valley Nature Notes, 179–185
Yreka, California, 10, 119
Yurok Tribal Council, 199, 216–217